Mastering SQL Server Profiler

By Brad McGehee

First published by Simple Talk Publishing 2009

Typeset by Chris Massey

CONTENTS

ABOUT THE AUTHOR

Brad McGehee is a MCSE+I, MCSD, and MCT (former) with a Bachelors degree in Economics and a Masters in Business Administration. Currently the Director of DBA Education for Red Gate Software, Brad is an accomplished Microsoft SQL Server MVP with over 13 years' SQL Server experience, and over 6 years' training experience.

Brad is a frequent speaker at SQL PASS, SQL Connections, SQLTeach, Code Camps, SQL Server user groups, and other industry seminars, where he shares his 13 years' cumulative knowledge.

Brad was the founder of the popular community site SQL-Server-Performance.Com, and operated it from 2000 through 2006, where he wrote over one million words on SQL Server topics.

A well-known name in SQL Server literature, Brad is the author or co-author of more than 12 technical books and over 100 published articles. His recent books include "How to Become an Exceptional DBA" and "Brad's Sure Guide to SQL Server 2008".

When he is not traveling to spread his knowledge of SQL Server, Brad enjoys spending time with his wife and young daughter in Hawaii.

INTRODUCTION

I have been a SQL Server DBA for about 14 years, and I regard Profiler as one of the most useful of SQL Server's "built-in" tools. Profiler records data about various SQL Server events. This data is stored in a trace file and allows you to view the communications sent from a client to SQL Server, in addition to giving you an insight into its internal workings. This information can be used to troubleshoot a wide range of SQL Server issues, such as poorly-performing queries, locking and blocking, excessive table/index scanning, and a lot more.

For such a potentially powerful tool, Profiler is surprisingly underused. This must be due, at least in part, to the fact that it is occasionally a frustrating tool. The user interface is poor, it lacks many important features, it is poorly documented and, unless you have a lot of experience as a DBA, it is often hard to analyze the data you capture. As such, many DBAs tend to ignore it and this is distressing, because Profiler has so much potential to make a DBA's life more productive.

This is why I wrote this book, *Mastering SQL Server Profiler*. My goal was to make it easier for you to learn how to use Profiler, analyze the data it provides, and to take full advantage of its potential for troubleshooting SQL Server problems.

WHICH VERSION OF SQL SERVER PROFILER IS COVERED IN THIS BOOK?

Most DBAs are still using SQL Server 2005, so all the examples in this book are based on SQL Server 2005 Profiler. However, the differences between SQL Server 2005 and SQL Server 2008 are minimal. While you may notice some minor cosmetic changes between the two editions, and discover that SQL Server 2008 includes a few new events, every example in this book will work with SQL Server 2008 and everything you learn here is applicable to both SQL Server 2005 and SQL Server 2008.

In fact, most of what is covered in this book also applies to SQL Server 2000, although you will want to use the SQL Server 2005 Profiler tool to access your SQL Server 2000 instances.

HOW THE BOOK IS STRUCTURED

If you are new to Profiler, you will want to start with the first three chapters, which provide the basic foundation you need to begin using Profiler. If you're already familiar with the basics of capturing traces with Profiler, then you can head straight to Chapter 4 and onwards. These chapters are self-contained and can be read in any order that you wish.

CHAPTER 1: GETTING STARTED WITH PROFILER

If you are new to Profiler, this is where you will want to start. This chapter covers all the basics you need to get you started using Profiler, such as:

- Understanding how Profiler works
- An introduction to Profiler terminology, such as events, data columns, filters and traces
- Learning the basics of how to create, control, and save a Profiler trace

CHAPTER 2: WORKING WITH TRACES AND TEMPLATES

This chapter delves deeper into the world of traces. It covers topics such as:

- How to build custom traces from scratch
- How to Save Profiler traces to a SQL Server Table
- How to trace Analysis Services activity
- How to create and modify reusable profiler trace templates

CHAPTER 3: PROFILER GUI TIPS AND TRICKS

At this point, you should have a good understanding of what Profiler can do and how it works. This chapter covers several Profiler tips that will make you more productive, such as:

- Tips on Selecting Profiler Events and Data Columns
- Tips on Using Column Filters
- Tips on Organizing Columns for Grouping and Analysis
- How the "Server processes trace data" Option Affects Traces
- How to Set Global Trace Options
- How to Schedule a Trace's Stop Time

- How to use the Auto Scroll Window
- How to Search for Data Inside a Trace File
- How to Set and Use Bookmarks

CHAPTER 4: HOW TO IDENTIFY SLOW RUNNING QUERIES

Now that you have mastered Profiler basics, you get the opportunity to start making practical use of Profiler. As DBAs, one of the problems we face on an almost daily basis is slow-running queries. These are the kind of queries that keep us up late at night, ruining our sleep and turning us into zombies. This chapter shows you how to:

- Create a Profiler trace to capture all the information you need to identify and analyze slow running queries
- Analyze the poorly-performing queries identified by Profiler

CHAPTER 5: HOW TO IDENTIFY AND TROUBLESHOOT SQL SERVER PROBLEMS

This chapter shows how to create and analyze Profiler traces that will help you uncover a multitude of different problems (possibly problems that you didn't even know you had!). In this chapter, you will learn:

- How to Identify Deadlocks
- How to Identify Blocking Issues
- How to Identify Excessive Auto Stats Activity
- How to Identify Excessive Statement Compilations
- How to Identify Excessive Database File Growth/Shrinkage
- How to Identify Excessive Table/Index Scans
- How to Identify Memory Problems

CHAPTER 6: USING PROFILER TO AUDIT DATABASE ACTIVITY

Many DBAs are tasked with auditing the activity within their databases. Although Profiler is not the ideal tool for auditing, it can still get the job done. This chapter covers:

- The pros and cons of using Profiler for auditing
- Available Audit events
- How to conduct an Audit Trace

CHAPTER 7: USING PROFILER WITH THE DATABASE ENGINE TUNING ADVISOR

In combination, Profiler and the Database Engine Tuning Advisor can make it much easier for DBAs to identify indexing issues in your databases. In this chapter, you learn:

- About the features and benefits of using the DTA
- How to create a trace for use by the DTA
- How to run a trace for use by the DTA
- How to Perform a Missing Index Analysis Using the DTA

CHAPTER 8: CORRELATING PROFILER WITH PERFORMANCE MONITOR

Data captured in Performance Monitor and Profiler can be combined and displayed within the Profiler GUI, making it possible to identify correlations between Transact-SQL execution and resource usage. In this chapter, you learn:

- How to collect Profiler data for correlation analysis
- How to collect Performance Monitor data for correlation analysis
- How to correlate SQL Server 2005 Profiler data with Performance Monitor data
- How to analyze correlated data

CHAPTER 9: HOW TO CAPTURE PROFILER TRACES PROGRAMMATICALLY

While most DBAs create and collect traces using the Profiler GUI, there are certain advantages to using T-SQL scripts and system stored procedures. In this chapter, you will learn:

- The pros and cons of capturing traces programmatically
- How to use T-SQL and system stored procedures to capture traces
- How to use the Profiler GUI to create T-SQL trace scripts
- How to use a trace function to perform SELECT queries directly against a physical trace file

CHAPTER 10: PROFILER BEST PRACTICES

There are many different ways to use Profiler to capture trace data. This chapter summarizes some of my thoughts on the most efficient ways to:

- Create Traces
- Run Traces
- Analyze Traces
- Use Performance Monitor with Profiler
- Use Database Engine Tuning Advisor with Profiler

CHAPTER 11: PROFILER EVENTS AND DATA COLUMNS EXPLAINED

We saved the longest chapter for last. It provides a reference source for each of the 21 Profiler event categories that Profiler has to offer, and to offer an explanation of how they can be used to troubleshoot many different SQL Server problems. It includes a description of those events in each category that will be of the most interest to the DBA along with a digest of the most important data columns.

HAVE FUN, AND LET THE PROFILER ADVENTURE BEGIN

Now that you know where you are going, jump in with both feet and begin your journey towards mastering Profiler. Learning is always a great adventure, and I hope you enjoy reading this book as much as I did researching and writing it. If you have any questions or feedback, please send them to brad.mcgehee@red-gate.com.

Chapter 1
GETTING STARTED WITH PROFILER

SQL Server 2005 Profiler is a powerful tool that allows you to capture and analyze events, such as the execution of a stored procedure, occurring within SQL Server. This information can be used to identify and troubleshoot many SQL Server-related problems.

Everybody has to start somewhere and, if you are new to Profiler, this is where you want to begin. In this chapter, we'll cover the basics of how Profiler works, its core terminology, and how to create and save basic Profiler traces.

If you have used Profiler a lot in the past, you may want to skip right to the later, more advanced chapters in the book where we start to put Profiler into action, analyzing slow performing queries, troubleshooting bottleneck, auditing database activity and so on.

After reading this chapter, you will know why Profiler is such an essential tool in the DBA's armoury, and will:

- Understand how Profiler works
- Be familiar with core Profiler terminology, such as events, data columns, filters and traces
- Understand the permissions required to use Profiler and how to start up Profiler
- Be able to create and control basic Profiler traces and then save a completed trace to a file

WHY MASTERING PROFILER CAN HELP MAKE YOU AN EXCEPTIONAL DBA

One of the things that separate mediocre DBAs from exceptional ones is that exceptional DBAs know how to take full advantage of the tools available to them. By mastering Profiler, the exceptional DBA can track down and fix SQL Server performance and other problems quickly and efficiently, and even spot potential problems before they cause real difficulties. In this section, we take a look at the many different ways we can use Profiler to help us out in our job.

While the following lists are not totally comprehensive, they do describe the majority of the ways Profiler can be used to help us out as DBAs or developers.

How Profiler can help DBAs

- Monitor the activity of the:
  - SQL Server Database Engine
  - Analysis Services
  - Integration Services
- Monitor and identify performance-related problems with front-end application, queries, T-SQL, transactions, and much more
- Perform query analysis of execution plans
- Monitor and identify SQL Server errors and warnings
- Capture and replay traces of activity to replicate problems
- Audit user activity
- Analyze trace results by grouping or aggregating them
- Create your own custom traces, and save them, for use whenever you wish
- Correlate Profiler trace events with System Monitor performance counters to identify what event(s) are hogging server resources
- Capture data for analysis in the Database Engine Tuning Wizard
- Save trace results to a file, a database table, or to XML for later analysis
- Trace Profiler events programmatically, instead of using only the Profiler GUI

How Profiler can help developers

- View how SQL Server works when interacting with a client
- Debug T-SQL code and stored procedures
- Perform stress testing
- Perform quality assurance testing

As discussed in the book's introduction, the focus of this book is on DBAs, not developers. Because of this, we will be focusing on the type of features described above that are targeted more toward DBAs.

The inner workings of Profiler

What may be a surprise to many DBAs and developers is that SQL Server Profiler is only a GUI designed to work with another feature of

SQL Server called **SQL Trace**. It is SQL Trace that is actually doing most of the work when it comes to capturing SQL Server events and storing them for later use. SQL Trace is a feature of SQL Server that can be accessed indirectly with the Profiler GUI, system stored procedures, or programmatically using Server Management Objects (SMO).

In essence, SQL Trace is a very simple tool. Its job is just to capture SQL Server-related communication between a client and SQL Server. It acts similarly to a specialized network sniffer that captures traffic on the network related to SQL Server and allows you to see exactly which events are being sent from the client to SQL Server.

Unlike a network sniffer, which allows you to see every byte transversing the network, SQL Trace only captures and processes SQL Server-specific events. Here's how it works.

SQL Server Profiler Architecture

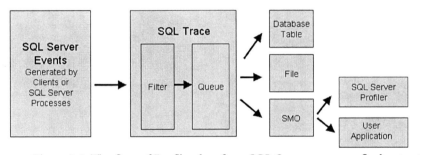

Figure 1-1: The flow of Profiler data from SQL Server events to final output.

First, a SQL Server-related event is created between a client or SQL Server process and SQL Server. Events include many different types of activities and will be described in more detail later. As these events are occurring in SQL Server, it is SQL Trace's job to capture specific SQL Server events that are of interest and to filter out those of no interest.

Once the events are captured, they are queued up in memory. At this point, they can be sent directly to a database table, to a physical file, or to an SMO-based application.

NOTE

Server Management Objects (SMO) is an object model that can be used to directly access SQL Server, including SQL Trace. In fact, the SQL Server Profiler GUI is actually a SMO-based application that interacts with SQL Trace.

In addition to SQL Server Profiler, SQL Server includes many system-stored procedures that use the SMO object model to interact with SQL Trace. We will discuss these system-stored procedures later on. Developers can also directly access SQL Trace using SMO objects, although this topic is not discussed in this book.

In effect, this means that SQL Trace is a black box that we can't directly access. All we can do is to interact with it indirectly with various tools. In our case, these tools will be Profiler and system-stored procedures.

PROFILER TERMINOLOGY

At school, I hated learning new terminology. Unfortunately, there is some basic Profiler terminology that we need to thoroughly understand before we can proceed any further. We will introduce four key terms now and expound on them later when appropriate.

These terms are:

- Events
- Data columns
- Filters
- Trace

EVENTS

I have already used this term several times, without properly explaining what an event is. Essentially, it is the occurrence of some defined action inside SQL Server. The execution of a stored procedure is one example of an event. SQL Server Profiler allows you to capture over 170 different SQL Server-related events. An **Event Category** is a group of related events. For example, the Stored Procedure event category groups together all events relating to the execution of a stored procedure. This event category will include events that, for example, allow you to capture information about when a procedure started executing, completed executing, and so on. The term **Event Class** refers to an event, and all of the **data columns** associated with it.

DATA COLUMNS

Every event that can be captured includes a group of related data that describes that event and is stored in what are called data columns. Think of an event as a row in a database and data columns as the columns in a worksheet. Different events are associated with different data columns, and not every data column is available for every event, as you can see in Figure 1-2.

Events	ApplicationName	BinaryData	ClientProcessID	DatabaseID	DatabaseName	Duration	EndTime
Stored Procedures							
Deprecated							
RPC Output Parameter	☐		☐	☐	☐		
RPC:Completed	☐	☐	☐	☐	☐	☐	☐
RPC:Starting	☐	☐	☐	☐	☐		
SP:CacheHit	☐		☐	☐	☐		
SP:CacheInsert	☐		☐	☐	☐		
SP:CacheMiss	☐		☐	☐			
SP:CacheRemove	☐		☐	☐	☐		
SP:Completed	☑	☑	☑	☑	☑	☑	☑
SP:Recompile	☐		☐	☐	☐		

Figure 1-2: The left column above shows some of the available events for the Event Class called Stored Procedures. The columns to the right are the data columns that include the data captured for each event.

Examples of the data columns for a stored procedure event include EventClass, TextData, ApplicationName, Reads, Writes, and Duration. Profiler offers 64 different event columns, although no event uses all of the available data columns. This data is very useful to the DBA or developer when analyzing specific events.

FILTERS

Many times you will want to capture information about a certain event, but only when it occurs under specific circumstances, rather than every single time the event occurs. For example, maybe you only want to capture events from a selected user, a specific application, or for a given database. Filters allow you to tell Profiler not to collect the events (rows) that you don't want to save or view.

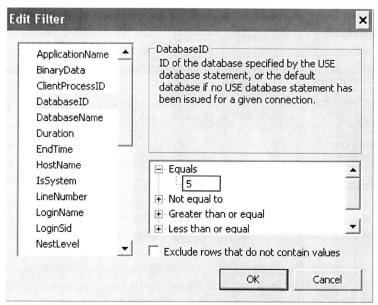

Figure 1-3: The above is an example of how you create a filter with Profiler. In the above example, we are filtering out all events that are not generated by the database with a DatabaseID of 5.

TRACES

A **trace** includes the events and data columns you collect and is usually stored in a physical file for later examination. A trace file can be saved in many ways.

It can be:

- Stored in memory of Profiler
- Exported to a proprietary Profiler file format
- Exported to a database table
- Exported to an XML file

In essence, your goal is to use Profiler to capture and save trace files for analysis.

EventClass	TextData	ApplicationName	NTUserName	LoginName	CPU	Reads	Writes	Duration
SQL:BatchStarting	select o.name, schema_...	SQLDMO_1	Brad	BRAD-LAPTOP\Brad				
SQL:BatchCompleted	select o.name, schema_...	SQLDMO_1	Brad	BRAD-LAPTOP\Brad	172	356	0	865
SQL:BatchStarting	select o.name, schema_...	SQLDMO_1	Brad	BRAD-LAPTOP\Brad				
SQL:BatchCompleted	select o.name, schema_...	SQLDMO_1	Brad	BRAD-LAPTOP\Brad	63	359	0	284
SQL:BatchStarting	exec sp_MShelptype nul...	SQLDMO_1	Brad	BRAD-LAPTOP\Brad				
SQL:BatchCompleted	exec sp_MShelptype nul...	SQLDMO_1	Brad	BRAD-LAPTOP\Brad	78	558	0	893
Audit Logout		SQLDMO_1	Brad	BRAD-LAPTOP\Brad	2735	19...	3	13093

Figure 1-4: This is a small example of an actual trace displayed in Profiler. It shows events as rows and data columns as columns.

GETTING STARTED WITH PROFILER

Now that we have covered the basics, we're going to start using the tool. You will get the most out of this book if you read it sitting in front of your computer, having access to a test or production SQL Server 2005 instance, Management Studio, and SQL Server Profiler. While you may be wary of working on a production instance, you need not be. Most of what we will do with Profiler will have minimal performance impact and can't hurt your production instance. There are a couple of exceptions to this, and I will clearly point them out at the appropriate time.

While a test server is perfectly adequate, the advantage of using a production instance is that you will be able to capture real and interesting events. If you only have access to a test SQL Server instance, you will want to write a script to simulate some database activity, so you can better follow the examples in this book. The following script, for example, does nothing special, except put a small load on your server so that you are able to capture some Profiler Events. As an alternative, there are several SQL Server stress tools on the market (Google "SQL Server stress test") that you may want to download and try. Most of these have free trial periods that will be more than adequate for simulating a SQL Server load for Profiler to trace while you are following the examples in this book.

```
USE [AdventureWorks]
EXECUTE dbo.uspGetEmployeeManagers 1
GO

SELECT   *
FROM     Production.Product ;
GO

SELECT   *
FROM     Production.Product
WHERE    [ReorderPoint] > 500
         OR [ReorderPoint] < 1000 ;
GO

SELECT   *
FROM     Production.ProductInventory ;
GO

SELECT   *
FROM     Sales.SalesOrderDetail ;
GO

SELECT   *
FROM     Production.TransactionHistory ;
GO
```

PERMISSIONS REQUIRED TO USE PROFILER

As you might imagine, you don't want just anyone to create, view, or play back a Profiler trace. If that were possible, anyone could see the data moving between client applications and SQL Server.

By default, only an SA, or a member of the SYSADMIN group, can create and run a Profiler trace, or replay an existing trace. In SQL Server 2005, it is now possible for SAs or SYSADMINs to grant Profiler permission to any SQL Server user. This, of course, is a potentially dangerous permission to assign, so it must be done with utmost discretion.

To assign SQL Server Login ID permission to use Profiler, an SA or member of the **SYSADMIN**s group must grant the **ALTER TRACE** permission, like this:

```
USE master;
GRANT ALTER TRACE TO LoginID;
GO
```

To remove this permission, use this statement:

```
USE master;
REVOKE ALTER TRACE FROM LoginID;
GO
```

HOW TO START UP PROFILER

There are a couple of ways you can start up the Profiler GUI. Use whichever option is more convenient for you and appropriate to the operating system you are using. The following example assumes that you are using Vista as your desktop OS to run Profiler.

If you are at the Desktop, go to:

Start → All Programs → Microsoft SQL Server 2005 → Performance Tools → SQL Server Profiler.

Or, if you have Management Studio or the Database Engine Tuning Advisor already open, then in each case you can go to:

Tools → SQL Server Profiler

Or, if you prefer the Command prompt, type in the following and press **ENTER.**:

profiler90

Personally, I think all of the above options are too much work. I prefer to create a Profiler shortcut and add it to my Quick Launch bar.

At this point, you can begin following along with me on your own computer. It is a great way to speed up your mastery of Profiler.

GETTING FAMILIAR WITH THE PROFILER GUI

In this section, we take a brief look at the Profiler GUI, so we have a frame of reference for when we drill down into the details of this tool. Once Profiler is launched, using any of the techniques described above, you get the less-than-intuitive and informational screen shown in figure 1-5:

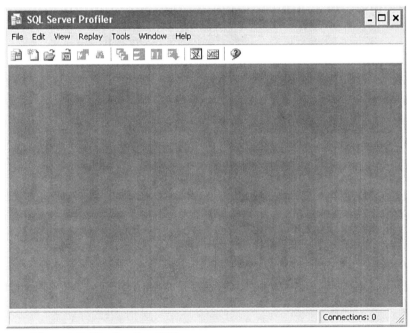

Figure 1-5: The Profiler GUI.

I'm betting that Microsoft must have spent over a million dollars just to design this screen, as it is so useful. Or maybe they saved a million dollars. I'm not sure which.

Seriously though, am I the only one who finds this user interface a little hard to figure out? For example, what's your first step? Even the icons at the top of the screen confuse me. But again, I have problems reading most street signs, so perhaps I am not a good person to offer an opinion.

To get Profiler up and running, click on the File menu (see Figure 1-6 below). From here, it gets easier, I promise.

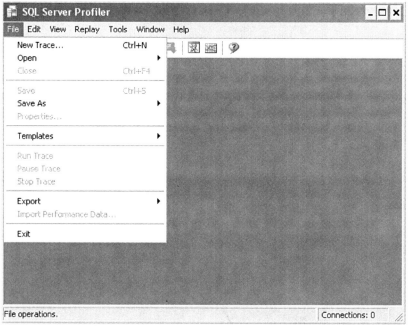

Figure 1-6: The File menu is where you begin using Profiler.

We will eventually examine all the options available in this menu, and the rest of the GUI, but for now, selecting "New Trace" is the best way to get started. After selecting "New Trace", you get a screen similar to the one shown in Figure 1-7.

Figure 1-7: You must always log in to Profiler before you can use it.

As we already discussed, not just anyone can use Profiler to capture SQL Server trace data. So before we can begin using Profiler for any task, we have to log in for SQL Server to verify that we have the proper permissions to use Profiler.

In order to log in, we must tell Profiler what kind of server we want to Profile (Database Engine or Analysis Services), the name of the server we want to access with Profiler, and the kind of authentication we want to use in order to have our credentials verified. This is all straightforward, and is exactly how we log in to Management Studio.

Assuming we have the proper credentials and have selected a running instance of SQL Server, we will see the following screen after clicking on "Connect."

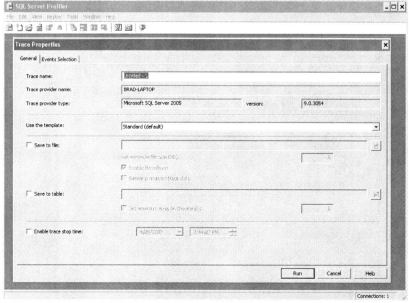

Figure 1-8: The Trace Properties screen is where you start to create a trace.

As you can see, there are lots of options on the first tab of this screen ("General"), and a second tab ("Events Selection") that we haven't even looked at yet. To keep things easy, we are going to start out by explaining the top two parts of this screen, then save the rest for later sections. No point overwhelming ourselves too soon.

So, let's first take a closer look at the top portion of the Trace Properties screen, as seen in Figure 1-9:

Figure 1-9: You should assign traces a name so you can easily refer to them.

One of the first things you need to do when you create a new Profiler trace is to give it a name. If you don't, then Profiler will automatically assign an easy-to-remember name (not), such as Untitled-1, for you. Assign a descriptive name that will make it easy for you to remember what this particular trace is for.

Notice that the next three boxes are grayed out. This is great; these are all filled in for you. If you are not in a big hurry, you might want to verify that the information is correct:

- **Trace Provider Name** should be the name of the SQL Server instance you are going to Profile
- **Trace Provider Type** should be the version name of the SQL Server instance Profile you are going to capture
- **Version** is the numerical version of the SQL Server instance you are profiling

Here's some "inside info". SQL Server Profiler can capture Profiler traces of both SQL Server 2000 and 2005. Events and data columns will vary somewhat with each version, but that is to be expected as the feature set between product versions is somewhat different.

If any of these is not what you expect, you probably logged in to the wrong instance and need to exit Profiler and start over again.

Now let's take a brief look at the second, "Use the template", section of this screen, as seen in Figure 1-10:

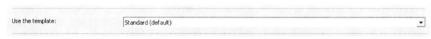

Figure 1-10: Templates are a powerful feature of Profiler.

So what exactly is a template? Remember when we defined events, data columns, filters, and traces earlier? Essentially, a template is a predefined trace, which includes predefined events, data columns, and filters. Profiler comes with a variety of templates you can use, or you can create your own. Once you create your own template, you can use it over and over again, saving a lot of time.

We are going to return to the theme of templates later chapters, but for now all you need to understand is that in Profiler, the Standard template is the default, which means that the events and data columns that define this template have already been selected and are ready for use. You can see which events are covered by this template by clicking on the "Events Selection" tab, although we will save the details of that to the next chapter.

This means that, without any further work, simply click the "Run" button and you can start collecting trace data, which is exactly what we will do next!

CAPTURING BASIC TRACES

Finally, we get to do some fun stuff! Up to this point, all we have covered is background information. Now we get to perform our first trace. The goal of this section is to show you how to start, pause, and stop traces, and learn when you should use each option. We will be using the Standard (default) predefined trace template, and accept all the Profiler default options.

NOTE

If you want to follow the examples, but don't have a production SQL Server to connect to, consider running the T-SQL code provided earlier. You will need to run it in Management Studio each time you want to simulate some SQL Server activity.

Please note before you start running any trace in Profiler, that the collected events are stored in the RAM of the computer where Profiler is running. So, if you are at the server, valuable RAM is being used by Profiler to store this data. That is why it is a good idea to run Profiler on a computer other than the SQL Server you are monitoring. This way, SQL Server doesn't have to compete for memory with Profiler. At some point, it is possible for your computer to run out of RAM to hold all the Profiler events. When this happens, your computer begins to use the Operating System swap file for additional memory, greatly slowing down your computer. Later in the book we will talk about how to avoid this problem. For now, just keep your traces short to prevent any unexpected problems.

HOW TO START A TRACE

Let's start at the beginning:

Step 1: Start Profiler.

Step 2: Select File→New Trace

Step 3: The "Connect to Server" screen appears. Log in to the SQL Server instance you want to profile. This can be any running SQL Server instance.

Step 4: You should now be at the "Trace Properties" screen. For now, we are going to leave all the options at their default setting. This is because our goal now is to learn how to start a trace, and nothing more.

Step 5: To start your first trace, click on "Run" at the bottom of the screen. Congratulations! You have just learned how to start a Profiler trace. The trace screen now appears (see figure 1-11). As new trace events occur, you will see them appear on the screen. As you can imagine, the events you see in the figure below will be different from the events you will be capturing.

While we are at this screen, there are a few things you need to learn. First, be aware that each row on the screen is an event that has been captured by Profiler. Second, each column on the screen represents a different data column. Notice again that not all events include all data columns. This trace has many data columns, and they are not all shown on this screen. You can scroll to the right to see them all.

The screen itself is divided into two areas. The top portion of the screen lists the events. The bottom portion of the screen (the gray area) shows you the complete contents of the **TextData** data column. If you can't see all the TextData in the lower window, you can choose to resize the height of the two windows, or you can scroll either of the two windows up and down to view the TextData.

At the very bottom left of this screen, notice the message "Trace is running" which tells you that the current state of the trace. Other messages that can appear here are "Trace is paused" and "Trace is stopped."

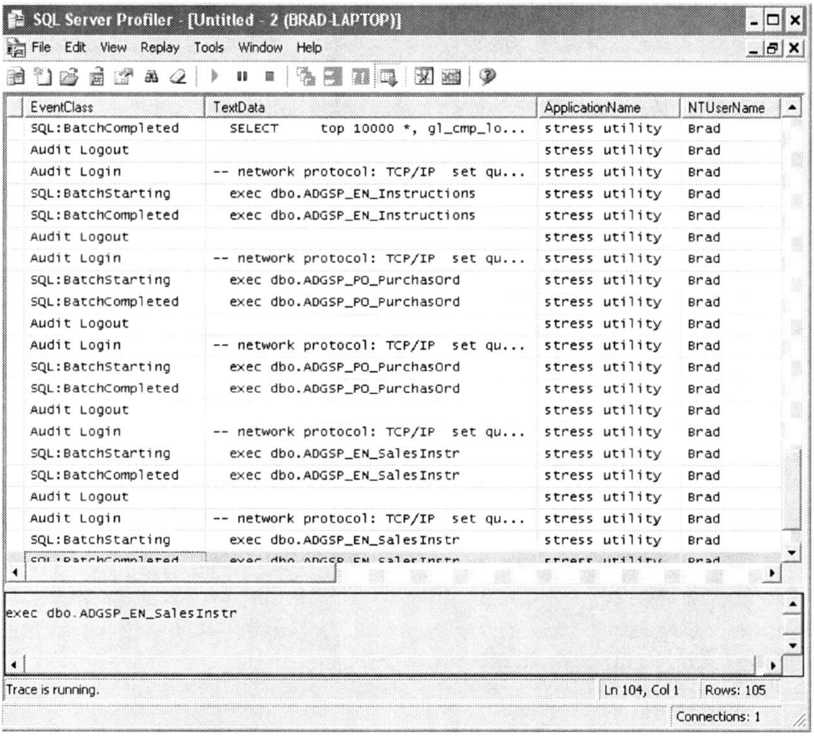

Figure 1-11: A partial screen shot of a running trace.

At the bottom right of the screen, you see several different types of information. First is the Line and Column number of the row that is currently selected by the cursor. In this case, it is Line 104 and Column 1. "Rows" refers to the total number of rows (or events) that have been captured so far. When a trace is running, this number generally increments very quickly.

As you view a live trace, new events are continually added and displayed on the screen. In our example, new events are being added to the bottom of the top window.

HOW TO PAUSE A TRACE

Pausing a trace means exactly what is says. When you pause a trace, you are telling Profiler to stop collecting events and wait until you either restart the trace or stop it. When you restart a paused trace, any events that occurred between the time you paused and unpaused it are gone and can't be recovered. But when you restart (unpause) the trace, Profiler will again begin collecting events, adding them to the screen from the moment you unpaused.

Pausing and unpausing a trace can be handy when you are trying to "capture" an event with the Profiler without collecting more events than you need. Think of pausing as a way as to control when you collect data, and when you don't, for short Profiler trace captures.

There are two ways to pause Profiler from the GUI. First, you can select the File menu at the top of the screen and select "Pause Trace." Or, you can click on the "Pause Trace" icon, which looks like this:

Figure 1-12: You can pause a trace by clicking on the Pause icon.

If you haven't done so already, give it a try and pause the trace. When the trace is paused, you will see "Trace is paused" at the bottom left of the screen.

To unpause a trace, you can either select the File Menu at the top of the screen and select "Run Trace", or you can click on the "Start Selected Trace" icon, which looks like this:

Figure 1-13: You can unpause a trace by clicking on the Start Selected Trace icon.

HOW TO STOP A TRACE

When you decide to stop a trace, you are telling Profiler that you are completely done with this trace and do not want to restart it later. If you attempt to start a trace after it has been stopped, it will delete the event data from the old trace from memory and start fresh. So, only stop a trace if you know that you don't want to restart it later.

There are two ways to stop a Profiler trace from the GUI. First, you can select the File menu at the top of the screen and select "Stop Trace." Or, you can click on the "Stop Trace" icon, which looks like this:

Figure 1-14: You can stop a trace by clicking on the Stop Trace icon.

After stopping a trace, you will see the message "Trace is stopped" at the bottom left of the screen. Once a trace is stopped, you can view it or save it for later viewing. We will learn how to save a trace later in this chapter.

HOW TO CLEAR A TRACE

Clearing a trace allows you to remove the current trace results from RAM. If you have saved these results, the saved results aren't affected by this option; only the RAM is cleared. I rarely need to use this option, as starting a new trace automatically clears the current trace.

There are two ways to clear a Profiler trace using the GUI. First, you can select the Edit menu at the top of the screen and select "Clear Trace Window." Or, you can click on the "Clear Trace Window" icon, which looks like this:

Figure 1-15: You can clear a trace from memory by clicking on the Clear Trace Window icon.

Once you have cleared a trace, you can start a new trace at any time.

HOW TO SAVE A COMPLETED TRACE TO A FILE

In many cases, you will want to save your Profiler traces. You may not have time right away to analyze the trace, you may want more time to analyze the data, you may want to share the data with others, or to archive the trace results so you can compare them to traces taken later. In this section, we take a look at how to save a trace after it has been captured and stored in RAM. In the next chapter, I'll explain how to save a trace as it is being run.

Traces can be stored in a trace file (.trc format) or directly in a database table. In almost all cases, you will want to store traces in the trace file format, as it is the most efficient way to store them. Should you decide you want to store your traces in a database table, we will show you how to do that in a later chapter.

If you are following on your computer, start the default trace we have already been discussing. Be sure that some trace events have been captured in the trace window.

Now, let's save the trace to a trace file.

Step 1: Stop the trace. While it is not required to stop a trace before you save it, it makes sense that you would only really need to save a trace once it is complete and has been stopped.

Step 2: From the main menu, select File → Save, and you will get a standard Windows save dialog box. You can choose to save trace files anywhere you want. By default, trace files are stored under My Documents. You must give the trace file a name. So choose any folder and filename that works for you, then click "Save," and the file is saved. If you have accidentally selected a name already used, you will be asked if you want to overwrite the older file.

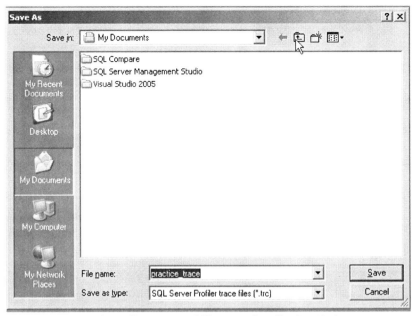

Figure 1-16: Trace files are saved like any other files in Windows.

The trace has now been saved. Notice that the trace is still in RAM. Saving a trace does not affect the trace currently in RAM. At this point, you can choose to clear the trace, start a new trace (which clears the current trace), or exit Profiler, which also clears the trace from RAM.

HOW TO LOAD A SAVED TRACE

Once you have created and saved a trace, it is very common for a user to want to reload it into the Profiler GUI for additional analysis. For our example, let's assume that we want to load the trace we just created in the previous section. If you are following on your own computer and have not done so yet, exit Profiler, so we can all start from the beginning.

Follow these steps to load an existing trace file.

Step 1: Start Profiler.

Step 2: Next, select File → Open → Trace File, as shown below.

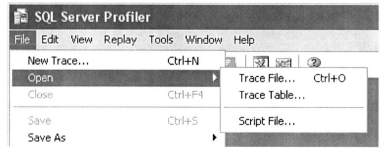

Figure 1-17: How to open an existing trace file.

Step 3: A new screen appears.

Select the trace you want to open and click on the "Open" button, and the trace will appear, just like it did after you did the initial trace capture.

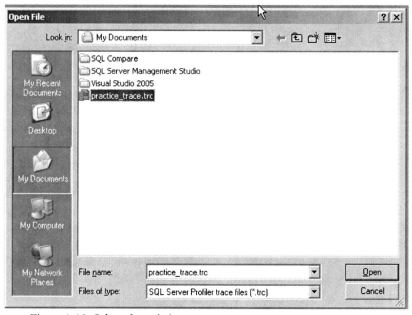

Figure 1-18: Select the existing trace you want to open.

SUMMARY

Believe it or not, you have just mastered the basics of getting Profiler up and running. Without wishing to scare you, though, it has to be said that we have barely scratched the surface of what Profiler is capable of and we have a long way to go. But we have made a good start.

Now, let's drill down and learn how to master this powerful, though inelegant, tool.

Chapter 2
WORKING WITH TRACES AND TEMPLATES

As you have probably guessed, there is a lot more to Profiler than using the default template and simply clicking "run". More usually, you'll want to create and save your own custom traces, tailored to the specific problem you are trying to solve.

The first goal of this chapter is to introduce you to the fundamentals of creating a new trace using a simple example. This will include selecting events and data columns, applying filters, ordering columns, as well as running the trace and saving it to a file or to a database table. Although this book is focused on profiling database engine events, I'll also briefly show you how you can apply the same knowledge of creating traces to profiling Analysis Server events.

We will then return to the topic of **templates**. Creating your own custom traces is a fundamental skill, but it would be a mistake to dismiss the built-in templates that Profiler provides, as they can save you a lot of time and effort.

We'll examine these built-in templates first, then investigate how to modify them to create your own custom templates, finally to build your own template from scratch. We'll even see how to import and export templates, as Exceptional DBAs often maintain a collection of Profiler Trace templates that they share with co-workers and other DBAs.

UNDERSTANDING THE EVENTS SELECTION OPTIONS

In Chapter 1, we spent all of our time on the "General" tab of the Profiler GUI, barely glancing at the "Events Selection" tab. Before we start creating custom traces, we need to quickly review this tab. Its name is not very accurate, since not only does it allow you to select events, but also to sort events, select data columns, and to filter events.

If you leave all the default options on the General tab, and switch over to Events Selection, you'll see the screen shown in Figure 2-1:

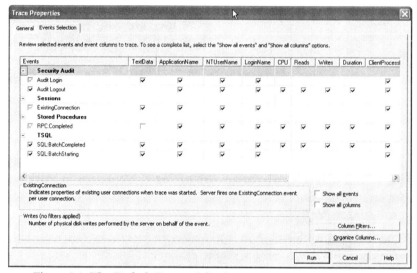

Figure 2-1: The Default Events Selection screen

NOTE:

Figure 2-1 is not quite the "default" Events Selection screen. I've expanded the data columns so you can read their names in full. You do this by simply dragging the right edge of the column across, or double-clicking on it. Unfortunately, changes in column width are not saved, so the next time you bring up Trace Properties window, you will have to repeat this step.

The first column on the screen is "Events". This is where you select one or more events to be captured in your trace. Here, we can see four event categories (in bold) and six events. All the remaining columns are the available data columns associated with each event. A checked box in a column means that the data column will be captured for that event. The existence of an empty box means that the data column in question is available for the given event, but is currently not set to collect data. For example, in figure 2-1, the **TextData** data column is available for the **RPC:Completed** event, but is not selected. If there is no box, then the data column is not available for that event – for example The **CPU, Reads, Writes** and **Duration** data columns are not available for the **ExistingConnection** event.

In Figure 2-1, Profiler is showing you a default selection of events and database columns: those that comprise the Default template. In fact, this is just a small subset of the events and data column that are available to you. In order to see them all, simply check the "Show all events" and the "Show all columns" check boxes in the lower right portion of the screen:

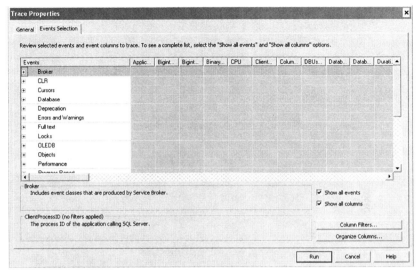

Figure 2-2: The Events Selection screen showing all events.

The screen is now showing you only "event categories," not specific events. This is why there are no longer any options to select or deselect the data columns. To see specific events, you have to click on the plus sign next to each event category, at which point the check boxes for the data columns will reappear.

Directly below the rows and columns that represent the event and column data to be collected are two Help boxes. In Figure 2-3 below, you see that the "Broker" event category is named in the top Help box, and below that is a brief description of the events found in this event category.

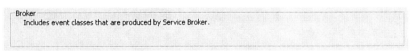

Figure 2-3: This Help box is for events.

In Figure 2-4 below, the bottom Help box says "ClientProcessID (no filters applied), with a short description below. This Help box describes the data column the mouse is hovering over. So if you move the mouse to other data columns, you will see different Help information for each different data column. The words "no filters applied" tell you that no filter has been applied to this data column. We will learn more about filters shortly.

Figure 2-4: This Help box is for data columns.

Now that we understand how the two Help boxes work, let's take a quick look at the remaining part of the Trace Properties screen, as shown in Figure 2-5 below.

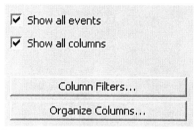

Figure 2-5: This portion of the Trace Properties screen allows you to perform many more tasks than you might imagine.

As we have seen, the top options shown in Figure 2-5 allow you to show, or not show, all the available events and data columns. I leave these options on when I am selecting which events and data columns to collect for a particular trace, so I can see what is available. I am getting old and can't remember as well as I used to, but once I have selected all the events and data columns I want to trace, I often deselect these two options. When you do this, only the events and data columns you have selected remain, making the screen a bit easier to read.

The "Column Filters..." button allows you to filter out any events (together with their data columns) that you don't want to capture. The "Organize Columns..." option is used to perform two tasks. First, you can use it to arrange the order of the data columns on the screen when a trace is running. Second, it allows you to group events by a single event type. Both these are large subjects and deserve their own sections; they are discussed later.

Now that you know your way around both tabs, we can move on to see how to create a new trace from scratch. While you don't have to follow the order I have outlined below, it is a practical approach and you might want to follow it closely until you have gained more experience with Profiler.

CREATING A CUSTOM TRACE FROM SCRATCH

In Chapter 1, we used all the default options and the default template to create a Profiler trace. In this section, you will learn the fundamentals of creating a new trace from scratch, using a simple example. In later chapters of this book, we will apply the fundamentals we learn here to more practical and complex solutions, but the fundamentals remain the same.

We won't look at every possible option, as there is no point confusing you with complex information before you have mastered the basics. Essentially, to create a new trace, you follow these steps:

1. Start Profiler and log in to a SQL Server instance
2. Create a new trace definition and assign it a name
3. Specify that you want to save the trace file, and how to save it
4. Select the specific events you want to trace
5. Select the data columns for each event you want to trace
6. Create any filters you might want to use
7. Order the data columns, along with deciding what column to group by
8. Start the trace
9. End the trace, once you have captured all the data you want to collect

STEP 1: START PROFILER

If you are following on your own computer, start Profiler using one of the options described in Chapter 1, so that the following introductory screen appears.

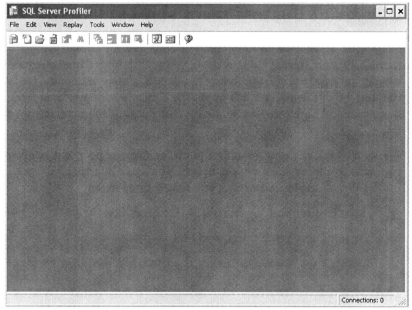

Figure 2-6: This is where we always start when creating a new trace.

STEP 2: CREATE A NEW TRACE DEFINITION

Next, select **File→ New Trace**, then log on to the SQL Server instance you want to practice with. Once you have logged in, the Trace Properties screen appears.

Now we can begin creating our own new trace. Next to "Trace Name" give this trace some name you will remember, such as **Profiler_Practice**, or whatever you prefer.

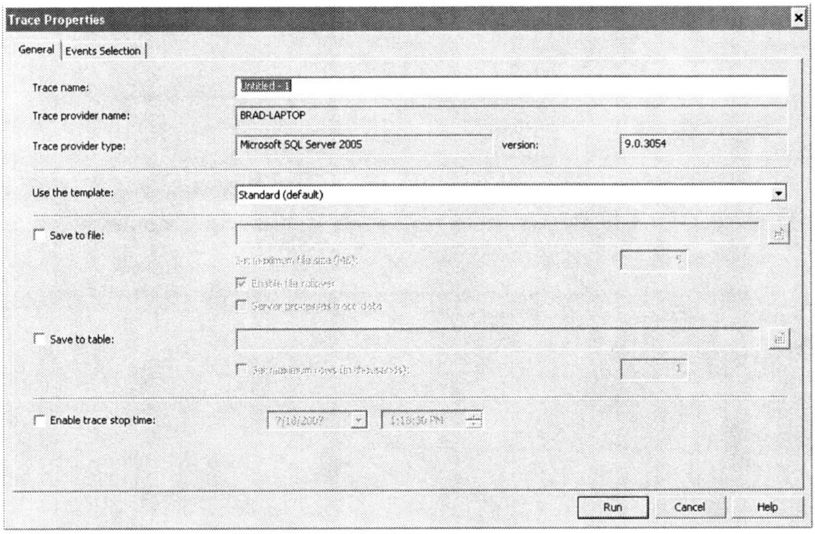

Figure 2-7: The Trace Properties screen is where we create new traces.

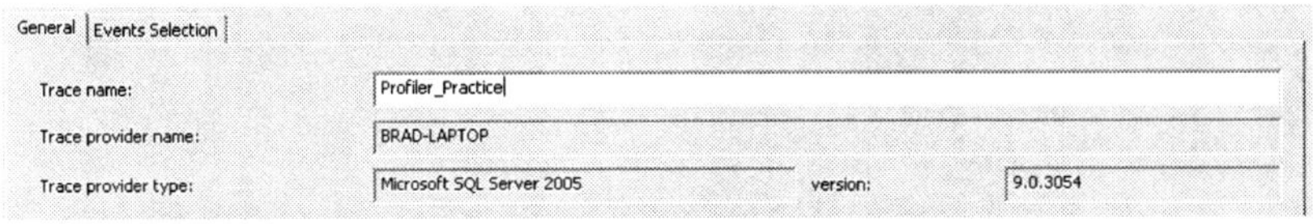

Figure 2-8: Enter a name for your first trace.

Next to "Use the template," use the drop-down menu to select "Blank."
This tells Profiler that you don't want to use a pre-existing template and
that you want to set all the trace options manually. The "Blank" option is
at the very top of the drop-down list, so you may have to scroll up to see
it.

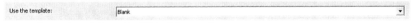

Figure 2-9: Select the "Blank" template.

STEP 3: SAVING THE TRACE TO FILE

Up to this point, we have not done much different from before. Now it
is time to do something new. In Chapter 1, as we were running the trace,
the data was stored only in RAM, which is the default behavior. Only
after the trace was complete did we save the results to file.

For this new trace, we want Profiler to store the results in a physical file
on a local hard disk, as well as in RAM, as the trace data is being
collected. As you gain more experience with Profiler, you will find

yourself wanting to save trace files, and specifying this now can save a little time.

NOTE:

A little later in the chapter, I'll show you how to save a trace directly to a database table (although this is not recommended, because of performance issues).

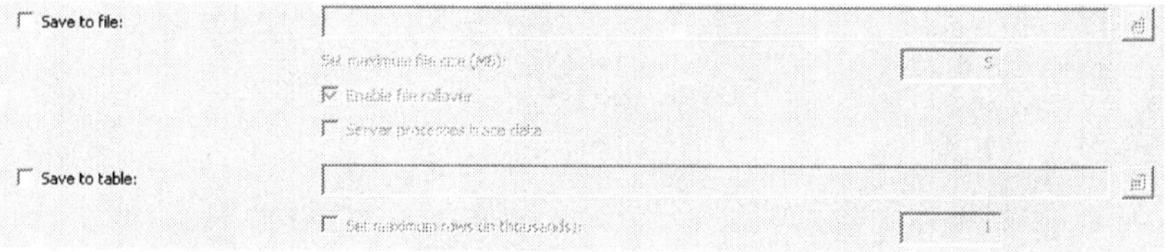

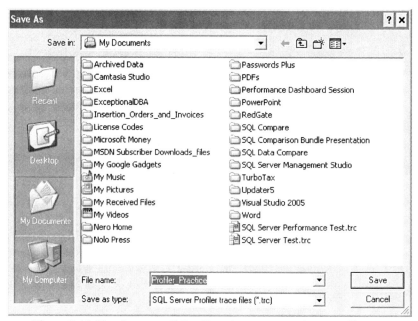

Figure 2-10: Automatically saving a trace to a file.

To tell Profiler that you want the trace to be automatically saved as a trace file, select the option "Save to File." When you click on this option, you immediately get a "Save As" dialog box:

Figure 2-11: You have to tell Profiler where to store the trace file.

By default, traces are stored under "My Documents". If you would prefer to store traces somewhere else, that's fine. Notice that the "File Name" for the trace is the same name you assigned the trace. You can use this name, or choose a different name, whichever option works best for you. In addition, trace files have a .trc extension. While the file format used to store trace data is proprietary, it is an efficient way to store traces. We can, as we will discover later, convert the trace data into different formats, but for now, we will stick with the .trc format, which works well.

Once you assign the trace file a name, you are returned to the Trace Properties screen, which now looks slightly different,

Figure 2-12: Once you choose to save a trace file, you have several options to choose from.

The first option you have available is to "Set maximum file size (MB)." The default value is 5 MB. Depending on how busy your server is, and how many events and data columns you are collecting, it doesn't take long for a trace file to get huge. This option allows you to control the size of the saved trace file. You can choose any file size you want, up to the available space on your disk.

The next option, "Enable file rollover" is directly related to the "Set maximum file size (MB)." By default, this option is selected. What this means is that when your trace file reaches 5 MB (or whatever size you specify), a new file will be created to store the trace data. The new file name will be the original .trc filename with a number appended to it, such as Profiler_Practice_1. This rollover effect will continue until you stop the trace or you run out of disk space. If you don't select this option, the trace will automatically stop when the maximum file size you specified is reached.

As a DBA, you must decide what the best compromise is between file size and file rollover. For now, I suggest you accept the defaults. When you have gained some experience, you will be in a better position to be able to determine what values work best for you.

However, be warned: when you begin practicing using Profiler, carefully watch the size and quantity of your rollover files. Depending on your server, you can create a lot of data very quickly, much faster than you might expect. You don't want to receive a nasty "Out of Disk Space" error. And one more tip: be sure to delete traces once you no longer need them. Again, they can take up a lot of disk space, potentially causing you future problems.

The next option is called "Server processes trace data," which we will save for the next chapter, as it is an advanced option.

STEP 4: SELECTING THE EVENTS TO TRACE

When I create a trace, the first thing I like to do is to select the events I want to capture. Since this is a practice trace, we don't want to select a lot of events. Our goal is learn the overall picture now, and we will focus on specific details later in this book. For our practice example, let's assume that we want to trace all Stored Procedure events. In order to select these events, we have to click on the plus sign next to the "Stored Procedures" event category, and the events specific to stored procedures are displayed on the screen. See Figure 2-12 below.

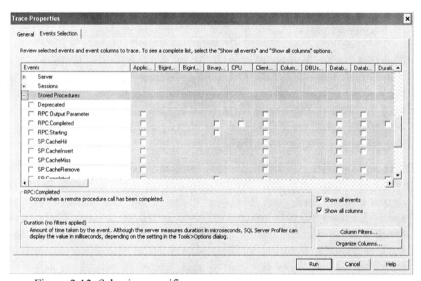

Figure 2-13: Selecting specific events to trace.

As you can see, the "Stored Procedures" event class has many specific events associated with it. In addition, you can see from the figure above that there are different data columns associated with each event.

To capture all the Stored Procedure events in the Stored Procedures category, click on each of the events as shown below. Not all are displayed on the screen, so you will need to scroll down a little to view and select them all.

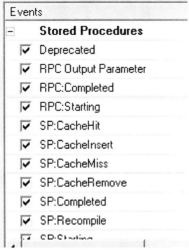

Figure 2-14: We have elected to trace all stored procedure events.

Essentially, that is all there is to selecting events to trace. You can select as many events as you want, although I should warn you that the more you select, the more data you collect and the more SQL Server resources you consume.

STEP 5: SELECTING THE DATA COLUMNS

Now that we have selected the events we want to trace, our next step is to select the data columns associated with the events we want to capture, for which we want to collect and store information. As you select your desired events, every data column available for that event is automatically selected.

While you can leave them all selected if you want, it is always a better choice to only select those you need, in order to minimize resource overhead. This means you need to deselect those columns you don't need.

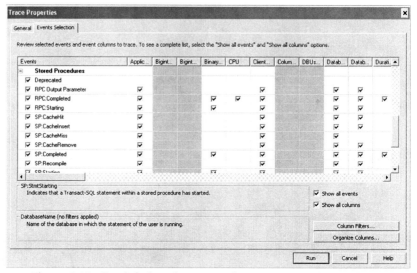

Figure 2-15: By default, when you select an event, all the data columns associated with that event are automatically selected.

However, to keep things simple for this example, let's keep all of the data columns selected. We will learn later in the book which data columns are the best selected, and which data columns are best not selected.

STEP 6: APPLYING FILTERS

Now we enter new territory. We are going to learn how to apply a filter to a trace. Remember, a filter is a way to reduce the number of events we collect in a trace. For example, if we only want to collect trace events for a single connection, or for a single database, we can do simply that. This reduces the amount of data that is stored in our trace. Using filters is optional, but very useful when isolating what data is collected during a trace.

To add a filter to a trace, click on the "Column Filters..." button, and the "Edit Filter" screen appears.

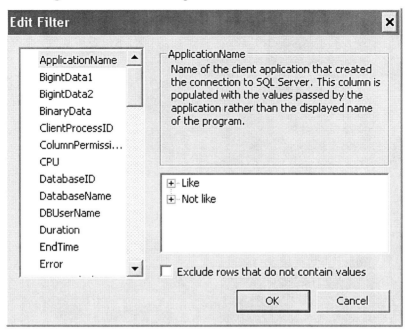

Figure 2-16: Select which trace events to capture using this screen.

On the left-hand side of this screen, you see all the available data columns for all the events you previously selected. On the right-hand side you see where you can add criteria to filter which events are selected and which are not.

You can apply a filter to any of the data columns available. A common filter column is DatabaseName, in order to collect events only from a given database, or to exclude other databases. For example, if Reporting Services is installed on the server you are profiling, you may find that you often use a "Not like ReportServer" filter on the DatabaseName column, in order to prevent your traces being cluttered with events fired on the ReportServer database.

In our practice example, let's choose a filter on the Duration data column, so that we only capture those events that have a duration longer than 100 milliseconds. This way, we filter out very short-running events and only see events than take more than 0.1 seconds to execute. To do this, select the Duration data column and enter 100 in the "Greater than or equal" box.

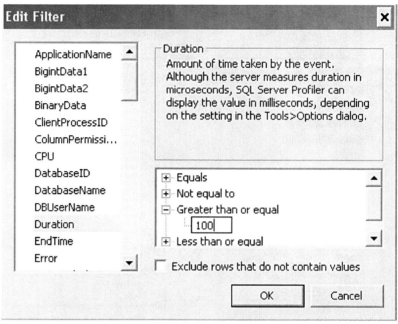

Figure 2-17: We have just added a filter based on the duration data column.

Once you have specified a filter, you can continue to add more. In our case we are done, so we click on "OK" and the filter has been saved for this trace. To verify this, you can click on the "Column Filters..." button again, and you'll see a filter icon next to the Duration column (not shown).

STEP 7: ORDERING THE DATA COLUMNS

Now that a filter has been added, our next step is to select the order in which we want the data columns to be displayed when the trace is run, and to specify whether we want to group events according to a given data column. This is an optional step, but one that you will find quite useful for many traces.

To organize columns, click on the "Organize Columns" button, and the following screen appears.

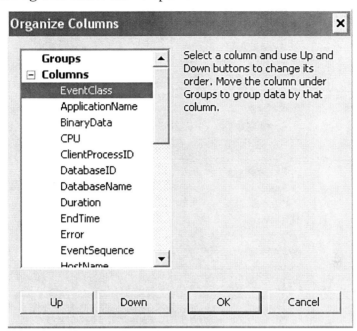

Figure 2-18: The Organize Columns screen

By default, when the Organize Columns screen appears, there is no grouping by events, and data columns are sorted alphabetically, with the exception of EventClass, which always appears first. If you wish to change the order in which the columns are displayed, simply select an event and click the "Up" or "Down" buttons.

For our practice trace, let's say that we want to group events by Duration and leave the remaining data columns in their default order. To group by Duration, click on Duration on the screen, and then click on the "Up" button until it moves up under "Groups," as shown in Figure 2-18:

Once you have completed this step, click on OK to return to the Trace Properties screen.

Can you believe it, we are now done creating our practice trace, and it is ready to run. So let's run it.

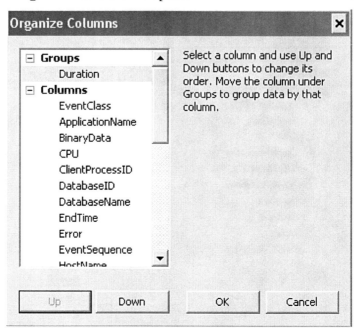

Figure 2-19: With the above setting, captured events will be grouped by duration.

STEP 8: RUNNING THE TRACE

To run your new trace, click on the "Run" button at the bottom of the screen, and the trace begins. You will see a screen similar to the one below, except that your events will look different, as I am using a different database and application than you are. If the server you are monitoring is not being accessed by stored procedures, or if all of them are faster than 0.1 seconds, or if your servers are not doing much, you won't see many results (because of the events and filter we selected). On the other hand, you may be seeing hundreds of events being collected very quickly. It all depends on your server's current workload.

In Figure 2-20, you see that events are sorted by duration, with the shortest running events shown at the top, the longest running at the bottom. The first figure in the Duration column is the elapsed time in milliseconds and it is followed, in brackets, by the number of events that ran in that duration.

The first row shows 35 events with what appears to be no duration. This is not really true. Some events don't have a specific duration. They occur, but their duration is not measured. Because of this, they have a duration of NULL and they show up at the top of the screen without any apparent duration.

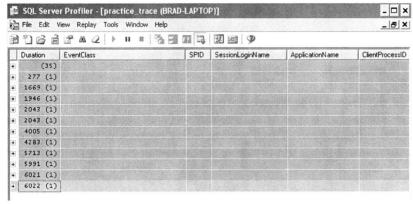

Figure 2-20: This is what a running trace looks like when it is grouped by duration. If you don't group by duration, the screen will look different, as we will see later.

After that, you see other events, starting with a duration of 277 milliseconds all the way to 6,022 milliseconds. In each case, only one event has run in each of these discrete time periods.

To view the actual events, you must click on the plus sign next to the row you want to examine. Let's start with clicking on the 35 events with a NULL duration.

Duration	EventClass	SPID	SessionLoginName	ApplicationName	(
	Trace Start				
	RPC:Starting	53	BRAD-LAPTOP\Brad	SQL Server P...	
	SP:CacheHit	53	BRAD-LAPTOP\Brad	SQL Server P...	
	SP:StmtStarting	53	BRAD-LAPTOP\Brad	SQL Server P...	
	SP:CacheHit	53	BRAD-LAPTOP\Brad	SQL Server P...	
	SP:Starting	53	BRAD-LAPTOP\Brad	SQL Server P...	
	SP:StmtStarting	53	BRAD-LAPTOP\Brad	SQL Server P...	
	SP:CacheMiss	52	BRAD-LAPTOP\Brad	stress utility	
	SP:CacheHit	52	BRAD-LAPTOP\Brad	stress utility	
	SP:Starting	52	BRAD-LAPTOP\Brad	stress utility	
	SP:StmtStarting	52	BRAD-LAPTOP\Brad	stress utility	
	SP:StmtStarting	52	BRAD-LAPTOP\Brad	stress utility	
	SP:CacheMiss	52	BRAD-LAPTOP\Brad	stress utility	
	SP:CacheHit	52	BRAD-LAPTOP\Brad	stress utility	
	SP:Starting	52	BRAD-LAPTOP\Brad	stress utility	

Figure 2-21: The above events don't have a discrete duration.

While I don't want to get into a lot of detail now, you can see that some of the events above represent a stored procedure being executed, and show whether its execution plan was found in SQL Server's buffer cache.

Let's now take a look at one of the discrete events that were captured:

277 (1)			
277	SP:StmtCompleted	52 BRAD-LAPTOP\Brad	stress utility

Figure 2-22: Here is an example of a stored procedure being completed. Note that the duration of this stored procedure execution was 277 milliseconds.

In the above figure, we see that a particular stored procedure ran for 277 milliseconds. Because of the small size of the screen, I can't show you all of the data columns. But if you are following on your computer, you can scroll over and see all the various data columns that have been collected.

STEP 9: STOPPING THE TRACE

Once you've collected enough data, stop the trace by clicking on the "Stop Selected Trace" icon.

Congratulations, you have now created and run your first trace. At this point, you would usually review the collected trace data to identify whatever issue you were looking for. Once you were done, you would exit Profiler. Because we gave the trace a name and saved it as a trace file, this file has automatically been saved on disk for us at the location previously specified.

So, if you exit Profiler now, Profiler will exit, but the trace you made is still saved and can be viewed any time you like by selecting File | Open | Trace File.

If you are done analyzing your trace, you can either archive the trace (store it somewhere so that you can find it again) or delete it to save space.

SAVING TRACES TO A SQL SERVER TABLE

Until this point, we have only talked about saving Profiler traces directly to disk. There is a good reason for this, and that is performance. For the least impact of using Profiler, traces should be originally stored on disk using the standard Profiler file format.

Is this the only option? No. Profiler also allows you to store a Profiler trace directly into a SQL Server table (see Figure 2-5), bypassing a disk file entirely. While this option works fine, it puts a lot of overhead on SQL Server that can negatively affect SQL Server's performance. Because of this, saving a Profiler trace directly to SQL Server is not recommended.

Now you ask, what if I want to store my Profiler traces in SQL Server, not only for the ease of querying the data, but to store it in order to maintain a baseline of Profiler activity? That's not a problem. Instead of saving Profiler trace data directly to a SQL Server database, you should first save it to disk. Then you can import the Profiler trace data into a SQL Server database later. While this is an extra step, it is necessary if you don't want to hurt the performance of the production SQL Server instances you trace. *What about a diff. SQL Server* Within the SQL Server Profiler GUI, it is very easy to save a Profiler *instance* trace to a SQL Server table. To begin, you have to have a trace loaded *If,* into Profiler. To save this file into a SQL Server table, go to the Main *allows* menu and select File | Save As | Trace Table. *this.*

Figure 2-23: Profiler traces can be saved in SQL Server tables using the Trace Table option.

Once you select this option, a new window appears (see figure 2-34 below) prompting you to log into the SQL Server instance where you have the database containing your Profiler traces.

Figure 2-24: Log into any SQL Server instance where you want to store Profiler traces.

Next, you must specify the name of a pre-existing database where you want to store the trace table (see figure 2-25 below). Ideally, you should have a database designed for this specific purpose. In addition, you have to assign the trace table a name. Give it a name that makes it obvious what it is so you can find it later.

Once you click the OK button, the file is automatically moved from Profiler to the database. A new table is automatically created for you, and the data stored in it.

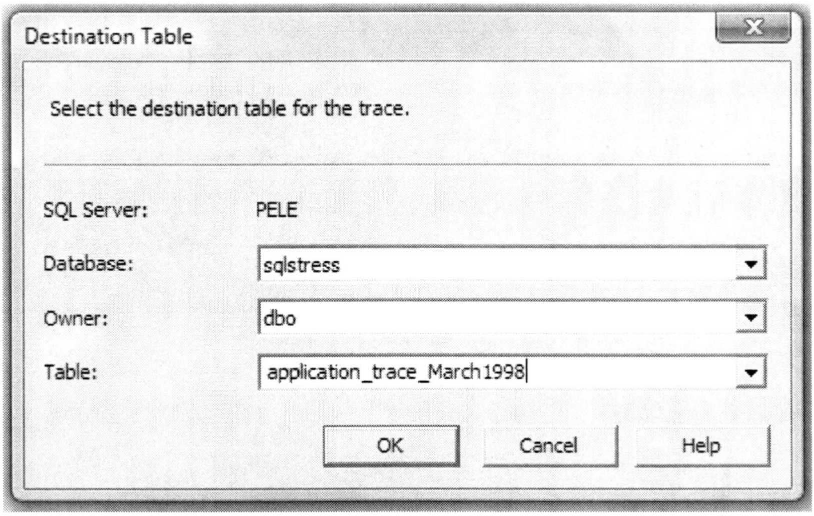

Figure 2-25: Select the database where you want to store Profiler traces.

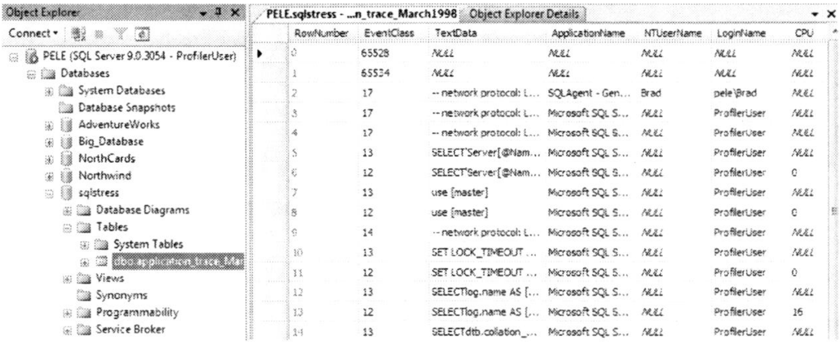

Figure 2-26: This is what the trace looks like inside a SQL Server table.

Once the data has been stored in a SQL Server database, you can access the data just as you would with any other SQL Server data. Many DBAs create their own scripts to analyze the data; others use Reporting Services to create custom reports.

CAPTURING ANALYSIS SERVER TRACES

The focus of this book is on administrative DBAs who work with the SQL Server engine, not Analysis Services. However, starting with SQL Server 2005, DBAs do now have the ability to capture Analysis Services traces, and the process is very similar to the one we've just seen, so what you have already learned can be reapplied here.

To start an Analysis Services Profiler trace, start Profiler and select File | New Trace, just as you do create any trace in Profiler. The only difference is that you select Analysis Services as the Server type:

Figure 2-27 When you start an Analysis Services trace, you must select the appropriate server type.

After you select the appropriate server and login information, click on "Connect" and the Trace Properties screen appears:

As you can see, the General tab is identical to what we have seen before. The only difference is that there are only two built-in templates, plus the blank template available.

Let's choose the Blank template and click on the "Events Selection" tab.

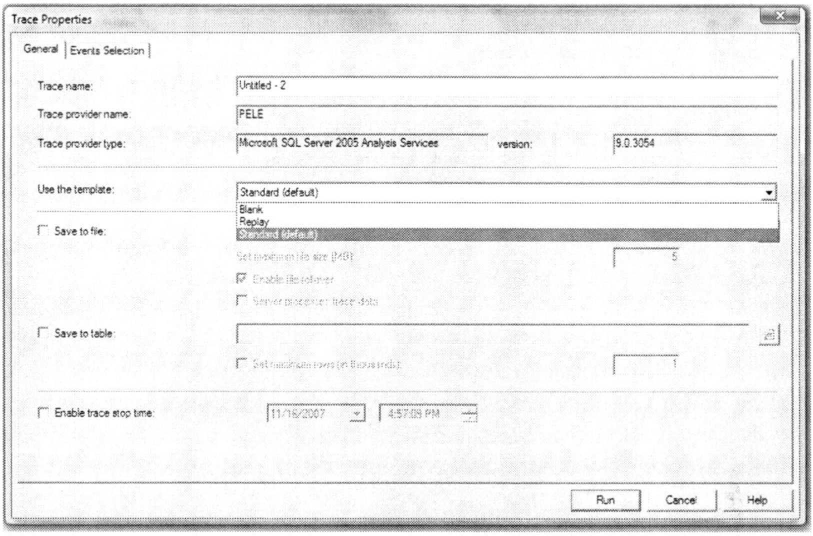

Figure 2-28: Gee, this screen looks familiar.

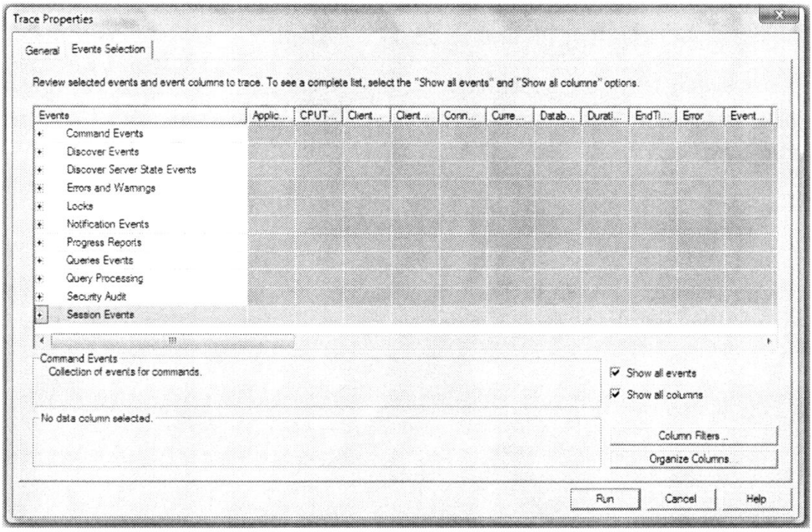

Figure 2-29: The "Events Selection" tab above works just like the "Events Selection" tabs we have seen throughout the entire book.

At first glance, this screen looks very similar to the "Event Selection" tabs we have already seen. In fact, it works identically, but what is different is that Analysis Services has its own set of unique events and data columns, distinct from the database engine, so in fact this is an entirely different world that we have not seen before.

We are confronted with 11 Event Categories, 42 events, and 32 data columns. There is enough material here for another book, and that's why we won't be discussing any of the details of the events and data columns available for Analysis Services.

However, all other aspects of using Profiler are identical so, if you want, you can use what you already know to start experimenting with Analysis Services traces and see how they can help make your data warehousing projects perform better.

CREATING AND USING TRACE TEMPLATES

Now that you know how to create your own trace, it's time to explore further the idea of trace templates. As you might expect, creating custom traces can be a lot of work, especially if you take the care to select only those events and data columns that you really need, apply the appropriate filters, organize the columns as you want them, and so on.

Once you've taken the time to define a trace exactly as you want it in order to investigate a certain SQL Server issue, you certainly would not want to have to go through all that work again next time the issue arose. Instead, you will want to save your custom trace as a trace template, so that you can run it again and again, as required.

Fortunately, Profiler provides a variety of built-in (predefined) templates, and also allows you to define you own. We'll start our investigations with the former.

PREDEFINED PROFILER TEMPLATES

From the General tab in Profiler, you can click on the down arrow of the "Use the Template" drop-down box to see all the available templates:

Figure 2-30: Predefined Profiler templates are listed.

Profiler comes with eight predefined templates for the Database Engine, plus the blank template. At first glance, you may or may not be able to guess what some of these templates are designed to capture. To be honest, until I played with each template, I couldn't figure out what each one was really designed to do, as the template names are not obvious.

To learn how to use predefined templates, we don't have to take an in-depth look at each one. What I want to do is to talk about the first two templates in some detail, so you fully understand the concepts behind templates. The last six templates will then only need a brief mention.

STANDARD (DEFAULT)

This template captures six different events in four event categories: **Security Audit, Sessions, Stored Procedures**, and **TSQL**. It also includes many different data columns, many of which are not included in this screen shot because there is not enough room to show them all.

Events	TextData	ApplicationName	NTUserName	LoginName	CPU	Reads	Writes	Duration	Client...	SPID
Security Audit										
✓ Audit Login	✓	✓	✓	✓					✓	✓
✓ Audit Logout		✓	✓	✓	✓	✓	✓	✓	✓	✓
Sessions										
✓ ExistingConnection	✓	✓	✓	✓					✓	✓
Stored Procedures										
✓ RPC:Completed	☐	✓	✓	✓	✓	✓	✓	✓	✓	✓
TSQL										
✓ SQL:BatchCompleted	✓	✓	✓	✓	✓	✓	✓		✓	✓
✓ SQL:BatchStarting	✓	✓	✓	✓					✓	✓

Figure 2-31: The Standard (default) template collects a wide variety of information.

As you might expect from a fairly complex, general purpose template, the resulting trace (below) can be reasonably complex.

EventClass	TextData	ApplicationName	NTUserNa...	LoginN...	CPU	Reads	Writes
Trace Start							
ExistingConnection	-- network protocol: LPC set quote...	SQLAgent - Generic Refresher	Brad	BRA...			
Audit Login	-- network protocol: TCP/IP set qu...	stress utility	Brad	BRA...			
SQL:BatchStarting	exec dbo.ADGSP_EN_BOLInstr	stress utility	Brad	BRA...			
SQL:BatchCompleted	exec dbo.ADGSP_EN_BOLInstr	stress utility	Brad	BRA...	1640	10028	0
Audit Logout		stress utility	Brad	BRA...	1640	10028	0
Audit Login	-- network protocol: TCP/IP set qu...	stress utility	Brad	BRA...			
SQL:BatchStarting	exec dbo.ADGSP_SO_LOADNOTSHIP	stress utility	Brad	BRA...			
SQL:BatchCompleted	exec dbo.ADGSP_SO_LOADNOTSHIP	stress utility	Brad	BRA...	1656	147309	32
Audit Logout		stress utility	Brad	BRA...	1656	147309	32
Audit Login	-- network protocol: TCP/IP set qu...	stress utility	Brad	BRA...			
SQL:BatchStarting	exec dbo.ADGSP_EN_Instructions	stress utility	Brad	BRA...			
SQL:BatchCompleted	exec dbo.ADGSP_EN_Instructions	stress utility	Brad	BRA...	4000	1859482	0
Audit Logout		stress utility	Brad	BRA...	4000	1859482	0
Audit Login	-- network protocol: TCP/IP set qu...	stress utility	Brad	BRA...			
SQL:BatchStarting	exec dbo.ADGSP_PO_PurchasOrd	stress utility	Brad	BRA...			
SQL:BatchCompleted	exec dbo.ADGSP_PO_PurchasOrd	stress utility	Brad	BRA...	5562	7121	0
Audit Logout		stress utility	Brad	BRA...	5562	7121	0
Audit Login	-- network protocol: TCP/IP set qu...	stress utility	Brad	BRA...			
SQL:BatchStarting	exec dbo.ADGSP_PO_PurchasOrd	stress utility	Brad	BRA...			
SQL:BatchCompleted	exec dbo.ADGSP_PO_PurchasOrd	stress utility	Brad	BRA...	5453	7121	0
Audit Logout		stress utility	Brad	BRA...	5453	7121	0
Audit Login	-- network protocol: TCP/IP set qu...	stress utility	Brad	BRA...			

exec dbo.ADGSP_EN_BOLInstr

Figure 2-32: A small sample of the events captured by the default trace template.

So why might you use this template? First, it lists all the currently existing connections to the server instance you are monitoring. In my example, there is only one connection. Second, it lists audit events, showing you when SQL Server Login IDs have logged into and out of the server.

Third, it captures stored procedure execution. Fourth, it captures T-SQL statements that are not part of stored procedures. In the data columns, you also see a little bit about the resources used by each event, which can help tell you how each event has affected the instance's resources. Oftentimes, I use this template when I want to do a "quick and dirty" profile without having to put a lot of thought into selecting what specific events or data columns I want to collect. This template identifies many common performance-related issues, and is a good starting point.

SP_COUNTS

This template is very different from the **Standard** template, including far fewer events and data columns. A point I want to make now is that templates can be very different from one another.

This simple template is designed to capture information whenever a stored procedure is first started. The results are then sorted by **EventClass**, **ServerName**, **DatabaseID** and **ObjectID**. This way, once the output has been collected, it can be sent to a SQL Server database where you can then perform a Transact-SQL count on the **ObjectName** in order to count how many times each stored procedure ran during the trace period.

For example, as you can see from the screen shot below, this template captures a single Event: **SP:Starting**.

Events		ServerName	DatabaseID	ObjectID	SPID	DatabaseName	ObjectName
–	**Stored Procedures**						
☑	SP:Starting	☑	☑	☑	☑	☑	☑

Figure 2-33: Events captured with the SP_Counts Profiler template.

The screen shot below shows a trace generated by the **SP_Counts** Profiler template

EventClass	ServerName	DatabaseID	ObjectID	SPID	DatabaseName	ObjectName
SP:Starting	PELE	1	508658945	52	master	sp_trace_getdata
SP:Starting	PELE	6	831810521	53	Big_Database	ADGSP_EN_Instructions
SP:Starting	PELE	6	1281879429	53	Big_Database	ADGSP_PO_PurchasOrd
SP:Starting	PELE	6	1281879429	53	Big_Database	ADGSP_PO_PurchasOrd
SP:Starting	PELE	6	1769577888	53	Big_Database	ADGSP_EN_SalesInstr
SP:Starting	PELE	6	1769577888	53	Big_Database	ADGSP_EN_SalesInstr
SP:Starting	PELE	6	1769577888	53	Big_Database	ADGSP_EN_SalesInstr
SP:Starting	PELE	6	1773443775	53	Big_Database	ADGSP_SO_LOADNOTSHIP
SP:Starting	PELE	6	1801578002	53	Big_Database	ADGSP_EN_BOLInstr
Trace Start						
Trace Stop						

Figure 2-34: An example of a trace produced by the SP_Counts Profiler template.

So how might you use this template? Let's say that you are interesting in identifying the top ten most run stored procedures in your application. By running this trace, and through a little Transact-SQL code, you can produce a report showing how many times each stored procedure ran during the trace period.

Now that you have seen a little detail about two of the predefined Profiler templates that come with Profiler, let's take a quick look at what the remaining templates do.

TSQL

This template is used to capture all T-SQL statements that are submitted to SQL Server by clients, along with time stamps. This might be used by developers to debug client applications.

TSQL_DURATION

The TSQL_Duration template is used to capture all T-SQL statements submitted to SQL Server by clients and their execution time. It groups the results by execution time duration. This template is often used to identify slow queries.

TSQL_GROUPED

This is used to capture all T-SQL statements submitted to SQL Server and the time they were submitted for execution. In addition, the statements are grouped by the user or client that submitted the statement. This is often used to investigate problem queries from a particular client or user.

TSQL_REPLAY

This is used to capture the appropriate events and data columns about T-SQL statements so the trace can be captured and later replayed back to SQL Server. This is often used to for iterative tuning, benchmark testing, or stress testing.

TSQL_SPs

This template captures detailed information about all executing stored procedures. It is often used to analyze the statements within stored procedures.

TUNING

This template captures information about stored procedures and T-SQL batch execution. This trace can be used as the raw data to feed into the Database Engine Tuning Advisor for index optimization.

As you can see, these templates are fairly limited in scope, but they are often a good starting place for a novice Profiler user. As you gain more experience, you will tend to skip these templates and create your own.

CUSTOM PROFILER TRACE TEMPLATES

As we've seen, a custom trace is one where you define the events and data columns to collect, the filters to apply and so on. A custom trace template is essentially the same thing, but you have the ability to reuse it again and again, without having to repeat all this work. So, if you think about it for a moment, every trace you create, apart form the very simplest, should be a custom trace template!

In this section we will be taking a look at the following topics:

- How to create a Trace Template from scratch
- How to create a Trace Template from a running trace
- How to create a Trace Template from a saved trace file or trace table
- How to modify a Trace Template
- How to execute a Trace Template
- How to import and export Trace Templates

CREATING A CUSTOM TRACE TEMPLATE FROM SCRATCH

Creating a trace template is as easy as creating a custom trace, although you use different Profiler options. To begin creating a trace template, from the Main menu, select File | Templates | New Template, as shown in figure 2-35:

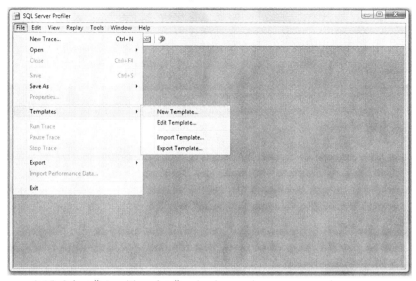

2-35: Select "New Template" to begin creating a new template.

After selecting the "New Template" option, the Trace Template Properties screen appears:

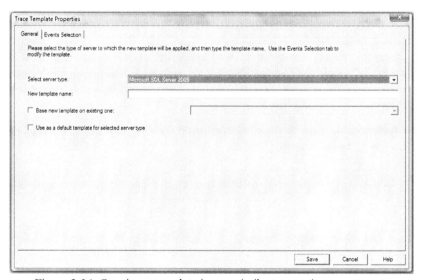

Figure 2-36: Creating a template is very similar to creating a custom trace.

This screen is very similar to the "Trace Properties" screen we see when we create a custom trace. There are two tabs: "General" and "Events Selection." While the "General" tab is slightly different from the "Trace Properties" screen, the "Events Selection" tab is identical.

Let's have a look at the "General" tab first. At the top of the screen is a drop-down box called "Select server type":

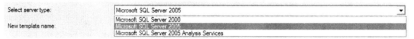

Figure 2-37: When you create a trace template, the first step is to choose the type of trace.

As you can see in figure 2-37 above, this option allows you to specify what kind of instance the trace will be running against. You need to make this choice because it affects the events and data columns that will be available on the "Events Selection" tab.

Next to "New template name" you enter the name of the template. Be sure to give it a descriptive name that not only you, but other DBAs, will be able to understand.

If you like, you can create a new template based on an existing one. To do this, check the "Base new template on existing one" checkbox and then select the predefined template you want to use as basis for your new custom template.

If you want to make your custom template the default Profiler template for the selected Server type, you can do this by checking the "Use as a default template for selected server type." The default Profiler template refers to which template is displayed, by default, next to "Use the template" from the "Trace Properties" screen. Generally, I don't bother with this option because I end up selecting some other template other than the default one listed on the screen.

Once you have made your choices (only the first two are required), click on the "Events Selection" tab.

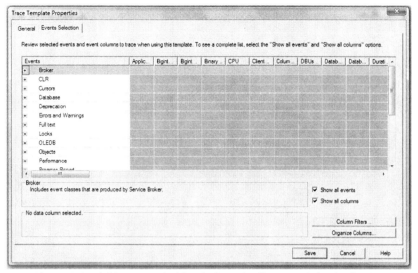

Figure 2-38: This screen is identical to the "Events Selection" tab we have used many times before.

Now you are ready to create your trace, selecting the events and data columns you want, including setting column filters and organizing columns, just you did before. Once you are done, click on "Save" to save the template. The template will be saved and will be available from the "Use the template" drop-down box on the "Trace Properties" screen.

CREATE A CUSTOM TRACE TEMPLATE FROM AN EXISTING OR SAVED TRACE FILE

Above, we discussed how to create a trace template from scratch. There are two other ways to create this template. One is to take a currently existing trace (loaded in Profiler, but not running) and convert it into a trace template. The other way is to load a pre-existing trace file from disk into Profiler, then create a trace template from that.

Let's say that you have created a custom trace (not a trace template) as we did earlier in the chapter, and are looking at the results on the Profiler screen. It is doing exactly what you need, but you did not create this originally as a template. Is there any way to save all this work as a template without having to create a template from scratch?

Yes. From the Main menu, select File | Save As | Trace Template, as you see in figure 2-39.

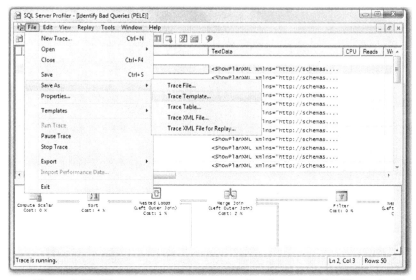

Figure 2-39: You can save a trace template by using the "Save As Trace Template" option.

Then the following screen appears, where you enter the name you want to assign to the template. After you have entered the new template name, click on OK and the trace is saved. See figure 2-40.

Figure 2-40: Name the new template.

If you want to create a custom template from a trace file previously saved to disk, simply open the trace file in Profiler (File | Open | Trace File) and follow the same steps.

If you had saved the file to a SQL Server database table instead of a file, you can also load it into Profiler by selecting File | Open | Trace table, which will allow you to select the table you want to load, and it will load into Profiler for viewing. At this point, you can save the file as a new template, just as in the previous example.

Sometimes, when you follow the above procedure and try to select File | Save As | Trace Template, the option will be grayed out, preventing you from saving your existing trace as a Trace Template. This can be caused by one of two things. First, be sure the existing trace has been stopped, and is not running. You cannot save a trace template of a running trace.

If this hasn't fixed the problem, then go to the Main menu and select View, and either "Aggregated View" or "Grouped View" will be selected. Deselect whichever option is selected. Now, to back to File | Save As | Trace Template, and try again. This time, it will not be grayed out and you can save the template. For whatever odd reason, you can't save a trace template unless both of these options are turned off.

MODIFYING CUSTOM TEMPLATES

If you decide later that you want to modify your custom template, this is also an easy task. Go to the Main menu and select **File | Templates | Edit Template**.

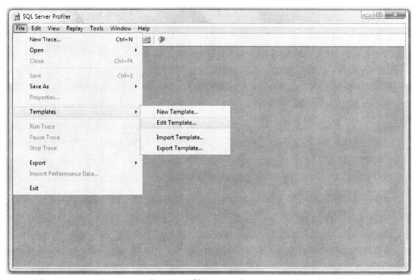

Figure 2-41: You can edit a Profiler template at any time.

Once you have made this selection, the following screen appears.

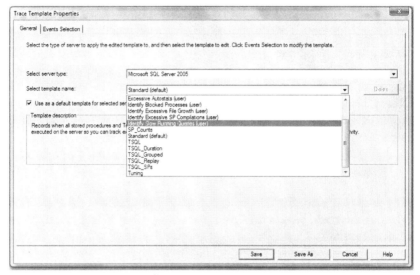

Figure 2-42: You can edit any template you want.

To select a template to edit, first choose "Select server type" for the type of template you want to edit. Notice that specific templates are associated with specific server types. This makes sense as each server type offers different Profiler trace events and data columns.

Once you have selected the server type, click on the "Select template name" drop-down box to select the template you want to edit. Notice in the drop-down list shown above (figure 2-42) that templates you create are labeled as "User" and that default templates that come with Profiler don't have any designation.

Once you have selected the template to edit, click on the "Events Selection" tab, where you can modify the template to your liking. When you are done modifying the template, save it by clicking on the **"Save"** button.

EXECUTING CUSTOM TRACE TEMPLATES

We execute custom-made templates like we would any template; simply select your custom template from the "Use the template" dropdown on the General tab.

If you like, you can modify a trace before you execute it. All you need to do is to go to the "Events Selection" tab and make any changes you want. These changes will not be saved to your template, and will only be in effect for this trace.

IMPORTING AND EXPORTING TRACE TEMPLATES

Once you have created many useful Profiler templates, you may want to share them with other DBAs. Or, perhaps, other DBAs have created trace templates that they have given to you for you to use. While you can locate the trace files on your computer and just copy them, it is easier to use the built-in features of Profiler that allows you to export and import trace template files.

To export a trace template, from the main menu of Profiler, select File | Templates | Export Template.

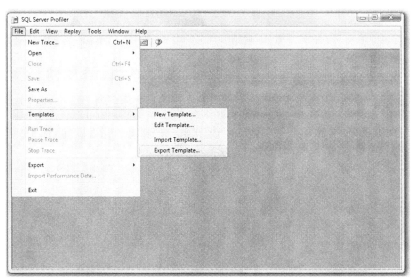

Figure 2-43: You can easily import and export Profiler trace templates.

Next, the following screen appears.

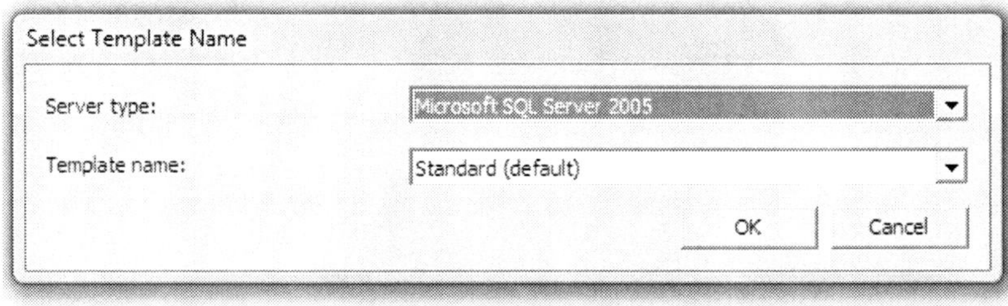

Figure 2-44: You can only export or import one template at a time.

Here, select the template you want to export. Notice that you can only export one Profiler trace template file at a time. When you click on

"OK," you are presented with a standard save screen, where you are able to choose the path where you want to export the trace file.

If you want to import a trace file, select File | Templates | Import Template, and you are presented with a standard open screen, where you can select the template you want to import.

SUMMARY

Having read this chapter, you now understand the basics of creating your own custom traces; you also know how to save them to file and subsequently to a database table for further analysis.

You have appreciated the advantages of creating reusable trace templates, either from scratch or based on existing pre-defined templates.

In the next chapter, we take a look at some tips and tricks that will allow you to use Profiler more efficiently. Once you master this chapter, you will know about every feature and option in Profiler. Then you will be ready for the rest of the book, where we focus on how to apply Profiler to our daily jobs as DBAs.

Chapter 3
PROFILER GUI TIPS AND TRICKS

By this stage in the book, you should have a good idea about what Profiler can do and how it works. Up to now we've tackled the GUI in a fairly "narrow" fashion, covering only those features that were directly necessary to us to achieve our goals of creating basic traces custom traces, template and so on.

There are quite a few options that we didn't cover, however, and quite a few tips and tricks that, once you know about them, can really help you use Profiler more efficiently.

So, in this chapter, we cover these topics:

- Tips on Selecting Profiler Events and Data Columns
- Tips on Using Column Filters
- Tips on Organizing Columns for Grouping and Analysis
- How the "Server processes trace data" Option Affects Traces
- How to Set Global Trace Options
- How to Schedule a Trace's Stop Time
- How to use the Auto Scroll Window
- How to Search for Data Inside a Trace File
- How to Set and Use Bookmarks

So let's get started.

TIPS ON SELECTING PROFILER EVENTS AND DATA COLUMNS

In the previous chapter, you learned how to select events and data columns in order to create a custom trace. This is a straightforward process and is more or less self-evident. The problem is not in the mechanics of selecting events but in deciding which of the 170 Profiler events and 64 data columns that really want to select and in making sure you haven't inadvertently included extraneous events and columns.

Our focus here is on tips and tricks to help you select which profiler events and data columns to capture in a trace.

Tip #1: Don't overload your traces

There is no easy way to decide which events or data columns you need to capture as part of a trace. It depends on the problem at hand, and it requires a good understanding of what events are available and what each one of them does.

NOTE:

We cover specific events and data columns in some detail in Chapter 11, *Profiler Events and Data Columns Explained.*

Your first inclination as a beginner will probably be to select more events and data columns than you need. This is very reasonable thing to do because the only real way learn about them, and especially how they apply to your SQL Server environment, is to experiment. I encourage you to experiment with different events and data columns, but with caution. Keep the following things in mind:

- Experimenting with too much data makes it hard to analyze the results. In other words, traces become very difficult to read if you collect too much data. You may get so overwhelmed that you become discouraged from wanting to learn how to master Profiler. For example, who would want to wade through several thousand Lock events (see Figure 3-1)?
- Returning too much data can put a performance hit not only on the SQL Server instance you are tracing, but on the local computer you are using to perform the trace.
- If, for some reason, you do need to collect a large number of events in a single trace, at least limit the length of the trace to a short period, say five minutes or less. This will allow you to collect a wide range of data, while at the same time not overwhelming resources.

So whether you are experimenting, or you are running actual traces, don't get carried away with collecting too much data. As you gain more experience with using Profiler, this will become easier and easier for you to do.

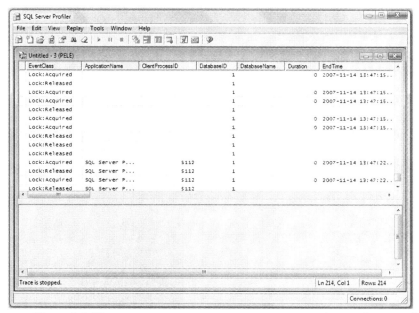

Figure 3-1: If you capture too many events, you can get lost, trying to make sense out of events that aren't really important. Who wants to see 5,000 **Lock:Acquired** and **Lock:Released** events?

TIP #2: EVENT CATEGORIES ARE A GUIDE ONLY

As we have already discussed, individual events are divided into categories of similar events. The purpose of this is to allow you to more easily locate the events you are looking for. However, it is *not* designed as a short cut to help you identify which events to select. For example, if you wish to diagnose a problem with a slow performing query, you might be tempted to assume it's as simple as selecting all the events in the Performance event category. Far from it. In most cases, you will need to carefully select trace events from multiple event categories. Rarely would you find yourself selecting all the events in a single event category (except those, of course, that only have one event associated with them).

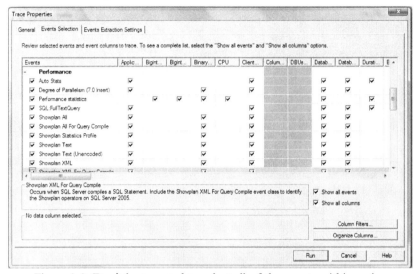

Figure 3-2: Don't be tempted to select all of the events within a given event category. You will only end up selecting events of little use, and missing other events that are important to your analysis.

TIP #3: DESELECT UNWANTED DATA COLUMNS

As we noted in Chapter 2, when you select an event, all the data columns for that event are automatically selected. In most cases, you will want to select only limited data columns, not all of them, meaning that you will have to deselect those data columns from the events you don't want.

A common mistake is to accidentally leave unnecessary data columns selected, and therefore clutter the resulting traces with unwanted data. In fact, the Profiler GUI offers you a helpful visual clue that can help you avoid this situation. Take a look again at Figure 3-2. You may not have noticed it at first, but there are two data columns in that figure that are empty, and grey in color. Every other column in the figure is selected for at least one event, and is white in color.

In other words, a white column is a visual cue to you that a data column has been selected for at least one event. So how is this helpful? Let's say that you are creating a new trace and have selected about a dozen events, as seen in the figure 3-7 below.

Events	Object...	Durati...	TextD...	CPU	Reads	Writes	DatabaseID	DatabaseName	Binary...	SPID
— Performance										
☑ Showplan XML	☑		☑				☑	☑	☑	☑
— Stored Procedures										
☑ RPC:Completed	☑	☑	☑	☑	☑	☑	☑	☑	☑	☑
☑ RPC:Starting	☑		☑				☑	☑	☑	☑
☑ SP:Completed	☑	☑	☑				☑	☑	☑	☑
☑ SP:Recompile	☑		☑				☑	☑		☑
☑ SP:Starting	☑		☑				☑	☑	☑	☑
☑ SP:StmtCompleted	☑	☑	☑	☑	☑	☑	☑	☑		☑
☑ SP:StmtStarting	☑		☑				☑	☑		☑
— TSQL										
☑ SQL:BatchCompleted		☑	☑	☑	☑	☑	☑	☑		☑

Figure 3-7: Often, you can't see all the events you selected on the same screen without scrolling through all of them.

As you select each event, every data column is selected for that event. However, let's say that you want to deselect the Database ID data column for all events, because it essentially duplicates information in the DatabaseName column. So, you deselect the DatabaseID column for every event you can find, as shown in Figure 3-8:

Events	Object..	Durati..	TextD...	CPU	Reads	Writes	DatabaseID	DatabaseName	Binary..	SPID ▲
— Performance										
☑ Showplan XML	☑		☑				☐	☑	☑	☑
— Stored Procedures										
☑ RPC:Completed	☑	☑	☑	☑	☑	☑	☐	☑	☑	☑
☑ RPC:Starting	☑		☑				☐	☑	☑	☑
☑ SP:Completed	☑	☑	☑				☐	☑	☑	☑
☑ SP:Recompile	☑		☑				☐	☑		☑
☑ SP:Starting	☑		☑				☐	☑	☑	☑
☑ SP:StmtCompleted	☑	☑	☑	☑	☑	☑	☐	☑		☑
☑ SP:StmtStarting	☑		☑				☐	☑		☑
— TSQL										
☑ SQL:BatchCompleted		☐	☐	☐	☐	☐	☐	☐		☐

Figure 3-8: After deselecting all the DatabaseID checkboxes, the column is still white.

What you will notice is that the column is still white. This is an immediate indication that there are still some events for which this column is selected:

Events	Object...	Durati..	TextD...	CPU	Reads	Writes	DatabaseID	DatabaseName	Binary...	SPID ▲
☑ SP:Completed	☑	☑	☑				☐	☑	☑	☑
☑ SP:Recompile	☑		☑				☐	☑		☑
☑ SP:Starting	☑		☑				☐	☑	☑	☑
☑ SP:StmtCompleted	☑	☑	☑	☑	☑	☑	☐	☑		☑
☑ SP:StmtStarting	☑		☑				☐	☑		☑
— TSQL										
☑ SQL:BatchCompleted		☑	☑	☑	☑	☑	☐	☑		☑
☑ SQL:BatchStarting			☑				☑	☑		☑
☑ SQL:StmtCompleted		☑	☑	☑	☑	☑	☑	☑		☑
☑ SQL:StmtRecompile	☑		☑				☑	☑		☑
☑ SQL:StmtStarting			☑				☑	☑		☑

Figure 3-9: I guess I didn't unselect all the events after all.

This visual cue can be very helpful when creating complex traces and when you want to ensure that you don't collect more data than you intended. Once you've deselected the column for the rogue events that you missed, the screen should look as shown in Figure 3-10:

Events	Object ..	Durati..	TextD...	CPU	Reads	Writes	DatabaseID	DatabaseName	Binary...	SPID
☑ SP:Completed	☑	☑	☑				☐	☑	☑	☑
☑ SP:Recompile	☑		☑				☐	☑		☑
☑ SP:Starting	☑		☑				☐	☑	☑	☑
☑ SP:StmtCompleted	☑	☑	☑	☑	☑	☑	☐	☑		☑
☑ SP:StmtStarting	☑		☑				☐	☑		☑
– **TSQL**										
☑ SQL:BatchCompleted		☑	☑	☑	☑	☑	☐	☑		☑
☑ SQL:BatchStarting			☑				☐	☑		☑
☑ SQL:StmtCompleted		☑	☑	☑	☑	☑	☐	☑		☑
☑ SQL:StmtRecompile	☑		☑				☐	☑		☑
☑ SQL:StmtStarting			☑				☐	☑		☑

Figure 3-10: The grey columns tell us that no events have been selected for this data column.

In actual fact, Profiler offers a second visual clue that can help you spot events for which all data columns are still selected. Did you spot it? Take a close look at the checkboxes to the left of the event names, in Figures 3-9 and 3-10. In Figure 3-9, the first five rows have a grayed-out check and the remaining events have a black check. If you see a black check, it means that all the data columns for that event have been selected. If you see a grayed-out check in the checkbox, it means that at least one of the data columns have been unselected. This can be useful to know as you create complex traces.

One more tip. If you want to select or deselect all the data columns for all the events listed on the Events Selection screen, right-click on the data column heading and choose either **"Select Column"** or **"Deselect Column."**

TIP #4: USE SHOW ALL EVENTS AND SHOW ALL COLUMNS

I mentioned this briefly in Chapter 2, but it's worth emphasizing again here. When you create a new trace, the easiest way is to start is with the Blank template, with the Show All Events and Show All Columns text boxes selected.

However, once you have selected the events and data columns you want, the screen soon becomes hard to read because it still shows events and data columns you did not select. In addition, since the size of the screen is limited, you can't see all the events you selected without scrolling up and down the screen. See figure 3-12 below.

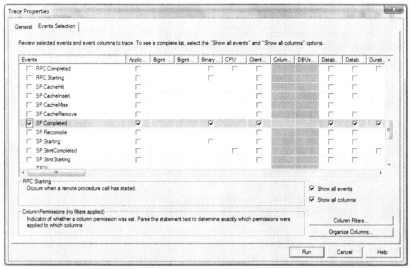

Figure 3-12: This Profiler screen makes it hard to see what events have been selected.

Once you have selected the events and data columns you want, it is much easier to see what you have selected if you deselect the Show All Events and Show All Columns checkboxes. When you do this, you only see those events and data columns, as shown in figure 3-13 below.

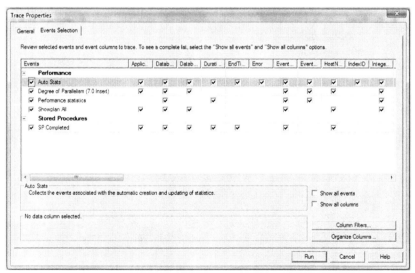

Figure 3-13: Now it is easy to see what events and data columns I have selected.

If you decide later to add more events or data columns, you can easily check the Show All Events and Show All Columns checkboxes, makes the changes you want, and then deselect the Show All Events and Show All Columns checkboxes again. If you have many events selected, you still may have to scroll to see them all, but it is still a lot easier than scrolling through 150+ events.

TIP #5: WHEN CREATING TRACES, YOU CAN ONLY CHANGE THE COLUMN ORDER USING ORGANIZE COLUMNS

As you select the data columns you want to capture for each event, it would often be handy to move the data columns in a different order. Unfortunately, you can't click and drag a data column from one location to another. If you want to rearrange the columns on the screen in any order other than alphabetical order, you have to do so by using the Organize Columns button on this screen. If you click on any of the data columns head, thinking you might be able to drag and drop them, or even to change the sort order of the events (which you can't), a box pops up that can be a little disconcerting.

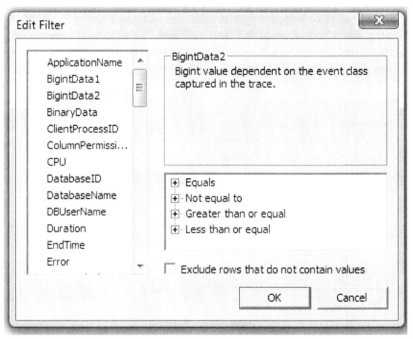

Figure 3-14: The Edit Filter window appears whenever you click on the name of any data column.

Clicking any of the data column names is the same as clicking on the Column Filters button. If you do this by accident, click "Cancel" to get rid of the screen.

However, note that once you are actually running a trace, then you can move the data columns into a different order, just by dragging and dropping.

TIP #6: THE SPID AND EVENTNAME DATA COLUMNS ARE MANDATORY

Let's say that you don't want the SPID data column to be captured for a given event and try to unselect it. It will produce an error message as in figure 3-16.

Figure 3-16: The SPID data column is required.

Of all the data columns, two are required and must be included in every trace. One is **EventName**, which is not even listed on the Events Selection screen, and SPID, which is listed. It seems a little odd that one required data column is not even shown, but that is the way Profiler has been designed, so just be aware of this peculiarity. You will see both the **EventName** and SPID column when you run a trace.

TIP #7: USE THE HELP TIPS!

You have probably already figured this out, but just in case you haven't, if you hover the mouse pointer over any event or data column name, you will see a help tip at the bottom of the screen.

In figure 3-17, I hovered my mouse pointer over the checkbox that intersects the event RPC:Completed and the ServerName data column. This way, I get two tooltips: one for the event and one for the data column. Or, you can just hover over the event or data column name to see a tooltip.

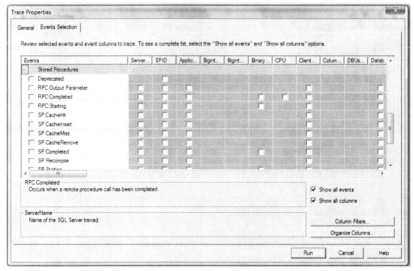

Figure 3-17: Tooltips are available for all events and data columns.

TIPS ON USING COLUMN FILTERS

Filters are a powerful tool because they allow you restrict which events are captured and which are excluded. For example, if you have selected the SQL:StmtCompleted event as part of your trace, you may only want to see Transact-SQL statements from a single database only, not from all the databases on your server. This is easily accomplished by creating a filter to limit the events to be captured to those that occur only in the database you select, not events occurring on other databases on the same SQL Server instance.

In this section, we look at some tips to help you make the most of this feature.

TIP #1: EDITING FILTERS

There are two different ways to display the Edit Filters window, which is used to add, modify, or remove column filters. The easiest option is to click on the Column Filters button. The other way is to click on any column name on the screen. If you choose the latter method, the column name you selected is automatically selected for you in the Edit Filters window.

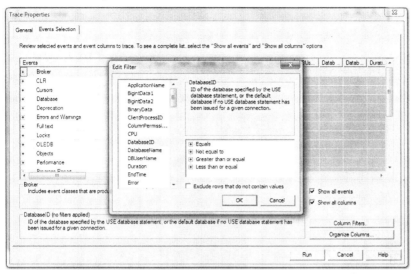

Figure 3-18: The Edit Filter window is used to create, modify, or remove column filters.

In figure 3-18 above, I clicked on the **DatabaseID** data column on the Events Selection tab of the Trace Properties screen and the Edit Filter window appeared, with **DatabaseID** preselected for me.

TIP #2: FILTERS DO NOT NECESSARILY REDUCE WORKLOAD

Many DBAs assume that by creating filters for a Profiler trace, that they are substantially reducing the workload on SQL Server. The assumption is that if you are collecting fewer events because you have added filters, that the workload should be less. Unfortunately, this assumption is often not true.

Here is what is happening. When you select an event for SQL Server to trace, SQL Trace (the SQL Server component that actually does the tracing work) has to look at every event that is occurring in order to identify a particular event as one you want to collect. If you don't add a column filter, then your trace will record data for every occurrence of that event in your instance of SQL Server. This alone is a lot of work.

When you add a column filter, every event is still captured, but then SQL Server also has to decide whether to keep the event (and store it in RAM and/or disk) or to toss it away.

But all is not lost. While the addition of a column filter does introduce additional CPU overhead, it does reduce the number of events that are stored in RAM and/or written to disk. This acts to reduce the amount of resources used to run Profiler. The hard part is gauging whether or not the extra resources needed to apply the filter are more, or less, than the resources saved by limiting the number of events collected.

TIP #3: CREATING MULTIPLE FILTERS

When you create a column filter for a trace, you can filter on a single data column or on multiple data columns. Each time you filter on an additional data column, a funnel icon appears next to the data column you are filtering on.

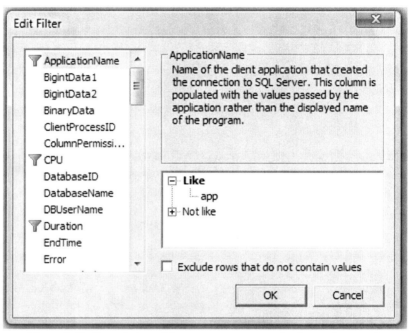

Figure 3-19: Funnel shaped icons appear next to the data columns where you have set up specific filters.

As you add filter criteria to a data column, only click the OK button if you have finished adding filters for this trace. If you want to create several data column filters at one sitting, create one filter, then press the TAB key to save the criteria, and then to proceed to add other filter criteria. Only when you are done should you click OK. If you click OK by mistake before you are done, the Edit Filter screen disappears, although you can still go back and change the filter; it just takes extra keystrokes.

TIP #4: FILTER CRITERIA

When adding filter criteria, keep the following in mind:

- Not all data columns can be filtered.

- Some data columns have different filter criteria than others. The available criteria are displayed for you, so you know what is available.

- You can use the % symbol as a wildcard for the **TextData** data column.

- The data you are filtering for has to exist. Not all data columns are always populated for the same event.

- If you filter on **StartTime** or **EndTime** data columns, use the format: YYYY/MM/DD hh:mm:sec.

TIP #5: EXCLUDING EMPTY ROWS

At the bottom of the Edit Filter window is a checkbox that says, "Exclude rows that do not contain values." This provides a way to filter out records that don't include any data for a specific data column.

When this filter is put into place, it only works on rows that have data columns that are actually empty. If there is a NULL value in a data column, the row will be returned. This option should not be combined with another filter for the same data column. If you try, the results may be unpredictable, due to a bug in the code that has not been fixed in SQL Server 2005.

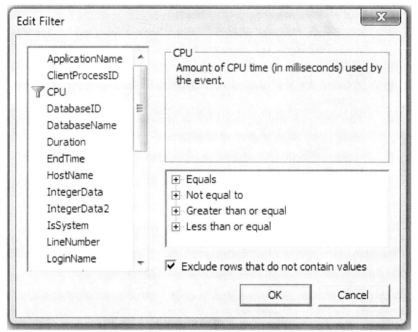

Figure 3-20: The "Exclude rows that do not contain values" option is data column specific.

TIPS ON ORGANIZING COLUMNS FOR GROUPING AND ANALYSIS

In chapter 2, we learned that the Organize Columns window allows you to perform two major functions:

- Change the default order of the data columns on the screen
- Group events based on a certain data column

This section covers some tips on how to make the most of these two features.

TIP #1: WHICH ARE THE MOST IMPORTANT DATA COLUMNS?

While you can choose any order in which to display data columns, I recommend that you put the most useful events toward the left, and the less useful toward the right of the trace screen. This way, when you read and analyze trace results, you will have to perform less scrolling to see the data you want to see.

There is no way to say, definitively, which are the most important columns, because it will vary according to what you are tracing. However, some of the data columns that I like to put on the left side, because I use them a lot, include TextData, Duration, CPU, Reads, Writes, ApplicationName, StartTime, and EndTime.

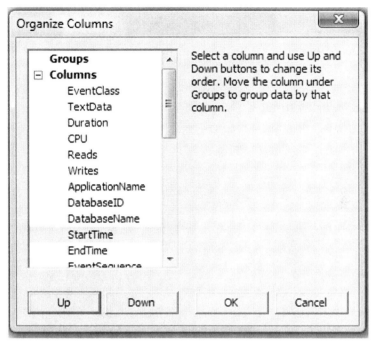

Figure 3-21: You should order data columns in the order that is of most important to you.

TIP #2: DATA IS ONLY AGGREGATED IF YOU GROUP ON A SINGLE COLUMN

If you decide to group rows by a data column, keep the following in mind:

- If you group a single data column, that data column will automatically be aggregated for you.
- If you group two or more data columns, the data will be sorted as you specify, but no aggregations are performed.

TIP #3: CONTROLLING AGGREGATION AND GROUPING

If you have specified that data columns be grouped, or aggregated, inside of the Organize Columns window, and are currently capturing or displaying data in Profiler, you can turn off grouping and aggregation by going to the VIEW menu and selecting the appropriate option.

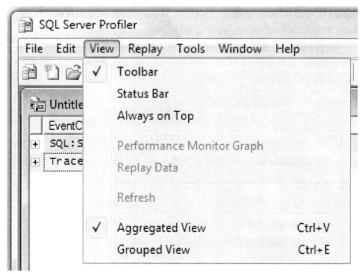

Figure 3-22: You can change the way events are grouped by selecting, or not selecting the Aggregated View or Grouped View options.

You can choose to turn off both Aggregated View and Grouped View, which means that all the data will be ungrouped and unaggregated.

If you turn the Aggregated View on and Grouped View off, then the results will be aggregated based on what data column you are grouping by.

If you turn the Aggregated View off and the Grouped View on, then all the results will be sorted on the data column you are grouping by.

For example, let's say that I am going to run a trace, and that I have specified that I want to group data by EventClass. When I run this trace, I will see all the data automatically aggregated for by EventClass. This is the default behavior.

Then I decide to change the View settings so that Aggregated View and Grouped View are turned off. In this case, the events are ordered in the order they actually occurred:

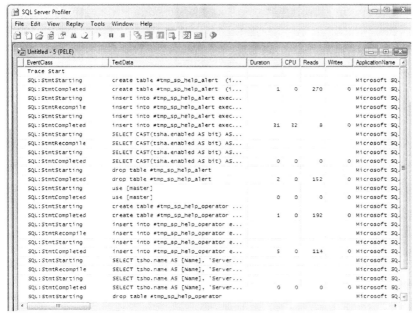

Figure 3-23: Both Grouped View and Aggregated View are turned off.

If I then decide to turn Grouped View on, but leave Aggregated View off, the data columns are sorted by **EventClass**:

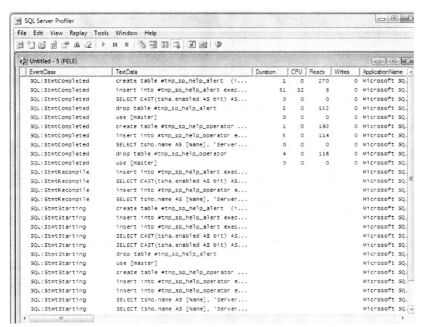

Figure 3-24: Grouped View is turned on and Aggregated View is turned off.

If Grouped View is turned off and Aggregated View is turned on, then rows are aggregated by EventClass. This returns us to our default view:

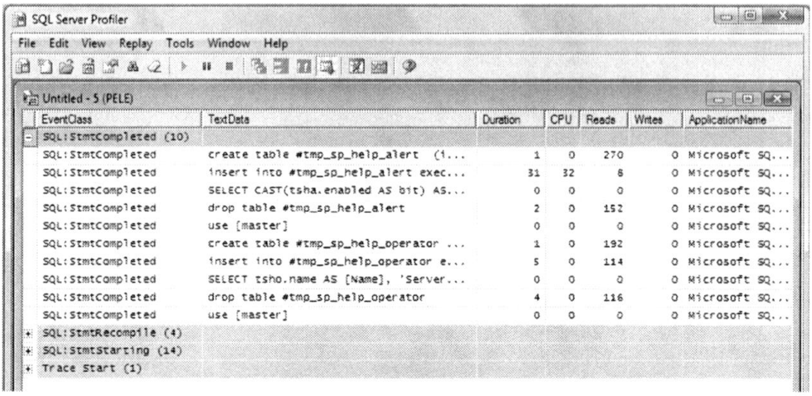

Figure 3-25: Grouped View is turned off and Aggregated View is turned on.

Keep in mind that this feature only works if already have an event under Groups in the Organize Columns window. In addition, you can switch between viewing modes as much as you like. What you can't do is to change the event you are grouping. That can only be done before you start a new trace, not after the trace has been created.

HOW THE "SERVER PROCESSES TRACE DATA" OPTION AFFECTS TRACES

In the General tab of the Trace Properties screen, if you select the "Save to file" option, an additional option becomes available, called "Server processes trace data."

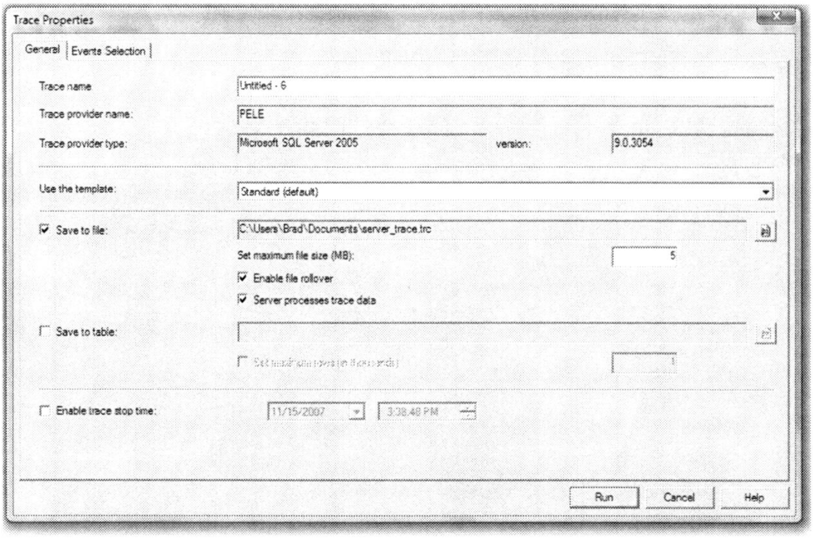

Figure 3-26: The "Server processes trace data" option

When this option is selected, Profiler ensures that all events are recorded, even if this means that the SQL Server instance's performance will be hurt. To accomplish this task, two separate trace processes are started that trace exactly the same events as each other. One trace process sends events to the Profiler GUI, and the other trace process sends the data to a local disk file. While this ensures that all events are captured, it also means that a significant burden may be put on SQL Server, hurting its performance. If the SQL Server instance is not busy, then the performance hit is not a problem. But if the instance is very busy, then the performance hit could be significant.

If this option is not selected, then Profiler does not guarantee that all events will be captured, and only one process is used to capture events. This reduces the performance burden on SQL Server significantly. If the SQL Server instance is not too busy, then there should be no loss of events. But if the server is busy, and Profiler thinks that capturing all events would hurt the performance of the instance, then events will be dropped as needed to prevent a significant performance hit.

So, should you use this option or not? In most cases, you will not want to select this option. If your server is not too busy, then all events will be captured anyway. If the server is very busy, you most likely don't want to add an additional performance burden to it. In most cases, missing some events won't affect your analysis, so this is not a problem. In the rare case where you run into a situation where you have a busy server, but you can't seem to find the events you need to resolve a problem because they are not being captured, consider turning this option on for short periods until you get the trace results you need. At the same time, ensure you are only collecting those events and data columns you really need, in order to reduce the performance hit as much as possible.

HOW TO SET GLOBAL TRACE OPTIONS

SQL Server Profiler allows you to control some general settings that affect how Profiler performs. In this section, we look at these options and how they should be set.

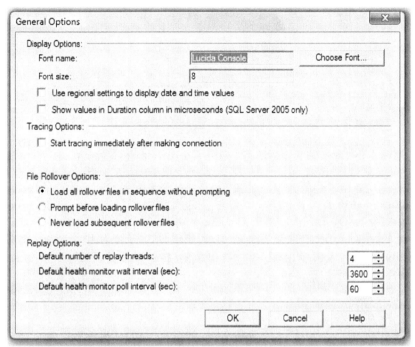

Figure 3-27: The General Options screen allows you to affect some global Profiler behavior.

DISPLAY OPTIONS

If you wish, you can change the font name and size used to display events in the Profiler trace window. By default, the font is Arial and the size is set to 8, which is about as small as you probably want to make it. If you want to make a change, click on the "Choose Font" button.

By default, date and time values displayed by Profiler use the fixed format used by SQL Server. If you want to use another format, you can select the "Use regional settings to display date and time values" checkbox, which will tell Profiler to use the regional date and time settings currently used by the OS.

In SQL Server 2005, duration is measured by Profiler in microseconds, but is displayed in Profiler in milliseconds by default. If you would prefer to see microseconds displayed instead of milliseconds in Profiler, select the "Show values in Duration column in microseconds" checkbox.

TRACING OPTIONS

I am not sure why anyone would want to use this option, but if the "Start tracing immediately after making connection" checkbox is selected, then the Default trace template is started immediately when Profiler is started.

FILE ROLLOVER OPTIONS

This option only applies when you load a pre-existing trace file for display by Profiler. By default, the option "Load all rollover files in sequence without prompting" is selected. This means that if you attempt to load a trace file that includes rollover files, then all the rollover files are loaded automatically in sequence. I prefer to use this option as it requires no extra keystrokes or mouse clicks to load a trace file.

If you choose the option "Prompt before loading rollover files," then you will be prompted to load each rollover file; you can choose to load it or not.

If you choose the option "Never load subsequent rollover files," this means that only the file you select is loaded, and other associated rollover files are ignored.

REPLAY OPTIONS

Replay options affect Profiler when you replay Profiler traces to a SQL Server instance.

The "Default number of replay threads" option determines how many threads are used to play back events. The default value if four, and should normally not be changed. Increasing this value will use more server resources.

The "Default health monitor wait interval" option affects the amount of time that a thread is allowed to run before it is turned off by the health monitor. The default value is 3,600 seconds, or 1 hour. The main purpose of this option is to prevent any trace replays from taking longer than you expect, and hurting performance.

The "Default health monitor poll interval" specifies how often the health monitor polls replays so it can determine how long they have been running. The default value is 60 seconds, and should normally not be changed.

HOW TO SCHEDULE A TRACE'S STOP TIME

Up to this point, we have been manually starting and stopping traces. While the SQL Server Profiler GUI won't allow you to schedule the start of a trace, it will allow you to schedule the stop time of a trace.

NOTE:

In a later chapter, we will discuss how you use system stored procedures to stop and start traces using a SQL Server Agent job.

Scheduling a trace stop time is very easy. Start by creating a trace as you normally would. At the bottom of the General tab on the Trace Properties screen is an option called "Enable trace stop time."

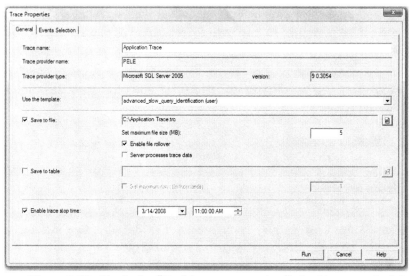

Figure 3-28: Check the "Enable trace stop time" checkbox to schedule a trace to stop.

Once you check this option, you can select a date and time for the trace to end automatically. After you start the trace manually, it will end at the time you specified.

The main thing you need to consider when using this option is how much data will you collect during this period, and will the storage location for the trace file have enough storage space for it? The last thing you want to do is to crash some system because you ran out of space. So don't use this option unless you are comfortable that your system won't run out of space. Otherwise, it is best to stick around during the trace, watching the size of the trace file to ensure it doesn't get too big.

HOW TO USE THE AUTO SCROLL WINDOW

When you are running a live trace and displaying the results in Profiler, you may have noticed that the Trace window automatically scrolls to the bottom, showing you the most recent events that have been captured. If you use your mouse to scroll the window up to see an earlier event while the trace is running, as soon as a new event has been captured, the screen immediately jumps down to the most recent event. This can be quite irritating if your goal is to look at an older event while the trace is running. This default behavior is called **auto scroll**.

Fortunately, there is an easy way to turn this default behavior off, which allows you to scroll anywhere you want inside the window without having to worry about new events jumping the screen to the bottom. There are two options available to turn off auto scroll.

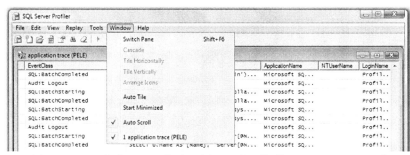

Figure 3-29: Going to Window|Auto Scroll allows you to turn the auto scroll feature off.

One option is to go to the Main menu and choose Windows, then click on Auto Scroll to turn it off.

Figure 3-30: Clicking on the Auto Scroll icon at the top of the screen will also turn auto scroll off.

The other option is to click on the Auto Scroll icon at the top of the Profiler screen. When a trace is running, you can turn off Auto Scroll on and off as much as you like. The sad part of this is that it is not remembered. So each time you start a new trace and you want to turn auto scroll off, you have to do so manually.

HOW TO SEARCH FOR DATA IN A TRACE FILE

Once you have created a trace file, it is often convenient to display it in Profiler for analysis. But as you know, Profiler can capture and display a huge amount of events, often making it difficult to find the specific event you are looking for. How do you find a single event out of thousands?

One option is to use Profiler's Find option. This primitive search tool allows you to search for a known string within all data columns, or within a specific data column, one event at a time.

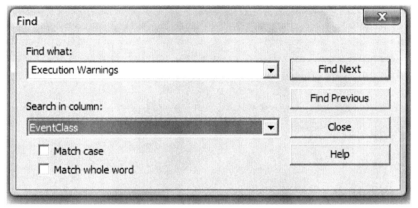

Figure 3-31: Use the Find option to locate specific records.

Anytime events are displayed in Profiler, you can go to Main menu and select Edit|Find, and the above window appears. Under "Find what," enter the string you are searching for, and under "Search in column," select a specific data column to search in, or select "All columns." When a match is found, the event is highlighted. You can look for additional matches by clicking on either "Find Next" or "Find Previous."

By default, the string you enter into the "Find what" box is a wildcard search. If you want to match case or match a whole word, you must select the appropriate option on the screen.

HOW TO SET BOOKMARKS

Sometimes, when you are analyzing events in a Profiler trace, it would be handy to mark the event so you can easily come back to it later. Profiler allows you to do this by bookmarking an event, and then jumping to the bookmark whenever you need to.

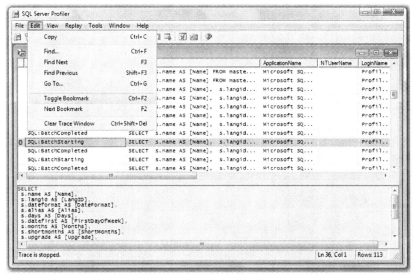

Figure 3-32: Use "Toggle Bookmark" to mark an event so you can easily return to it.

To bookmark an event, first click on the event you want to bookmark. Then, from the Main menu, select Edit|Toogle Bookmark. This will cause a small blue square to appear next to the event. You can bookmark as many events as you like. If you want to unmark an event, click on the event, then choose Edit|Toggle Bookmark again. This toggles the bookmark off.

To jump to a bookmarked event, from the Main menu, choose Edit|Next Bookmark, and you will jump to the next bookmarked event, and so on.

SUMMARY

At this point, you know about everything that is important to know about the mechanics of using SQL Server Profiler. From the next chapter onwards, we focus on how to use Profiler to troubleshoot and resolve specific SQL Server-related problems. In other words, while chapters 1-3 focused on the mechanics of using Profiler, the rest of the book focuses on how to apply Profiler to identifying and resolving common SQL Server problems.

Chapter 4
HOW TO IDENTIFY SLOW RUNNING QUERIES

As DBAs, one of the problems we face on an almost daily basis is slow-running queries. These are the ones that:

- Take 1 minute, 5 minutes, even 30 minutes to complete.
- Spike CPU utilization to 90% or more.
- Block other users from getting their work done.
- Result in your boss being called by an end-user's boss to find out why the problem hasn't been fixed yet.

Most of all, however, these are the kinds of queries that keep us up late at night, ruining our sleep and turning us into zombies. What can we do to fix this problem, once and for all? The answer: employ SQL Server 2005 Profiler, and our experience as a DBA.

One of the most powerful ways to use Profiler is to identify slow running queries; what's more, it is a simple and straightforward process that every DBA can master very quickly. Once poorly performing queries are identified, we need to figure out how to speed them up. This is not as easy as finding them in the first place, but Profiler can provide a lot of information that can help diagnose and resolve these performance problems.

So, in this chapter, we discuss the following:

- How to create a Profiler trace to capture all the information we need to identify and analyze slow running queries
- How to analyze the poorly-performing queries identified by Profiler

CREATING A TRACE TO IDENTIFY SLOW RUNNING QUERIES

This section covers the mechanics of how to create a Profiler trace template to capture and analyze slow running queries. The same approach can be applied to resolving many other SQL Server problems, so what you learn here can be applied to Profiler-based troubleshooting generally.

SELECTING EVENTS

Before you can choose which events to include in your trace, you first need to decide what information you want to capture. Well, we already have said we want to capture slow-running queries. Isn't that enough information to go on? Not really. Queries can come to a SQL Server instance in the form of stored procedures, batches of queries, or individual queries, so it's essential that you include the necessary events to capture all three forms in which a slow-running query can appear.

Also, keep in mind that stored procedures can be executed in two different ways:

- An RPC event – i.e. as a result of a Remote Procedure Call
- A Transact-SQL event – i.e. as a result of a call to the T-SQL EXECUTE statement

So you might need to capture both types of stored procedure events.

Last of all, you need to include any additional events that will provide clues *why* a particular query is slow, such as events that provide information about how a query performs, and "context" events that help put the query in perspective. Context events are those events that happen directly before and after other events, helping us understand more fully what is going on inside SQL Server.

So which events should you select? There is no single "correct combination" of events to include in a trace such as this. While one DBA may want to use seven different events to identify and analyze slow running queries, another DBA might use nine events, or only five. As the DBA, you must know Profiler events well enough in order to determine which events are needed for a particular situation.

NOTE:

See Chapter 11, *Profiler Events and Data Columns Reference*, for descriptions of all the events and data columns likely to be of interest to the DBA.

In this case, I am going to describe the events I think are needed to identify long-running queries. Feel free to modify my suggestions when performing your own traces. Just keep in mind that in order to minimize the load the trace will put on your SQL Server instance, you should minimize the number of events you collect.

When I troubleshoot slow-performing queries, I like to capture the following events:

- RPC:Completed
- SP:StmtCompleted
- SQL:BatchStarting
- SQL:BatchCompleted
- Showplan XML

Let's look at each one to see what the event does, and why I have chosen to collect it for this particular trace.

RPC:COMPLETED

The RPC: Completed event fires after a stored procedure is executed as a remote procedure call.

This event includes useful information about the execution of the stored procedure, including the Duration, CPU, Reads, Writes, together with the name of the stored procedure that ran. If a stored procedure is called by the Transact-SQL EXECUTE statement, then this event will not fire. In addition, this event does not fire for Transact-SQL statements that occur outside a stored procedure.

SP:STMTCOMPLETED

The SP:StmtCompleted event tells us when a statement within a stored procedure has completed.

It also provides us the text (the Transact-SQL code) of the statement, along with the event's Duration, CPU, Reads, and Writes. Keep in mind that a single stored procedure may contain a single, or many, individual statements. For example, if a stored procedure executes five SELECT statements, then there will be five SP:StmtCompleted events for that stored procedure. This event does not fire for Transact-SQL statements that occur outside a stored procedure.

SQL:BATCHSTARTING

A SQL: BatchStarting event is fired whenever a new Transact-SQL batch begins. This can include a batch inside or outside a stored procedure.

I use this as a context event because it fires anytime a new stored procedure or Transact-SQL statement fires, allowing me to better see where a new chain of query-related events begins.

SQL:BATCHCOMPLETED

The SQL: BatchCompleted event occurs when a Transact-SQL statement completes, whether the Transact-SQL statement is inside or outside a stored procedure.

If the event is a stored procedure, SQL:BatchCompleted provides the name of the stored procedure (but not the actual Transact-SQL code), together with the Duration, CPU, Reads, and Writes of the statement. It may seem as if this event is somewhat redundant, in that it produces very similar results to the SP:StmtCompleted event. Unfortunately, you need to capture both events: SQL:BatchCompleted to provide Duration, CPU, Reads, and Writes event data when a Transact-SQL statement is run outside a stored procedure, and SP:StmtCompleted to see more easily what the code is inside a stored procedure.

SHOWPLAN XML

This event displays the graphical execution plan of a query.

While ShowPlan XML is not required to identify slow running queries, it is critical to understanding why a query is performing poorly and it needs to be included with the trace.

If you are a little confused about what each of these event do, don't worry, as we will see them in action very soon, when their use will make much more sense.

ANALYZING CAPTURED EVENTS

Figure 4-1 shows an example trace, displaying the captured events relating to the firing of a single stored procedure. Let's examine each event in turn and see how they "fit" together.

NOTE:

This example focuses on tracing a stored procedure called by the EXECUTE statement, and not called as a Remote Procedure Call (RPC).

Duration	EventClass	ObjectName	TextData	CPU	Reads	Writes
	SQL:BatchStarting		exec dbo.ADGSP_SO_LOADNOTSHIP			
	ShowPlan XML	ADGSP_SO_LOADNOT...	<ShowPlanXML xmlns="http://sc...			
4493	SP:StmtCompleted	ADGSP_SO_LOADNOT...	SELECT DISTINCT so_hdr_...	3244	158114	157
4493	SQL:BatchCompleted		exec dbo.ADGSP_SO_LOADNOTSHIP	3244	158120	157

Figure 4-1: Trace results of a stored procedure.

Row 1 shows the SQL:BatchStarting event. The main reason I use this context event is because it indicates when a stored procedure is called, along with its name. In this case, the stored procedure is dbo.ADGSP_SO_LOADNOTSHIP.

Row 2 shows the Showplan XML event, which provides a graphical execution plan of the Transact-SQL statement shown in the next event (Row 3). We'll discuss graphical execution plans in more detail a little later in this chapter.

Row 3 is the SP:StmtCompleted event, which shows the actual code that has run (you can see part of it in the TextData data column in figure 4-1 above), together with the time taken by the event (Duration), the amount of CPU time, and the number of logical Reads and physical disk Writes. While this example has a single SP:StmtCompleted event, as noted earlier, if a stored procedure has more than one statement in it, you will see a SP:StmtCompleted event for each individual statement within the stored procedure.

The SQL:BatchCompleted event in Row 4 indicates that this stored procedure has completed, and that all statements within it have fired. It also displays the name of the stored procedure (again), and the Duration, CPU, Reads, and Writes for the entire stored procedure. Since there is only a single statement in the stored procedure, the values for the Duration, CPU, Reads, and Writes for the SQL:BatchCompleted event are very similar to those for SP:StmtCompleted event in row 3. If there were multiple statements within the stored procedure, then the Duration, CPU, Reads, and Writes for the SQL:BatchCompleted event would be the sum (or a very close approximation) of all the SP:StmtCompleted events that occurred during the execution of the stored procedure.

Let's now look at a different example. Figure 4-2 show a captured event related to the firing of a single Transact-SQL statement that is *not* inside a stored procedure.

Duration	EventClass	ObjectName	TextData	CPU	Reads	Writes
	SQL:BatchStarting		SELECT top 50000 *, g1_...			
	Showplan XML	Dynamic SQL	<ShowPlanXML xmlns="http://sc...			
212	SQL:BatchCompleted		SELECT top 50000 *, g1_...	218	2782	0

Figure 4-2: Traces results of a query not inside a stored procedure.

When this single T-SQL query executes, it generates three events.

Row 1 shows the SQL:BatchStarting event, but because we're looking at the execution of a single T-SQL statement, rather than a stored procedure, the TextData data column of the SQL:BatchStarting event shows the T-SQL code of the query that is executing, not the name of a stored procedure, as we saw in the previous example.

Row 2 shows the Showplan XML event, which provides a graphical execution plan of the Transact-SQL statement that was executed.

Row 3 shows the SQL:BatchCompleted event, which repeats the T-SQL code in the TextData data column we saw in the SQL:BatchStarting event in Row 1, but it also includes the Duration, CPU, Reads, and Writes for the event.

By this time, hopefully you are beginning to see why I have selected the events I did, and how they are used. The more you use Profiler to analyze trace results like this, the easier it will for you to become familiar with the various events and how they can best provide the information you need when analyzing them.

SELECTING DATA COLUMNS

Having discussed the Profiler events needed to identify slow queries and why, it's time to do the same for the data columns. I reiterate: it's important to select only those data columns you really need, in order to minimize the amount of resources consumed by the trace. The fewer data columns you select, the less overhead there is in collecting it.

As with events, the data columns regarded as necessary will vary from DBA to DBA. In my case, I choose to collect these data columns when identifying slow queries:

- Duration
- ObjectName
- TextData
- CPU
- Reads
- Writes
- IntegerData
- DatabaseName
- ApplicationName
- StartTime
- EndTime
- SPID
- LoginName
- EventSequence
- BinaryData

Let's look at each one to see what it collects. While I might not use all the information found in all columns for every analysis, I generally end up using all of them at some point in time as I analyze various queries.

DURATION

This very useful data column provides the length of time in *microseconds* that an event takes from beginning to end, but what is curious is than when Duration is displayed from the Profiler GUI, it is shown, by default, in *milliseconds*. So internally, SQL Server stores Duration data as microseconds, but displays it as milliseconds in Profiler. If you want, you can change this default behavior by going to Tools|Options in Profiler and select "Show values in Duration column in microseconds". I prefer to leave it to the default display of milliseconds, as it is easier to read. All the examples in this book will be shown in milliseconds.

Since our goal in this trace is to identify long-running queries, the Duration data column is central to our analysis. Later, we will create both a filter and an aggregation on this data column to help with our analysis.

Note that the Duration data column only exists for the RPC:Completed, SP:StmtCompleted and SQL:BatchCompleted events.

OBJECTNAME

This is the logical name of the object being referenced during an event. If a stored procedure is being executed, then the name of the stored procedure is displayed. If an isolated query is being executed, then the message "Dynamic SQL" is inserted in this data column. This column therefore provides a quick means of telling whether or not a query is part of a stored procedure.

Note that this data column is not captured for the **SQL:BatchStarting** or **the SQL:BatchCompleted** events.

TEXTDATA

As our previous examples have indicated, the contents of the TextData column depend on the event that is being captured and in what context.

For the SQL:BatchStarting or SQL:BatchCompleted events, the TextData column will either contain the name of the executing stored procedure or, for a query outside a stored procedure, the Transact-SQL code for that query.

If the event is SP:StmtCompleted, the TextData column contains the Transact-SQL code for the query executed within the stored procedure.

For the Showplan XML event, it includes the XML code used to create the graphical execution plan for the query.

CPU

This data column shows the amount of CPU time used by an event (in milliseconds). Obviously, the smaller this number, the fewer CPU resources were used for the query. Note that CPU data column is only captured for the RPC:Completed, SP:StmtCompleted, and the SQL:BatchCompleted events.

READS

This data column shows the number of *logical* page reads that occurred during an event. Again, the smaller this number, the fewer disk I/O resources were used for the event. Note that Reads are only captured for the RPC:Completed, SP:StmtCompleted and the SQL:BatchCompleted events.

WRITES

This data column shows the number of *physical* writes that occurred during an event and provides an indication of the I/O resources that were used for an event. Again, Writes is only captured for the RPC:Completed, SP:StmtCompleted and the SQL:BatchCompleted events.

INTEGERDATA

The value of this column depends on the event. For the SP:StmtCompleted event, the value is the actual number of rows that were returned for the event. For the ShowPlan XML event, it shows the estimated number of rows that were to be returned for the event, based on the query's execution plan. The other events don't use this data column. Knowing how many rows a query actually returns can help you determine how hard a query is working. If you know that a query returns a single row, then it should use a lot less resources than a query that returns 100,000 rows. If you notice that the actual number or rows returned is significantly different that the estimated value of rows returned, this may indicate that the statistics used by the Query Optimizer to create the execution plan for the query is out of date. Out of date statistics can result in poorly performing queries and they should be updated for optimal query performance.

DATABASENAME

This is the name of the database the event occurred in. Often, you will want to filter on this data column so that you only capture those events that occur in a specific database.

APPLICATIONNAME

This is the name of the client application that is communicating with SQL Server. Some applications populate this data column; others don't. Assuming this data column is populated, you can use it to filter events on a particular application.

STARTTIME

Virtually every event has a StartTime data column and, as you would expect, it includes the time the event started. Often, the start time of an event can be matched to other related events to identify their order of execution. It can also be compared to the stop time of events to determine the differences in time between when one event started and another completed.

ENDTIME

The EndTime data column is used for those events that have a specific end time associated with them. It can be used to help identify when a particular query or transaction runs at a specific point in time.

SPID

This data column is mandatory for every event, and contains the number of the server process ID (SPID) that is assigned to the client process creating the event. It can help identify what connections are being used for an event, and can also be used as a filter to limit the number of events returned to those of particular interest.

LOGINNAME

Most events include the LoginName data column. It stores the login of the user that triggered the event. Depending on the type of login used, this column can contain either the SQL Server Login ID or the Windows Login ID (domain\username). This very useful data column helps you identify who is causing potential problems. It is a good column to filter on, in order to limit trace results to those of a specific user.

EVENTSEQUENCE

Every event produced by SQL Server Profiler is assigned a sequence number that indicates the order that events occurred in SQL Server. Much of the time, you will capture traces in default order, which means the events are displayed in the order they occurred in the Profiler GUI. EventSequence numbers appear in ascending order.

However, should you choose to apply a custom grouping, based on a certain data column such as Duration, then the EventSequence data column makes it easier for you to see which events occurred before, or after, other events.

BINARYDATA

This data column is only populated for the Showplan XML event and includes the estimated cost of a query, which is used for displaying the graphical execution plan of the query. This data is not human-readable, and is used by Profiler internally to help display the graphical execution plan.

CREATING A FILTER

When creating a trace to identify long-running queries, I generally include two or more filters in order to minimize the number of rows returned in my trace.

The first, and most important, filter I create is on the **Duration** data column, which returns the length of time it takes for a particular event (query) to run. I use this filter to exclude queries that execute very quickly (which is most queries). The hard part is determining the threshold at which a query becomes "long-running". For example, is a long-running query one that takes more than 1 second, more than 5 seconds, more than 15 seconds?

I generally use 5000 milliseconds (5 seconds), although this is just a personal preference and you will want to adjust this to best meet your needs. In this example, however, I am going to use 100 milliseconds as my limit, just because it is easier to create illustrative examples using a smaller value.

In addition to the Duration filter, I generally add additional ones in order to reduce the number of events captured. For example, I might only want to collect queries for a specific database, a specific application, or a specific user. In this example, I have created a second filter on the **DatabaseName** column, in order to limit my trace data to events raised in a specific database, as shown in Figure 4-3:

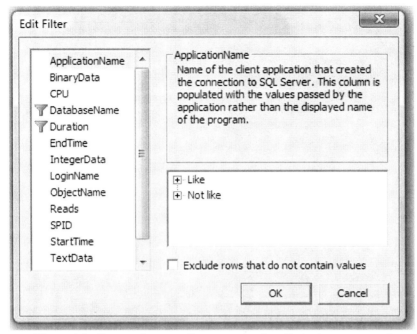

Figure 4-3: Create whatever filters you need to limit the amount of events returned.

ORGANIZING COLUMNS

When you use the "Organize Columns" window, you have two major decisions to make:

- Whether or not you want to group any of the data columns and aggregate the results
- The order in which you want the data columns arranged when the trace results are returned.

Judicious column organization can make the analysis of the results much easier to perform. When creating a trace to identify long running queries, I always group by Duration, as shown in figure 4-4, so that I can quickly identify the longest-running queries:

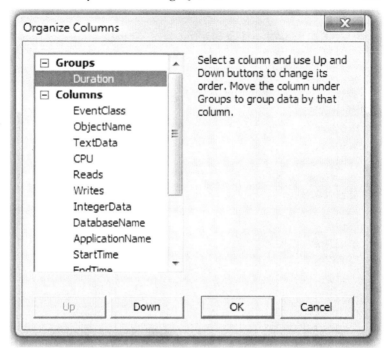

Figure 4-4: I like to group by Duration, and arrange the other data columns in the order that makes the most sense for me.

I also like to rearrange the order of the data columns so that the most useful columns appear to the left, and the less useful columns to the right. Figure 4-4 above shows my personal preferences.

CREATING A TEMPLATE

I run this trace a lot, so I have created it as a custom trace template, which includes all the events, data columns, column filters and column organization described previously. I suggest you do the same, as described in the "Custom Profiler Trace Templates" section of Chapter 2.

RUNNING THE TRACE

Once you have created your trace template, it is time to run it. Ideally this will be on a production server, otherwise on a test server and a stress test tool, or a simple load-generation script (see Chapter 1).

Keep the following in mind when you run this trace to identify slow running queries:

- Select a day that represents a typical workload.

- Run the trace for an entire day. This might seem like a long time, but if your filters are effective, you should not collect too much data. If this is the first time you have run it, you may want to monitor the trace file size throughout the day to ensure that it is not using up too much space.
- Before you start the trace, choose to save it to a file as the trace runs.
- Start the trace manually and set it to stop automatically after 24 hours.
- Up to this point, we have only discussed running traces from the Profiler GUI. However, you can also run this same trace using system stored procedures. By doing so, you will reduce the load on the server. You will learn how to use system-stored procedures to run a trace later in this book, in the chapter on "How to Capture Profiler Traces Programmatically".

Once you have captured the trace, you are ready to analyze it.

ANALYZING THE POORLY PERFORMING QUERIES IDENTIFIED BY PROFILER

Let's assume that you have just created and run a trace similar to the one just described. What do the results look like, and how do you use this trace to identify and troubleshoot slow-performing queries?

The following sections set out my preferred way of performing an analysis on slow-performing queries. As always, through practice, you will develop a methodology that works best for you.

THE BIG PICTURE

Before drilling down into statement-level analysis, I always start by looking at the big picture. When I ran our example trace template on my sample database, I got trace screen that looked as shown in Figure 4-5:

Duration	EventClass	ObjectName	TextData
+	(157)		
+ 165 (1)			
+ 206 (1)			
+ 206 (1)			
+ 206 (1)			
+ 207 (1)			

Duration	EventClass	ObjectName	TextData
+ 9951 (1)			
+ 9952 (1)			
+ 9954 (1)			
+ 10230 (1)			
+ 10232 (1)			
+ 12592 (1)			
+ 12594 (1)			
+ 14602 (1)			
+ 14604 (1)			
+ 15086 (1)			
+ 15088 (1)			

Figure 4-5: After you have completed the trace, scroll through the events to get a feeling for the results you got back.

Note that, since the events are grouped by Duration, each event is aggregated by Duration. Also, all one can see are the Duration times; no other data. Given the absence of any data beyond duration, you may be tempted to drill quickly down to individual events. However, it is definitely worth spending a little time analyzing this "big picture" screen.

In Figure 4-5, for ease of presentation, I've actually split one big screen into two smaller ones. The top screen shows 5 events that marginally exceeded the 100-millisecond threshold and the lower screen shows 11 events that exceeded it substantially. This information, on its own, can be informative. What if, for example, there were several hundred events that "marginally" exceeded the threshold? You would very quickly be overwhelmed with data – an indication that the Duration threshold on your filter is not set appropriately. The next time you run this trace, you should increase the Duration threshold on your filter so that you can focus your efforts on a manageable number of events and on those that need the most urgent attention. Having fixed these queries you can then rerun the trace with a lower Duration limit and start work on the slow-running queries that did not make the first cut.

Conversely, you may find that only very few events have been captured. If this is the case, then you may want to rerun the trace using a lower Duration threshold, in order to identify more queries. Of course, this also may be a sign that you don't have any long-running queries, which would be a good thing.

FINDING SLOW-RUNNING PROCEDURES AND QUERIES

The next step is to review each event in the trace, starting with those at the bottom – i.e. the slowest-running events that took the most time to execute. To do this, click on the plus sign next to each of the events you want to examine, as shown in figure 4-6:

Duration	EventClass	ObjectName	TextData	CPU	Reads
10230 (1)					
10230	SP:StmtCompleted	ADGSP_PO_PurchasOrd	SELECT DISTINCT dbo.po_...	12027	14595
10232 (1)					
10232	SQL:BatchCompleted		exec dbo.ADGSP_PO_PurchasOrd	12027	14608
12592 (1)					
12592	SP:StmtCompleted	ADGSP_PO_PurchasOrd	SELECT DISTINCT dbo.po_...	15148	14595
12594 (1)					
12594	SQL:BatchCompleted		exec dbo.ADGSP_PO_PurchasOrd	15148	14608
14602 (1)					
14602	SP:StmtCompleted	ADGSP_PO_PurchasOrd	SELECT DISTINCT dbo.po_...	20623	14595
14604 (1)					
14604	SQL:BatchCompleted		exec dbo.ADGSP_PO_PurchasOrd	20623	14608
15086 (1)					
15086	SP:StmtCompleted	ADGSP_PO_PurchasOrd	SELECT DISTINCT dbo.po_...	19782	14595
15088 (1)					
15088	SQL:BatchCompleted		exec dbo.ADGSP_PO_PurchasOrd	19782	14608

Figure 4-6: Once the events are revealed, an entirely different representation of your data may appear.

The first thing to do is analyze this screen for any obvious "patterns".

NOTE:

The rows highlighted in blue aren't events, but aggregated results of events. The rows in white are the actual events captured by Profiler and this is where you should focus your attention.

The most obvious pattern is that the same stored procedure, ADGSP_PO_PurchasOrd, occurs in the ObjectName data column for each of the four SP:StmtCompleted events, including the longest running event, which takes over 15 seconds. This is a strong indication that this stored procedure would be a good place to start your investigations.

The second pattern, a little more subtle, is that each execution of this stored procedure appears to be associated with two events: SP:StmtCompleted and SQL:BatchCompleted. The first SP:StmtCompleted event in Figure 4-6, for example, is related to completion of the execution of a SELECT DISTINCT…query within the ADGSP_PO_PurchasOrd stored procedure. Its duration was 10230, the CPU time was 12027 and there were 14595 reads. Following that is a SQL:BatchCompleted event relating to completion of the execution of the the ADGSP_PO_PurchasOrd stored procedure, with a duration of 10232, CPU time of 12027 and 14608 reads.

If the Duration, CPU and Reads times for these two events look suspiciously similar. That is because, in this case, they are in effect the same event. So, the 8 events that we see here represent the execution of 4 queries – not 8 queries, as you may initially suspect. In fact, what we are seeing here is 4 executions of a stored procedure that contains a single T-SQL statement. The SP:StmtCompleted is fired when the Transact-SQL statement within the stored procedure has completed; the SQL:BatchCompleted event is fired whenever a Transact-SQL statement is fired, whether or not it is inside or outside a stored procedure, and it also fires at the end of the execution of every stored procedure. In this case, these two events occur more or less simultaneously.

You may be thinking that this is an unnecessary duplication of data, and we should just collect one event or the other. However, there are several reasons why it is essential to capture both events. The most obvious one is that, if we omitted the SQL:BatchCompleted event, then we would miss any T-SQL statements that occurred outside of a stored procedure.

Furthermore, consider a different set of trace results, as shown in Figure 4-7:

Duration	EventClass	ObjectName	TextData	CPU	Reads
	Trace Start				
	SQL:BatchStarting		EXECUTE dbo.test		
	Showplan XML	test	<ShowPlanXML xmlns="http://schemas....		
2809	SP:StmtCompleted	test	SELECT top 50000 *, ...	218	2782
	Showplan XML	test	<ShowPlanXML xmlns="http://schemas....		
2399	SP:StmtCompleted	test	SELECT top 50000 *, ...	218	2782
	Showplan XML	test	<ShowPlanXML xmlns="http://schemas....		
2924	SP:StmtCompleted	test	SELECT top 60000 *, ...	141	3339
	Showplan XML	test	<ShowPlanXML xmlns="http://schemas....		
4760	SP:StmtCompleted	test	SELECT top 70000 *, ...	327	3695
	Showplan XML	test	<ShowPlanXML xmlns="http://schemas....		
4430	SP:StmtCompleted	test	SELECT top 80000 *, ...	375	4456
17324	SQL:BatchCompleted		EXECUTE dbo.test	1279	17257
	Trace Stop				

Figure 4-7: This is an example with a stored procedure that has five queries within it.

Here, we see:

1. One SQL:BatchStarting event, relating the start of the execution of a dbo.test stored procedure

2. Five SP:StmtCompleted events, each with a different duration, and each representing the execution of a separate query within a single stored procedure

3. One SQL:BatchCompleted event relating the end of the execution of a dbo.test stored procedure

If you add up the Duration, CPU, and Reads for each query within the stored procedure, the sum total will be very close to the total found in the SQL:BatchCompleted event.

This is another example of why it is important to include both the SQL:BatchCompleted (and SQL:BatchStarting) event as well as the SP:StmtCompleted event, when performing an analysis of slow-performing queries. The former gives you the big picture for the stored procedure and the latter the details.

To summarize what we have learned so far: we have identified eight events that took over 10 seconds each to execute. We discovered that a single stored procedure was the cause of all 8 events that exceeded 10 seconds. We then drilled down into the data and discovered that there were not really eight queries but only four, as each execution of the stored procedure was represented by two events and what we were seeing was four executions of a stored procedure containing a single T-SQL statement.

While, for our simple example, it seemed as if we were collecting duplicate data, we also saw that for more complex traces it was vital to collect all these events, in order to get the complete picture.

FINDING QUERIES AND PROCEDURES THAT EXECUTE FREQUENTLY

It is important not only to identify long-running queries, but also to identify those queries that execute the most often. For example, which is worse, a query that runs once an hour and takes 30 seconds to run, or a query that runs 100 times a second that takes 1 second to run? I think you would agree that the shorter query would probably have more effect on the overall performance of the system than the longer one.

So how do we determine how often a query runs? Unfortunately, the tools that accompany SQL Server don't make this easy. One option would be use the SQL Server 2005 SP2 Performance Dashboard tool. This tool automatically calculates the twenty most resource-hogging queries that are currently in the plan cache. It does this by summing up the total duration of queries each time they run, which identifies those queries that use the most resources overall. The problem with this tool is that it only accounts for queries that are currently in the plan cache. This means that the results don't fairly represent all the queries that have run all day on your SQL Server instance.

Alternatively, we can export our profiler trace data into a SQL Server table, as described in Chapter 2, and use a little SQL code to produce the report we need, as shown in figure 4-8:

```
SELECT    [ObjectName],
          COUNT(*) AS [SP Count]
FROM      [dbo].[Identify_query_counts]
WHERE     [Duration] > 100
          AND [ObjectName] IS NOT NULL
GROUP BY  [ObjectName]
ORDER BY  [SP Count] DESC
```

	ObjectName	SP Count
1	ADGSP_EN_SalesInstr	17
2	ADGSP_PO_PurchasOrd	16
3	ADGSP_SO_LOADNOTSHIP	9
4	ADGSP_EN_BOLInstr	9
5	ADGSP_EN_Instructions	9

Figure 4-8: You can manually perform your own analysis on trace data stored in a SQL Server table.

NOTE:

This code sample only counts stored procedures, not other T-SQL that may have been captured in your trace. You will need to modify the query in order to extract information on these queries.

This code simply counts the number of times a stored procedure has run with a duration longer than 100 milliseconds. We can immediately see that the ADGSP_PO_PurchasOrd stored procedure, which we identified as the home of our longest running queries, is the second most commonly run query in this trace. This is a confirmation that this procedure, and the query within it, needs our attention

Once we have dealt with it, we can then use the information from figure 4-6 (long-running queries) and figure 4-8 (how often queries run) to help us prioritize what other queries we should focus on.

As you can see, you have many options about how to analyze your data. It is impossible to explore them all. What I hope to accomplish is for you to be aware of your options and then, based on your current skill set and available tools, for you decide the best approach to identify those queries that need the greatest attention.

ANALYZING PROBLEM QUERIES

Now that we have identified a specific stored procedure, ADGSG_PO_PurchasOrd, that needs work, let's start analyzing it so that we can identify what is the cause of its slowness, with the presumption that it will enable us to fix the problem.

DRILLING IN TO THE TRACE DATA

At this point, within Profiler, our data has been aggregated by Duration. This is a useful way to get started on our analysis, as we have already discovered. In the next step, what I often do is to disaggregate the data, so that the events are displayed in the order they actually occurred. This allows me to examine the stored procedure in question in the context of actual events occurring on the server.

To disaggregate trace data, select from the main menu, View | Aggregated View, as shown in Figure 4-9:

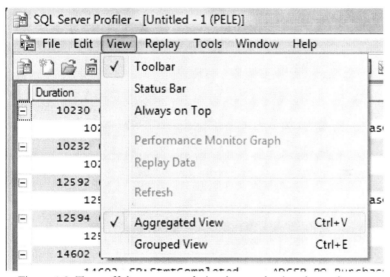

Figure 4-9: Turn off the aggregated view by unselecting the option.

This will remove the checkmark next to "Aggregated View" and the data you see in Profiler changes appearance, as shown in Figure 4-10:

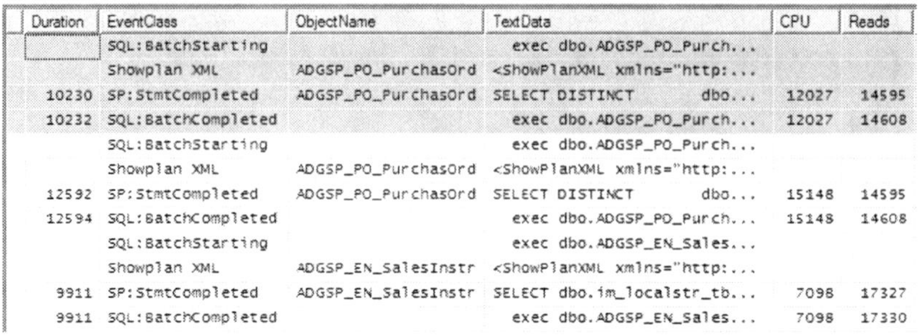

Duration	EventClass	ObjectName	TextData	CPU	Reads
	SQL:BatchStarting		exec dbo.ADGSP_PO_Purch...		
	Showplan XML	ADGSP_PO_PurchasOrd	<ShowPlanXML xmlns="http:...		
10230	SP:StmtCompleted	ADGSP_PO_PurchasOrd	SELECT DISTINCT dbo...	12027	14595
10232	SQL:BatchCompleted		exec dbo.ADGSP_PO_Purch...	12027	14608
	SQL:BatchStarting		exec dbo.ADGSP_PO_Purch...		
	Showplan XML	ADGSP_PO_PurchasOrd	<ShowPlanXML xmlns="http:...		
12592	SP:StmtCompleted	ADGSP_PO_PurchasOrd	SELECT DISTINCT dbo...	15148	14595
12594	SQL:BatchCompleted		exec dbo.ADGSP_PO_Purch...	15148	14608
	SQL:BatchStarting		exec dbo.ADGSP_EN_Sales...		
	Showplan XML	ADGSP_EN_SalesInstr	<ShowPlanXML xmlns="http:...		
9911	SP:StmtCompleted	ADGSP_EN_SalesInstr	SELECT dbo.im_localstr_tb...	7098	17327
9911	SQL:BatchCompleted		exec dbo.ADGSP_EN_Sales...	7098	17330

Figure 4-10: Events are now ordered in the way they were captured.

In Figure 4-10, I have scrolled the window to display three distinct stored procedure events. The first one is highlighted in blue, which shows all the events we captured that are associated with the ADGSP_PO_PurchasOrd stored procedure. We also see another four events associated with a second execution of the same stored procedure, and we see a third stored procedure that's not related to our current analysis. To keep our analysis simple, let's focus on the four events highlighted in blue.

Together, these four events describe what happens to the stored procedure as it is executed. In row 1, we see that a SQL:BatchStarting event has occurred. By expanding the TextData column, or just by clicking on the event row and examining the window in the bottom half of the Profiler screen, as shown in Figure 4-11, we can see that it relates to the execution of our problem ADGSP_PO_PurchasOrd stored procedure:

```
exec dbo.ADGSP_PO_PurchasOrd
go
```

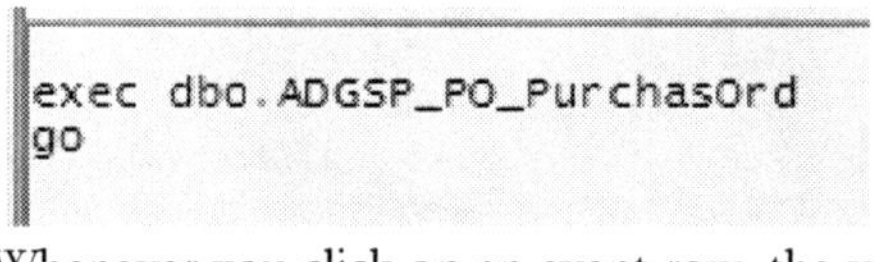

Figure 4-11: Whenever you click on an event row, the value of the TextData data column is displayed in the window at the bottom of the Profiler screen.

As mentioned earlier in this chapter, the SQL:BatchStarting event is a context event. It is not strictly required for analysis of slow queries, but it helps us to keep track of where we are in an analysis.

Row 2 in Figure 4-10 is a Showplan XML event, providing a graphical execution plan of the Transact-SQL that is about to be executed. To view the graphical execution plan, click on this row and you will see it at the bottom of the screen, as shown in Figure 4-12:

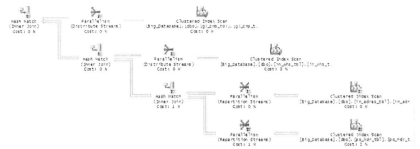

Figure 4-12: This figure only shows part of the execution plan. The entire plan would not fit on the screen.

The graphical execution plan is our main tool for determining why a particular query may be slow. For the moment, however, let's hold off on how to interpret it and look at row 3 of Figure 4-10.

Row 3 shows the SP:StmtCompleted event, indicating the end of a Transact-SQL statement within a stored procedure. It also includes the Duration, CPU, Reads and Writes for the statement. What is useful about this event is found in the TextData column. When you click on this row, the code that just ran is displayed at the bottom window of the screen, as shown in Figure 4-13:

```
SELECT DISTINCT
    dbo.po_hdr_tbl.gl_cmp_key AS Company,
    dbo.po_hdr_tbl.so_brnch_key AS Branch,
    dbo.po_hdr_tbl.po_hdr_key AS [Purchase Order No],
    dbo.po_hdr_tbl.ap_delfm_key AS [Vendor No],
    dbo.po_hdr_tbl.po_hdr_revno AS [Change Order No],
    dbo.po_hdr_tbl.po_hdr_revdt AS [Change Order Date],
    dbo.po_hdr_tbl.po_hdr_via AS [Ship Via],
    dbo.po_hdr_tbl.in_whs_key AS [Whse Key],
    dbo.po_hdr_tbl.ar_terms_key AS [Terms Key],
    dbo.po_hdr_tbl.in_buyc AS [Buyer Key],
    dbo.po_hdr_tbl.po_hdr_confm AS [Confirmed-by Name],
    dbo.po_hdr_tbl.en_carr_key AS [Carrier Key],
    dbo.po_dtl_tbl.po_dtl_key AS [Detail Line no],
    dbo.po_dtl_tbl.in_item_key AS [Item No],
    dbo.po_dtl_tbl.po_dtl_uom AS [Detail UOM],
    dbo.po_dtl_tbl.po_dtl_cmmts AS [Detail Comments],
    dbo.po_dtl_tbl.po_dtl_entdt AS [PO Date],
    dbo.po_dtl_tbl.po_dtl_prqty AS Quantity,
    dbo.po_dtl_tbl.po_dtl_quotc AS [PO Price],
    dbo.po_dtl_tbl.po_dtl_quotcf AS [PO Price Foreign],
    dbo.po_dtl_tbl.en_uom_pruom AS [Pricing UOM],
    dbo.po_dtl_tbl.po_dtl_taxf AS [Detail Tax Flag],
    dbo.po_dtl_tbl.po_dtl_reqdt AS [Required Date],
    dbo.in_whs_tbl.in_whs_name AS [Ship To Name],
    dbo.in_whs_tbl.in_whs_adr1 AS [ShipAddress 1],
    dbo.in_whs_tbl.in_whs_adr2 AS [ShipAddress 2],
    dbo.in_whs_tbl.in_whs_city AS [Ship City],
    dbo.in_whs_tbl.in_whs_state AS [Ship State],
    dbo.in_whs_tbl.in_whs_postc AS [Ship Zip],
    dbo.in_whs_tbl.in_whs_telex AS [Tax exempt no],
    dbo.in_buyc_tbl.in_buyc_desc AS [Buyer Name],
    dbo.ar_terms_tbl.ar_terms_desc AS Terms,
    dbo.im_adres_tbl.im_adres_name AS [Vendor Name],
    dbo.im_adres_tbl.im_adres_line1 AS [Vendor Addr1],
    dbo.im_adres_tbl.im_adres_line2 AS [Vendor Addr2],
    dbo.im_adres_tbl.im_adres_line3 AS [Vendor Addr3],
    dbo.im_adres_tbl.im_adres_city AS [Vendor City],
    dbo.im_adres_tbl.im_adres_state AS [Vendor State],
    dbo.im_adres_tbl.im_adres_pczip AS [Vendor Zip],
    dbo.en_carr_tbl.en_carr_desc AS [Carrier Desc],
    dbo.po_hdr_tbl.en_fob_key AS FOB,
    dbo.en_fob_tbl.en_fob_desc AS [FOB Desc],
    a.en_itdsc_desc AS [Ext Description 0],
    b.en_itdsc_desc AS [Ext Description 1],
    c.en_itdsc_desc AS [Ext Description 2],
    d.en_itdsc_desc AS [Ext Description 3],
    e.en_itdsc_desc AS [Ext Description 4],
    f.en_itdsc_desc AS [Ext Description 5],
    g.en_itdsc_desc AS [Ext Description 6],
    h.en_itdsc_desc AS [Ext Description 7],
    i.en_itdsc_desc AS [Ext Description 8],
    j.en_itdsc_desc AS [Ext Description 9],
    dbo.po_hdr_tbl.po_hdr_orddt AS [Order Date],
    dbo.in_item_tbl.in_desc AS [Item Description],
    dbo.in_item_tbl.in_type_key AS [Item Type Key],
    dbo.po_hdr_tbl.po_hdr_frtf AS [PO HDR FOBF],
    dbo.en_fob_tbl.en_fob_desc AS [PO HDR FOBDSC],
    dbo.po_hdr_ext.po_hdr_a_cmmt_txt AS [PO HDR Comments],
    dbo.po_hdr_ext.po_hdr_b_po_pallet_txt AS [Nbr Pallet]
```

Figure 4-13: The code for this stored procedure is so long that only a small portion of it appears in this figure.

If I did not collect this event as part of my trace, then I would have to manually go to Management Studio, find the stored procedure code within the stored procedure itself, and then look at it there. As it is now displayed in Profiler, I can view the full T-SQL code right alongside the execution plan, which we will soon find is very useful.

Row 4 is the SQL:BatchCompleted event; it includes the Duration, CPU, Reads, and Writes data columns summed for the entire stored procedure. In this case, since there is only one Transact-SQL statement in the stored procedure, the SP:StmtCompleted and SQL:BatchCompleted events are almost identical.

In these cases, I use the values from the SQL:BatchCompleted event as they tend to be a little larger than the same values from the SP:StmtCompleted event. However, in reality, the differences between them are so small it is unimportant which one you end up using.

DOES A QUERY RUN SLOWLY EVERY TIME?

Let's recap what we know for certain at this stage:

- We know that the longest-running T-SQL statement (>15 seconds) arose from the execution of the ADGSP_PO_PurchasOrd stored procedure (Figure 4-6).
- We know for sure that this stored procedure ran 16 times over our examination period (Figure 4-8)
- We know which four events make up the execution of this stored procedure

What we don't know is whether this procedure *always* runs slowly, or just occasionally. Generally, we would expect the same Transact-SQL code to run in about the same amount of time each time it runs, although we would have to allow for variations in the overall server load.

However, what if we discovered cases where the duration was radically different? For example, we know the longest time it ran was about 15 seconds, but what if we found that sometimes this stored procedure only takes 1 second to run? This is important to know.

Assuming the trace is not large, one quick and dirty way to find out the 16 individual durations for each execution of ADGSP_PO_PurchasOrd stored procedure would be to search for the stored procedure name in the Profiler trace, using the "Find" command. For example, from the main menu, select Edit|Find, then type in ADGSP_PO_PurchasOrd and have Profiler search the ObjectName Column, as shown in Figure 4-14:

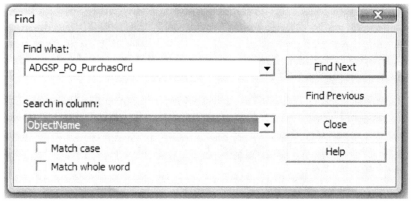

Figure 4-14: Use the Find option to search through your trace from within Profiler.

Having found the first instance of the stored procedure, note its Duration and then click "Find Next" until you have recorded each of the 16 durations for that stored procedure, as shown in Figure 4-15:

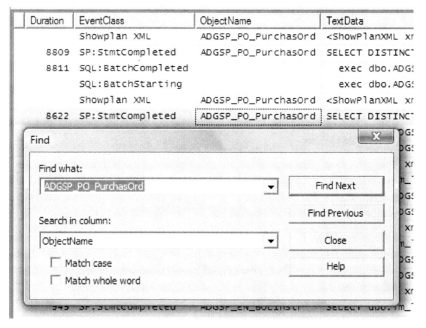

Figure 4-15: Use "Find Next" to continue searching through the trace.

In my example, I recorded 8901 milliseconds as the fastest time in which the stored procedure ran, and 15088 milliseconds as the slowest. This duration range, from 8901 through 15088, may or may not be significant. The only way to know for sure is to investigate further.

NOTE:

As traces increase in size, using "Find" becomes more laborious. It is easier to create some Transact-SQL code yourself and run it against the trace data, stored in a database table, to identify the duration of each execution of the stored procedure.

The next step in the investigation is to compare the CPU, Reads, Writes, Transact-SQL code and the execution plans for the slowest and fastest durations, as shown in figure 4-16 and 4-17:

Duration	EventClass	ObjectName	TextData	CPU	Reads	Writes
	SQL:BatchStarting		exec dbo.ADGSP_PO_Purch...			
	Showplan XML	ADGSP_PO_PurchasOrd	<ShowPlanXML xmlns="http:...			
15086	SP:StmtCompleted	ADGSP_PO_PurchasOrd	SELECT DISTINCT dbo...	19782	14595	0
15088	SQL:BatchCompleted		exec dbo.ADGSP_PO_Purch...	19782	14608	0

Figure 4-16: The four events that make up the longest-running instance of the stored procedure.

	SQL:BatchStarting		exec dbo.ADGSP_PO_Purch...			
	Showplan XML	ADGSP_PO_PurchasOrd	<ShowPlanXML xmlns="http:...			
8900	SP:StmtCompleted	ADGSP_PO_PurchasOrd	SELECT DISTINCT dbo...	9280	14595	0
8901	SQL:BatchCompleted		exec dbo.ADGSP_PO_Purch...	9280	14608	0

Figure 4-17: The four events that make up the shortest-running instance of the stored procedure.

The most obvious difference is in the CPU times. The CPU time for 8900-duration execution is about half the 15088-duration. So, how do we account for these differences in Duration and CPU, and are they significant?

Examining the data more closely, we see that the Reads in each case are identical. Though I am not showing all the screens here, the TextData columns for the Sp:StmtCompleted event reveal the code executed to be identical in each case, as are the execution plans. Also, the same number of rows, 72,023, is returned each time (more on this shortly).

Given all this, it is fair to assume that the differences in Duration and CPU time are based on different server loads at the time of each execution, not on differences in the query, or how the query was executed.

NOTE:

Another possible explanation why there was a difference in duration between different executions of the same query is that blocking may be affecting some executions of a query, but not other executions of the same query. In the next chapter, you will learn how to identify potential blocking issues.

Now, if we had seen differences in the code (different input parameters), a different execution plan, different numbers of logical Reads, and different numbers of rows returned, then our conclusion would be different. These observations would indicate that SQL Server is doing different work (using different resources) each time the stored procedure is run. This could mean that column or index statistics may not have been updated as they should, or perhaps they were updated between runs of the instances. It could mean that the parameters of the stored procedure affected the amount of work needed, and so on. In other words, we would need to investigate further the root cause of these differences.

In our simple case, however, we can assume these variations in duration are insignificant and can move on to our next step, which is evaluating the query for performance; we can also assume that the work we do for a single instance of the stored procedure will affect all other instances of its running in a similar way.

TUNING SLOW QUERIES

Now that we have established that we need to tune our single stored procedure, what information does Profiler provide? For the most part, we have already talked about the most useful data, namely the Duration, CPU, Read and Writes columns, the actual code, and the execution plan. All this information is helpful in determining why a particular query may be slower than it needs to be.

In addition, one of the first things I look at is how many rows are returned by the query. You can obtain this data from the IntergerData column, as shown in Figure 4-18:

Duration	EventClass	ObjectName	TextData		CPU	Reads	Writes	IntegerData
15086	SP:StmtCompleted	ADGSP_PO_PurchasOrd	SELECT DISTINCT	dbo...	19782	14595	0	72023

Figure 4-18: The IntegerData data column of the SP:StmtCompleted event shows you how many rows were actually returned by the query.

It is important to realize that the IntegerData column shows the *actual* number of rows returned by the query, while the execution plan, which we will look at next, only provides the *estimated* number of rows returned.

The next step is to figure out if the number of rows returned seems reasonable. Time and again, I see queries that return tens, or hundreds, of thousands of rows that aren't needed by the client application. So SQL

Server has to do all this extra work returning unnecessary rows and then the client application filters out only the handful it really needs.

In this particular example, 72023 rows are returned. On the surface, this sounds like a high number. Rarely would you need to return this many rows to a client application; of course, there are always exceptions.

Nevertheless, this number of rows sets alarm bells ringing and I would investigate further the purpose of this query. In this particular case, the purpose of the stored procedure is to return all the line items for a single purchase order. I really doubt that there are any purchase orders that have 72023 rows of detailed information. Returning too much data tells me something very important: it tells me that the WHERE clause of the query is not well written, allowing too many rows to being returned and slowing the query.

When too many rows are being returned, you need to look at the WHERE clause of the query to see how it is written. Here's the WHERE clause for this stored procedure.

```
WHERE dbo.po_hdr_tbl.in_buyc <> ''
```

Figure 4-19: This is the entire WHERE clause for this query.

If you have any experience at all with writing queries, it is obvious that this WHERE clause has problems. It tells SQL Server to return all rows where the "in_buyc" column is not empty. This is not a very restrictive WHERE clause because it is based on a single column, and because it is essentially looking for an either/or condition. One way to improve the performance of this query would be to rewrite the WHERE clause so that is it more restrictive, so fewer rows are returned.

Another major problem is that the WHERE clause is non-sargeble. This means that it cannot make use of an index to find the data it needs to return. In other words, an index scan will be performed to return the data. While the specifics of how to write a sargeble WHERE clause is beyond the scope of this book, it is worth noting that any time you use a "not equals" in a WHERE clause, the query optimizer must review every record in the table to find out whether or not each row satisfies the not equals condition.

To support the conclusion that the WHERE clause is not sargeble, let's look at the graphical execution plan that is provided to us from the Profiler trace.

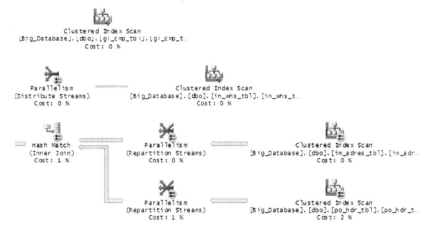

Figure 4-20: This is only a small portion of the entire execution plan for this query.

While figure 4-20 only shows part of the graphical execution plan, notice that there are four index scans occurring in this small portion of the query plan. Index scans occur when a clustered index has to be scanned, row by row, one row at a time, in order to identify the rows that need to be returned.

At this point, it may seem that analyzing why this query is performing slowly is complete. As usual, it depends. On one hand, we have barely looked at the code or the execution plan. There is still a lot of useful information that can be gleaned from it. How to do this is outside the scope of this book, as our goal here is to show you how to gather the data you need help you troubleshoot slow-performing queries, not to be able to analyze all of it. On the other hand, we have discovered two key pieces of information that, if acted on, could greatly speed up the query without doing any further analysis. First, we learned that too much data is being returned and that we need to make the WHERE clause more restrictive. Second, we learned that the current WHERE clause is non-sargeble, so we need to find a way to make it sargeble (assuming we can). With just these two pieces of data, we have a good start on what needs to be done to optimize the performance of this query.

SUMMARY

Let's review what we have learned in this chapter.

- We learned how to create a trace that can be used to help identify slow-running queries.
- We learned how to take the results of our trace and analyze them in such a way that we can identify which queries are slow-running.

- We have learned that Profiler can provide us with a wealth of information about our slow-running queries that can be used to help troubleshoot and optimize them.

As you can see, while Profiler is a great tool for uncovering problems, it still requires knowledge and experience on the part of the DBA or developer to analyze its output. The more you practice, the better you will become.

In the next chapter, we continue our quest on how to create and analyze traces to identify a wide variety of SQL Server problems.

Chapter 5
HOW TO IDENTIFY AND TROUBLESHOOT SQL SERVER PROBLEMS

While the previous chapter focused on a single topic, how to identify slow-running queries, this chapter shows how to create and analyze Profiler traces that will help you uncover a multitude of different problems – possibly ones you didn't even know you had!

Specifically, we will cover the following topics.

- How to Identify Deadlocks
- How to Identify Blocking Issues
- How to Identify Excessive Auto Stats Activity
- How to Identify Excessive Statement Compilations
- How to Identify Excessive Database File Growth/Shrinkage
- How to Identify Excessive Table/Index Scans
- How to Identify Memory Problems

In many of the sorts of traces presented in this chapter, you will be faced with a lot of *numbers*, such as the number of statement recompiles that occurred or the number of Sort Warnings, and you will need to decide whether these numbers are "good" or "bad". The only way you can really decide is if you know what these numbers look like during "normal operation" of your SQL Server. In other words, it's important that you capture these traces not just when problems have arisen, but when things are fine, so that you have a "baseline case" for comparison.

HOW TO IDENTIFY DEADLOCKS

Deadlocking occurs when two or more SQL Server processes have locks on separate database objects and each process is trying to acquire a lock on an object that the other processes have previously locked. For example, process one has an exclusive lock on object one, process two has an exclusive lock on object two, and process one also wants an exclusive lock on object two, and object two wants an exclusive lock on object one. Because two processes can't have an exclusive lock on the same object at the same time, the two processes become entangled in a deadlock, with neither process willing to yield of its own accord.

Since a deadlock is not a good thing for an application, SQL Server is smart enough to identify the problem and ends the deadlock by killing one of the processes – usually the process that has used the least amount of server resources up to that point. The aborted transaction is rolled back and the infamous "deadlock victim" error message is sent to the application. The other process can then continue to run as normal.

If the application is deadlock aware, it can resubmit the killed transaction automatically and the user may never know the deadlock happened. If the application is not deadlock aware, then most likely an error message appears on the application's screen and you get a call from a disgruntled user. Besides irritating users, deadlocks can use up SQL Server's resources unnecessarily as transactions are killed, rolled back, and resubmitted again.

Deadlocks have been the bane of many a DBA. While rare for a well-designed and written application, deadlocks can be a major problem for – how can I say this delicately? – "less efficient" application code. What is even more frustrating is there is not much the DBA can to do prevent deadlocks, as the burden of preventing them in the first place is on the application developers. Once an application is designed and written, it is hard for the DBA to do anything other than identify the offending code and report it back to the developers for fixing.

In SQL Server 2000 and earlier, the most common way to track down deadlock issues was to use a trace flag. In SQL Server 2005, trace flags can still be used (1204 or 1222), but it isn't always easy to do. When SQL Server 2005 was introduced, new events were added to the SQL Server Profiler that makes identifying deadlocks very easy. In this section, we learn how to use SQL Server Profiler to capture and analyze deadlocks.

DEADLOCK EVENTS

While there are many different combinations of events you can use to trace deadlocks using SQL Server Profiler, you may want to consider the following. For education purposes, I have included more events here than you really need, but they have been included for completeness.

The events you might consider collecting include:

- Deadlock graph
- Lock: Deadlock
- Lock: Deadlock Chain
- RPC:Completed
- SP:StmtCompleted
- SQL:BatchCompleted

- SQL:BatchStarting

Events	TextData	ApplicationName	DatabaseName	ServerName	Duration	SPID	LoginName	CPU	Reads
Locks									
Deadlock graph	✓			✓		✓	✓		
Lock:Deadlock	✓	✓	✓	✓	✓	✓	✓		
Lock:Deadlock Chain	✓		✓	✓		✓			
Stored Procedures									
RPC:Completed	✓	✓	✓	✓	✓	✓	✓	✓	✓
SP:StmtCompleted	✓	✓	✓	✓	✓	✓	✓	✓	✓
TSQL									
SQL:BatchCompleted	✓	✓	✓	✓	✓	✓	✓	✓	✓
SQL:BatchStarting	✓	✓	✓	✓		✓	✓		

Figure 5-1: I like to include extra context events to help better understanding of what is happening with the code.

I'm only going to focus here on the three lock-related events. The remaining four events were covered in Chapter 3 and 4, so I assume you are already familiar with them.

Deadlock Graph

The only event you must have when identifying deadlocks is the Deadlock Graph event. It captures, in both XML format and graphically, a drawing that shows you the code responsible for the deadlock. We will examine how to interpret this drawing shortly.

Lock:Deadlock

This event is fired whenever a deadlock occurs, also every time the Deadlock Graph event is fired, producing redundant data. I have included it here because it makes it a little easier to see what is happening but, if you prefer, you can drop this event from your trace.

Lock:Deadlock Chain

This event is fired once for every process involved in a deadlock. In most cases, a deadlock only affects two processes at a time, so you will see this event fired twice, just before the Deadlock Graph and the Lock:Deadlock events fire.

SELECTING DATA COLUMNS

You don't need to select many data columns to capture enough data for analyzing deadlocks. I generally select the following data columns, in the order they are listed below:

- Events
- TextData
- ApplicationName
- DatabaseName

- ServerName
- SessionLoginName
- SPID
- LoginName
- EventSequence
- BinaryData

If you are in doubt about what information these data columns collect, see chapter 11.

SELECTING A COLUMN FILTER

I may or may not use column filters when I am tracing deadlocks. If I do, I may consider filters on one or more of the following data columns:

- ApplicationName (if available)
- DatabaseName
- ServerName
- LoginName or SessionLoginName
- SPID

COLUMN ORGANIZATION

I don't generally perform any grouping or aggregation when tracing for deadlocks, but I generally order the data columns so that they are presented on the screen in an easily readable format. If you don't want to bother doing this, use the default data column organization.

RUNNING THE TRACE

One of the problems with troubleshooting deadlocks is that it is hard to predict when they will occur, so you may have to run your deadlock trace for a substantial period of time (24 hours or more).

If you run a trace for long periods on a busy production SQL Server, you can end up collecting a huge amount of data and the trace itself will produce some burden on the server. If you are facing this situation, you can choose to either collect for shorter periods of time (e.g. only when deadlock events are occurring, assuming you know when this happens), capture the trace programmatically using SQL Trace (See chapter 9), or limit yourself to only collecting the Deadlock Graph event. You may have to experiment to see what works best for your particular situation.

ANALYZING THE TRACE

Figure 5-2 shows example trace results, collected by running a trace template as described above:

EventClass	TextData	ApplicationName	DatabaseName
Trace Start			
SQL:BatchStarting	USE [AdventureWorks]	Microsoft...	AdventureWorks
SQL:BatchCompleted	USE [AdventureWorks]	Microsoft...	AdventureWorks
SQL:BatchStarting	BEGIN TRAN --Update One: Run 1st...	Microsoft...	AdventureWorks
SQL:BatchCompleted	BEGIN TRAN --Update One: Run 1st...	Microsoft...	AdventureWorks
SQL:BatchStarting	USE [AdventureWorks]	Microsoft...	AdventureWorks
SQL:BatchCompleted	USE [AdventureWorks]	Microsoft...	AdventureWorks
SQL:BatchStarting	BEGIN TRAN --Update: Run 2nd (...	Microsoft...	AdventureWorks
SQL:BatchStarting	--Update Two: Run 3rd UPDATE sale...	Microsoft...	AdventureWorks
Lock:Deadlock Chain	Deadlock Chain SPID = 55 (010086470...		AdventureWorks
Lock:Deadlock Chain	Deadlock Chain SPID = 54 (010086470...		AdventureWorks
Deadlock graph	<deadlock-list> <deadlock victim=...		
Lock:Deadlock	(010086470766)	Microsoft...	AdventureWorks
SQL:BatchCompleted	BEGIN TRAN --Update: Run 2nd (...	Microsoft...	AdventureWorks
SQL:BatchCompleted	--Update Two: Run 3rd UPDATE sale...	Microsoft...	AdventureWorks
Trace Stop			

Figure 5-2: These are the results of capturing a deadlock using the events recommended above.

To create a deadlock for demonstration purposes, I ran two separate transactions in two different processes that I knew would create a deadlock. These are represented by the eight SQL:BatchStarting and SQL:BatchCompleted events at the beginning of the above trace.

When SQL Server determines that a deadlock has occurred, the first event that denotes this is the Lock:Deadlock Chain event. There are two of these in the above trace, for SPID 55 and SPID 54. Next, the Deadlock Graph event is fired. Lastly, the Lock:Deadlock event is fired.

Once SQL Server detects a deadlock, it picks a loser and a winner. The SQL:BatchCompleted event that immediately follows the Lock:Deadlock event is the transaction that was killed and rolled back, and the following SQL:BatchCompleted event is the one that was picked as the winner and was successfully run.

If you have trouble following the above example, don't worry, as it will all make more sense when we take a close look at the Deadlock Graph event.

When you click on the Deadlock Graph event in Profiler, the deadlock graph appears at the bottom of the Profiler screen, as shown in Figure 5-3:

EventClass	TextData	ApplicationName	DatabaseName
Trace Start			
SQL:BatchStarting	USE [Adventureworks]	Microsoft...	Adventurework:
SQL:BatchCompleted	USE [Adventureworks]	Microsoft...	Adventurework:
SQL:BatchStarting	BEGIN TRAN --Update One: Run 1st...	Microsoft...	Adventurework:
SQL:BatchCompleted	BEGIN TRAN --Update One: Run 1st...	Microsoft...	Adventurework:
SQL:BatchStarting	USE [Adventureworks]	Microsoft...	Adventurework:
SQL:BatchCompleted	USE [Adventureworks]	Microsoft...	Adventurework:
SQL:BatchStarting	BEGIN TRAN --Update: Run 2nd (...	Microsoft...	Adventurework:
SQL:BatchStarting	--Update Two: Run 3rd UPDATE sale...	Microsoft...	Adventurework:
Lock:Deadlock Chain	Deadlock Chain SPID = 55 (010086470...		Adventurework:
Lock:Deadlock Chain	Deadlock Chain SPID = 54 (010086470...		Adventurework:
Deadlock graph	<deadlock-list> <deadlock victim=...		
Lock:Deadlock	(010086470766)	Microsoft...	Adventurework:
SQL:BatchCompleted	BEGIN TRAN --Update: Run 2nd (...	Microsoft...	Adventurework:
SQL:BatchCompleted	--Update Two: Run 3rd UPDATE sale...	Microsoft...	Adventurework:
Trace Stop			

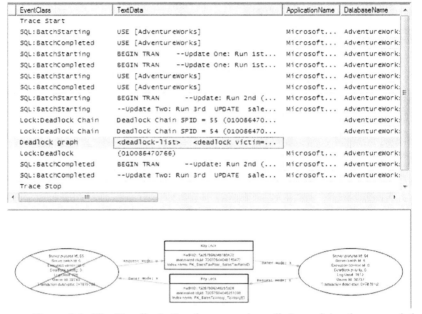

Figure 5-3: The Deadlock Graph summarizes all the activity that caused the deadlock to occur.

You can't read the graph details in Figure 5-3, but it does give you a good sense of the general layout. The ovals on the left and right hand side of the graph each represent a **Process Node** – in other words, a process that performs a specific task, such as an INSERT, UPDATE, or DELETE. If you move the mouse pointer over either oval, a tooltip appears. The left oval on the graph, with the blue cross, represents the transaction that was chosen as the deadlock victim by SQL Server. The Process Node on the right represents the successful transaction.

The two rectangular boxes in the middle are called **Resource Nodes**, which they represent a database object, such as a table, row, or an index. In this case, these Resource Nodes represent the indexes that each process was trying to get an exclusive lock on.

The arrows you see pointing from and to the ovals and rectangles are called **Edges**. An Edge represents a relationship between processes and resources. In this case, they represent the types of locks each process has on each Resource Node.

Now that you have a basic understanding of the big picture, let's drill down to the details. We'll start with the Process Node that represents the successful transaction, on the right side of our Deadlock Graph:

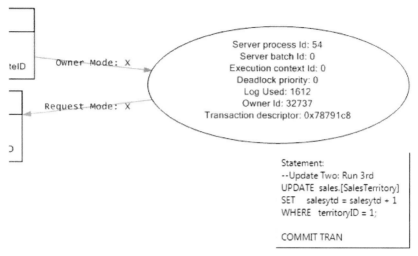

Figure 5-4: This transaction was selected as the winner

As you can see in Figure 5-4, there are a number of new terms listed inside the Process Node:

1. **Server Process ID:** This is the SPID of the process.

2. **Server Batch ID:** This is the internal reference number for the batch in which this code is running.

3. **Execution Context ID**: This is the internal reference number of the thread for the above SPID. A value of 0 represents the main, or parent, thread.

4. **Deadlock Priority:** By default, no one transaction has a greater or smaller chance of becoming a deadlock victim than the other (before they begin executing). However, if you use the SET DEADLOCK PRIORITY command for a particular session, then this session can be assigned a value of Low, Normal, or High, thereby determining the priority of this session's transaction over that of another session. This allows the DBA or developer to control which session is more important than another if a deadlock arises. A value of 0 indicates no priority has been assigned to this process.

5. **Log Used:** This is the amount of log space used by the transaction up to the point the deadlock occurs. SQL Server uses this information to help determine which transaction has used up the most resources so far. Generally, the transaction that has used the least resources is killed and rolled back,

helping to minimize the overhead required to deal with the deadlock.

6. **Owner ID:** This is the internal reference number for the transaction that is occurring.

7. **Transaction Descriptor:** This is an internal reference number that indicates the state of the transaction.

A lot of data is provided here, but not all of it is useful, unless you have an intimate knowledge of the internal workings of SQL Server. More immediately useful is the tooltip, which lists the Transact-SQL code that was executed to cause the deadlock to occur and allows us to trace the event to specific problematic code.

The Edges that we can see in Figure 5-4 provide further information. In this case, they tell us that this Process Node has an exclusive lock on the top Resource Node (the X represents an exclusive lock) and that it has requested another exclusive lock on the bottom Resource Node. When you look at this Process Node in isolation, this is not a big deal. The problem occurs when this transactions bumps heads with another transaction, as we find out next.

On the left side of the Deadlock graph (figure 5-5) is the other Process Node, tooltip, and Edges:

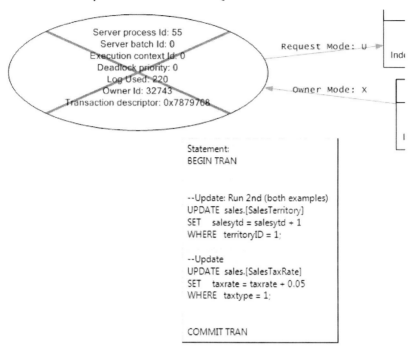

Figure 5-5: This transaction is the deadlock victim.

This information tells us the following:

1. It was the losing transaction (indicated by the blue cross)

2. The Transact-SQL code that contributed to the deadlock.

3. It has an exclusive lock on the bottom Resource Node.

4. It has requested an update lock (U) on the top Resource node.

We'll talk more about the locking conflicts shortly, but for now, let's look at the two Resource Nodes shown in Figure 5-6:

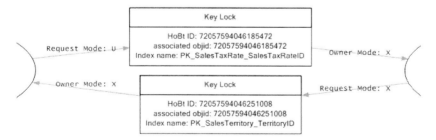

Figure 5-6: The resource nodes tell us what resources the transactions were fighting over.

Both of these Resource Nodes represent indexes, which the two transactions both needed access to in order to perform their requested work. Like Process Nodes, Resource Nodes have some new terms that we need to consider:

- **HoBt ID:** This number refers to a subset of data/index pages within a single partition. These may be in the form of a heap or a B-Tree. In SQL Server 2005, the HoBt ID is identical to the Partition ID found in the sys.partitions table.
- **Associated Objid:** This is the object ID of the table associated with this index.
- **Index Name:** The name of the index.

The top Resource Node represents the **PK_SalesTaxRate_Sales TaxRateID** index and the bottom Resource Node represents the **PK_SalesTerritory_TerritoryID** index.

Having discussed all the details of this Deadlock graph, let's bring all the pieces together.

- SPID 54 started a transaction, then requested, and received, an Exclusive lock on the PK_SalesTaxRate_SalesTaxRateID index.
- SPID 55 started a transaction, then requested an Exclusive lock on the PK_SalesTerritory_TerritoryID index.
- SPID 55, as part of the same transaction, then requested an Update lock on the PK_SalesTaxRate_SalesTaxRateID index. However, this lock was not granted because SPID 54 already had an Exclusive lock on the index. In most cases, this means that SPID 55 has to wait its turn before it can get an Update lock on PK_SalesTaxRate_SalesTaxRateID. At this point, SPID 54 is causing a blocking lock on SPID 55.
- As the above blocking lock is continuing, SPID 54 wants to complete its transaction. In step 1 above, it had only started the transaction, not completed it. Now, SPID 54 wants to complete the transaction. In order to do this, it must get an Exclusive lock on PK_SalesTerritory_TerritoryID. The problem is that it can't get a lock on this index because SPID 55 already has an Exclusive lock on it. Now we have a deadlock. Neither SPID can continue because each transaction is preventing the other from finishing.
- SQL Server examines the two transactions and decides to kill the one that has used up the least amount of resources so far. In this case, SPID 55 has used up 220 units of the Log and SPID 54 has used 1612 units of the log.
- SQL Server kills SPID 55 and the transactions are rolled back, which releases the Exclusive lock on

PK_SalesTerritory_TerritoryID, now allowing SPID 54 to get an Exclusive lock on it and to complete the transaction.

There is a lot of information to digest here, but once you grasp what the Deadlock Graph is telling you, you will be in a strong position to identify and fix the code and/or objects that are causing the deadlock.

In most cases, fixing the problem will require developers to get involved. Fortunately, you now have the information you need to share with the developers so they can remedy the problem. Below are some suggestions on how to eliminate, or at least mitigate, deadlocking problems in your applications. This list is only a starting point and should not be considered a complete list of the options you have to prevent or reduce deadlocking.

- Ensure the database design is properly normalized.
- Have the application access database objects in the same order every time.
- Keep transactions as short as possible.
- During transactions, don't allow any user input.
- Avoid cursors.
- Consider reducing lock escalation by using the ROWLOCK or PAGLOCK hint.
- Consider using the NOLOCK hint to prevent locking.
- Use as low a level of isolation as possible for user connections.

HOW TO IDENTIFY BLOCKING ISSUES

Whereas deadlocks should be rare events, a certain level of blocking is normal for SQL Server. In other words, SQL Server often intentionally prevents one process from accessing an object if another process has a lock on it. This means the second process is blocked from continuing until the first process releases the lock on the object to which the second process needs access.

Of course, the purpose of this is to prevent one process from interfering with another, in cases where data corruption is possible. With proper database design, table indexing, and application code, blocking is generally limited to milliseconds and users aren't even aware that it is occurring.

Nevertheless, few database designs, table indexing, and application code are perfect, and it's quite common for a DBA to see blocking that lasts 10 seconds, 60 seconds, even 6,000 seconds. Obviously, this kind of blocking will significantly affect the performance of SQL Server and its users. As DBAs and developers, we need to be able to identify these types of blocking issues so they can be fixed, or their occurrence minimized.

In SQL Server 2000 and earlier, identifying blocking issues was not an easy task. One option was to use Enterprise Manager to view existing connections to see if any blocking was occurring, or using the **sp_who** or _**sp_who2** commands. If you were really ambitious, you could write some code to extract blocking data from system tables.

In SQL Server 2005, the situation has improved. Besides Management Studio, stored procedures, and system tables, we also have DMVs and even the Performance Dashboard. However, most importantly, we have a new SQL Server Profiler event, **Blocked Process Report**. This event does a great job of helping you to identify blocking issues and, at the same time, provides you with much of the information you need to help correct the problem.

The Blocked Process Report Event

You will like this. You only need one Profiler event to capture all the information you need to identify long-running, blocked processes. The Blocked Process Report event does all the work for you and you don't even need to capture any context events.

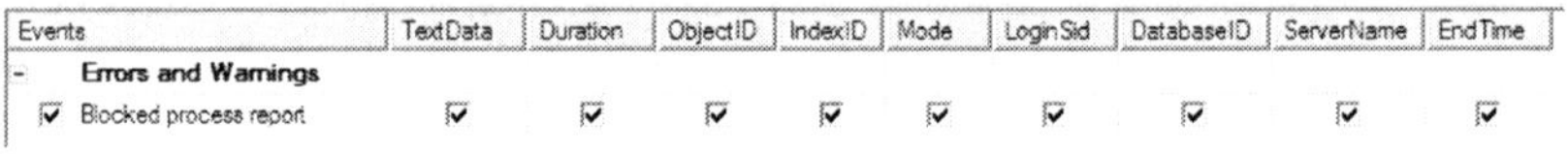

Events	TextData	Duration	ObjectID	IndexID	Mode	LoginSid	DatabaseID	ServerName	EndTime
Errors and Warnings									
☑ Blocked process report	☑	☑	☑	☑	☑	☑	☑	☑	☑

Figure 5-7: Only a single event is needed to capture information on blocked processes.

However, you may not like this. Up to this point when we selected events to identify a SQL Server issue, we just selected the event and the event was automatically collected for us when the trace ran. This is not the case with the Blocked Process Report event. In other words, if you select this event and run a trace, you will never collect any events. No, this is not a bug in Profiler; it has been designed to run this way.

This is not as big a deal as it may seem, but using the Blocked Process Report event requires you do perform an extra, non-Profiler-related task. You just have to keep this in mind, because if you forget about it, you will be pounding your head on your desk trying to figure out why this particular event doesn't work.

The fact is that collecting information about blocked processes in SQL Server 2005 is resource-intensive and so, by default, the Blocked Process Report event is turned off. This way, if you don't use this event, it is not wasting valuable server resources. Ideally, you will turn the feature on when you need it and turn it off when you don't.

You turn the Blocked Process Report event on and off using the **SP_CONFIGURE 'blocked process threshold'** command. By default, this option is set to 0, which means that the Blocked Process Report event is turned off. The **SP_CONFIGURE 'blocked process threshold'** command is an advanced **SP_CONFIGURE** command, which means that the **SP_CONFIGURE 'show advanced options'** command must be run first in order to be able to turn on the **SP_CONFIGURE 'blocked process threshold'** command, assuming this had not been done previously. In addition, as with most **SP_CONFIGURE** commands, you have to run the **RECONFIGURE** command afterwards to activate them.

The following code turns on the **'show advanced options'** – again, assuming you have not already done so.

```
SP_CONFIGURE 'show advanced options', 1 ;
GO

RECONFIGURE ;
GO

Now that the advanced options are on, the Blocked
Process Report can be turned on, using this code:
SP_CONFIGURE 'blocked process threshold', 10 ;
GO

RECONFIGURE ;
GO
```

After the **SP_CONFIGURE 'blocked process threshold'** command there is a value – in this case, the number 10. Setting this number allows you to control how often you want to look for blocked processes, since it determines how often the Blocked Process Report event is fired. In this example, the Blocked Process Report event will fire repeatedly, every 10 seconds. If any blocked processes occur within that 10 second period, they will be displayed as part of the report. Once you have finished running the Blocked Process Report, you will want to turn it off with the following command.

```
SP_CONFIGURE 'blocked process threshold', 0 ;
GO

RECONFIGURE ;
GO
```

We will talk more about how the report works when we get to the section on how to analyze the trace.

SELECTING DATA COLUMNS

Unlike many other events, the Blocked Process Report event doesn't offer you many data columns to choose from. At the very minimum, I select these data columns, and order them as they are ordered below:

- Events
- TextData
- Duration
- IndexID
- Mode
- LoginSid
- DatabaseID
- ServerName
- EndTime

We have talked about all the above columns filters before, except for one, and that is **Mode**. The content of the Mode data column varies depending on the nature of the event. For the Blocked Process Report Event, here are the possible values:

- 0=NULL
- 1=Sch-S
- 2=Sch-M
- 3=S
- 4=U
- 5=X
- 6=IS
- 7=IU
- 8=IX
- 9=SIU
- 10=SIX
- 11=UIX
- 12=BU
- 13=RangeS-S
- 14=RangeS-U
- 15=RangeI-N
- 16=RangeI-S
- 17=RangeI-U
- 18=RangeI-X
- 19=RangeX-S
- 20=RangeX-U

- 21=RangeX-X

Each value represents a type of lock that was received or requested for the event.

NOTE:

If you are not familiar with lock types, you can learn about them in SQL Server 2005 Books Online. This information might be useful to you when trying to figure out why a particular blocking lock occurred.

SELECTING A COLUMN FILTER

You can choose to filter by any of the available data columns. In most cases the only data column I ever filter by is DatabaseID. While not required, it does limit your trace to one database at a time, which may be useful if your server has many databases.

COLUMN ORGANIZATION

I don't normally perform any grouping or aggregation when running this trace and I generally order the data columns in a way that works best for me

RUNNING THE TRACE

Running a Blocked Process Report event trace can noticeably affect a server's performance, so it is important that you after you have performed the trace, you then turn it off. On the other hand, it is often hard to predict when blocking will occur. If you have a feel for the time of the day when blocking problems most often arise, then that is the time you should pick for conducting your trace. If you aren't able to pinpoint a time range, you might have to perform a trace for a 24-hour period. If you do this, be sure that you set the time period for the Blocked Process Report to run at a large number, such as 1800 (30 minutes). This will help to minimize the load and reduce the number of times the event is fired. You may also want to monitor the trace visually for a while to see what kind of results you are getting. If you get many blocked events, you may want to change the trace collection time to one more appropriate to your environment.

ANALYZING THE TRACE

Figure 5-8 shows the information collected in a typical trace, from the blocked process report event:

EventClass	TextData	Duration	ObjectID	IndexID	Mode	LoginSid	DatabaseID	ServerName
Trace Start								
Blocked process report	<blocked-process-report...	14710	722101613	0	8 - IX	0X01	5	PELE
Blocked process report	<blocked-process-report...	24710	722101613	0	8 - IX	0X01	5	PELE
Blocked process report	<blocked-process-report...	16766	126	256	4 - U	0X01	5	PELE
Blocked process report	<blocked-process-report...	34710	722101613	0	8 - IX	0X01	5	PELE
Blocked process report	<blocked-process-report...	28766	126	256	4 - U	0X01	5	PELE
Blocked process report	<blocked-process-report...	44709	722101613	0	8 - IX	0X01	5	PELE
Trace Stop								

```
<blocked-process-report monitorLoop="19685">
 <blocked-process>
  <process id="process2cd6898" taskpriority="0" logused="0" waitresource="OBJECT: 5:722101613:0 " waittime="14710"
ownerId="184543" transactionname="user_transaction" lasttranstarted="2007-12-07T12:17:37" XDES="0x7e95960" lockMode="IX"
schedulerid="2" kpid="3156" status="suspended" spid="54" sbid="0" ecid="0" priority="0" transcount="3">
lastbatchstarted="2007-12-07T12:24.44.013" lastbatchcompleted="2007-12-07T12:24.44.013"
lastattention="2007-12-07T12:23:12.787" clientapp="Microsoft SQL Server Management Studio - Query" hostname="PELE"
hostpid="5832" loginname="Profileruser" isolationlevel="read committed (2)" xactid="184543" currentdb="5"
lockTimeout="4294967295" clientoption1="671090784" clientoption2="390200">
   <executionStack>
    <frame line="4" stmtstart="68" sqlhandle="0x02000000a5155c2cb85ee89a270f471ceb11c6da7aff9a46"/>
   </executionStack>
   <inputbuf>
--This code is being blocked
BEGIN TRAN
UPDATE sales.[SalesOrderHeader]
SET    [DueDate] = GETDATE()
   </inputbuf>
  </process>
 </blocked-process>
 <blocking-process>
  <process status="suspended" waittime="21777" spid="55" sbid="0" ecid="0" priority="0" transcount="2">
lastbatchstarted="2007-12-07T12:24:35.393" lastbatchcompleted="2007-12-07T12:24:35.393" clientapp="Microsoft SQL Server
Management Studio - Query" hostname="PELE" hostpid="5832" loginname="Profileruser" isolationlevel="read committed (2)"
xactid="184490" currentdb="5" lockTimeout="4294967295" clientoption1="671090784" clientoption2="390200">
   <executionStack>
    <frame line="6" stmtstart="196" sqlhandle="0x02000000441a4ce18bcdae97ede7fd52f83ea77b512be8ebb"/>
   </executionStack>
   <inputbuf>
--Begin Lock of Table
BEGIN TRAN
SELECT *
FROM    Sales.SalesOrderHeader WITH ( HOLDLOCK )
WAITFOR DELAY &apos;00:05:00&apos;
   </inputbuf>
  </process>
 </blocking-process>
</blocked-process-report>
```

Figure 5-8: This is an excerpt from a Blocked Process Report that runs every 10 seconds.

In row 2, the first Blocked Process Report event is fired. Notice that the event has a duration of 14710 (about 15 seconds). This tells us that there has been a blocking lock occurring for about 15 seconds from(?) the time this event fired (which, in our example is once every 10 seconds). While the other data columns can sometimes provide us with useful information, the most important data column is TextData, which contains XML describing the blocking event, displaying both the code that is causing the blocking and the code that is being blocked, together with a lot of other detail.

For this blocked process event, the code that is causing the blocking is shown in figure 5-9:

```
--Begin Lock of Table
BEGIN TRAN
SELECT  *
FROM    Sales.SalesOrderHeader WITH ( HOLDLOCK )
WAITFOR DELAY &apos;00:05:00&apos;
```

Figure 5-9: This code is causing the blocking.

This blocking code is found at the bottom of the window, near the bottom of the XML code. Since I was creating sample code, I added a comment to the blocking code to make it obvious in the XML code. If you look toward the middle of the XML data, you will find the code this is being blocked, as shown in figure 5-10:

```
--This code is being blocked
BEGIN TRAN
UPDATE   sales.[SalesOrderHeader]
SET      [DueDate] = GETDATE()
```

Figure 5-10: This code is being blocked.

By examining the blocking and the blocked code, you should be able to eventually determine why the blocking is occurring. It might be because too much data is being returned, which takes time; or it might be caused by a missing index; or maybe even a poor locking choice made by SQL Server. Sometimes the problem will be obvious; at other times it will require additional investigation. For example, you may need to take a look at the code's graphical execution plan to figure out what exactly is going on. If you read the XML, there is additional information that may be helpful, such as the isolation level used for the connections, SPID, username, current state, and so on.

Now that we have looked at a single Blocked Process Report event, let's look at several others so that you better understand what you are viewing. Take a look at the first two Blocked Process Report events in figure 5-11:

EventClass	TextData	Duration	ObjectID	IndexID	Mode
Trace Start					
Blocked process report	<blocked-process-report...	14710	722101613	0	8 - IX
Blocked process report	<blocked-process-report...	24710	722101613	0	8 - IX
Blocked process report	<blocked-process-report...	18766	126	256	4 - U
Blocked process report	<blocked-process-report...	34710	722101613	0	8 - IX
Blocked process report	<blocked-process-report...	28766	126	256	4 - U
Blocked process report	<blocked-process-report...	44709	722101613	0	8 - IX
Trace Stop					

Figure 5-11: Notice that the first two events are 10 seconds apart and represent the same ObjectID.

The first of the two events has a duration of 14710 milliseconds indicating that, at the time the event fired, there was a blocked process that had been blocked for 14710 milliseconds, and it affected ObjectID 722101613.

The second of the two events has a duration of 24710 milliseconds indicating a blocked process for 24710 milliseconds, affecting the same object. Notice that this is exactly 10 seconds longer than for the first event and that, in our example, the event fires every 10 seconds.

In other words, the second event is a repeat of the first event and it's just telling us that the same blocking lock still existed 10 seconds later. If the block had cleared before the blocked process report event fired a second time, then we would not have seen that second row in the trace. So keep the following point in mind: at every time interval (which you set), all currently blocked events will be displayed.

Now it gets a little more complex. Take a look at Figure 5-12:

EventClass	TextData	Duration	ObjectID	IndexID	Mode
Trace Start					
Blocked process report	<blocked-process-report...	14710	722101613	0	8 - IX
Blocked process report	<blocked-process-report...	24710	722101613	0	8 - IX
Blocked process report	<blocked-process-report...	18766	126	256	4 - U
Blocked process report	<blocked-process-report...	34710	722101613	0	8 - IX
Blocked process report	<blocked-process-report...	28766	126	256	4 - U
Blocked process report	<blocked-process-report...	44709	722101613	0	8 - IX

Figure 5-12: This Blocked Process Report event represents a different blocking lock.

The third row has a duration of 18766 milliseconds and affects a different object. This is actually a second blocking event that occurred during the same time frame as the event in row two. In other words, rows two and three are blocking(?) events that were occurring during the second 10-second cycle of the Blocked Process Report.

When the third 10-second event fires, rows four and five appear on the trace. From the durations and the object they affect, you can see that the same two blocking events that existed the second time are still causing an issue the third time. You could also verify this by looking at the TextData data column.

As blocking starts and stops, each 10-second (in our example) interval may have different blocking events. In this example there are only two. But on a production system, you could easily have blocking events come and go, which makes reading the report quite tricky. The key is to identify those blocked processes that are blocked the longest (Duration), identify how often this happens, and examine the code causing the event. Once you have all this information, you should be ready to determine the cause of the blocking lock, and hopefully resolve it.

How do you resolve blocking locks? While the way to resolve blocking lock problems vary, some of the ones you may one to consider include:

- Identify problematic code and rewrite it.
- Ensure that all transactions are as short as possible.
- Only return the absolutely minimum amount of data needed.
- Identify and add missing indexes.
- Ensure column and index statistics are kept current.

- Use hints to modify locking behavior.
- Use the lowest isolation level acceptable.

HOW TO IDENTIFY EXCESSIVE AUTO STATS ACTIVITY

In order for the query optimizer to make good decisions about what execution plans to select, the query optimizer needs to know about the distribution of the data in the indexes and columns. In addition, these statistics need to be frequently updated because the distribution of data in a table often changes over time. By default, SQL Server automatically creates and updates these statistics for us.

The **AUTO_UPDATE_STATISTICS** database option, which is turned on by default for all newly created SQL Server databases, is responsible for keeping statistics updated. Using an internal algorithm, index and column statistics are automatically updated as necessary. However, like all algorithms, the auto stats feature is not perfect. Sometimes, statistics are:

- Not updated often enough, causing poor execution plans to be used.
- Updated more often than they need to be, wasting resources.
- Updated at inappropriate times, such as during the busiest time of the day for your SQL Server, causing queries to stall until the auto stats process completes.

Some DBAs find that auto stats causes more problems than it solves, and they turn off the **AUTO_UPDATE_STATISTICS** database option. If you do make this choice, bear in mind that you must then determine a way of updating statistics that better meets your needs, such as scheduling index rebuilds (which automatically update statistics), or updating statistics through SQL Server Agent jobs.

Auto stats exhibits two different types of behavior, depending on how your database is configured. In default mode, auto stats only runs when the query optimizer determines that it is time for statistics to be updated. This occurs when a query is about to be executed, and the query optimizer determines that the statistics needed to optimize the execution plan for the query are out of date. At this point, the query is held back from running until the auto stats process completes. Depending on the size of the table, this could be milliseconds, or many seconds. This default behavior is referred to as a **synchronous statistics update**. In most cases, the occasional delay in executing the query while the stats are updated is a good thing, because the query optimizer will then have all the data it needs to make a good query plan selection. However, if the auto update process takes a long time, it may slow down the execution of some queries. This can become frustrating if a query normally executed in milliseconds, but sometimes takes many seconds, as statistics are being updated.

Starting with SQL Server 2005, you can now run auto stats asynchronously. This feature is turned on by setting the **AUTO_UPDATE_STATISTICS_ASYNCHRONOUSLY** database option to **TRUE**. In this mode, query execution is not delayed when the query optimizer determines that it is time for statistics to be updated. Instead, the query is executed immediately, using old statistics. Auto stats runs in the background, so that the next time a query runs that needs the same statistics, it will use an execution plan based on the new statistics.

While asynchronous auto stats is effective in some cases, it can also present its own problems, such as using additional SQL Server resources, and allowing queries to execute using less than ideal execution plans.

THE AUTO STATS EVENT

Both the default synchronous and the optional asynchronous auto stats options can be monitored using SQL Server Profiler with a single event: Auto Stats. No context events are necessary.

Events	Duration	ObjectID	DatabaseName	EventSubClass	TextData	IndexID	IntegerData	Success	SPID	StartT...
Performance										
☑ Auto Stats	☑	☑	☑	☑	☑	☑	☑	☑	☑	☑

Figure 5-13: The Auto Stats event is found under the Performance Event category.

The purpose of the Auto Stats event is to determine how often statistics are updated. In other words, the Auto Stats event fires every time database statistics are updated. If you are using asynchronous auto stats, you can also find out about the status of the auto update. The information provided by this event can be used to help the DBA to determine if statistics are not being updated often enough, or more often than required. It can find out how long it takes to update statistics, if statistics are being updated at inappropriate times, or how well asynchronous auto stats is performing.

SELECTING THE DATA COLUMNS

You can capture a wide range of data columns for the Auto Stats event. I generally select the following:

- EventClass
- Duration

- ObjectID
- DatabaseName
- EventSubClass
- TextData
- IndexID
- IntegerData
- Success
- SPID
- StartTime
- EndTime
- ApplicationName
- LoginName
- ServerName

You will be familiar with most of the events listed above, but there are a couple that are new, or are specific to the Auto Stats event:

- **EventSubClass**: This data column can have one of four different values, each indicating a different variation of this event:

    o 1: Statistics have been created or updated synchronously.
    o 2: An asynchronous statistics update job was queued.
    o 3: An asynchronous statistics update job was started.
    o 4: An asynchronous statistics update job was finished.

- **TextData**: If the EventSubClass is 1, then the statistics that were created or updated are listed. If the EventSubClass is 2, 3, or 4, the value is a NULL.
- **IntegerData**: Returns the number of successfully updated statistics collections.
- **Success**: Returns a 0 if an error occurred or a 1 if the event was successful.

SELECTING A COLUMN FILTER

You can choose to filter by any of the available data columns. Most often, I filter on the DatabaseName data column, so that I can analyze one database at a time.

SELECTING COLUMN ORGANIZATION

I don't normally perform any grouping or aggregation when tracing this event, and I generally order the data columns in a way that works best for me. On the other hand, sometimes you might find it beneficial to group and aggregate by the Duration data column if you want to see how often Auto Stats events take place in your database and how long they take.

RUNNING THE TRACE

This is a very lightweight trace and there is no problem with running it for a 24-hour period if you want to see what is happening throughout the day. I would not recommend you run this trace when you are rebuilding your indexes or running an update statistics job, as both of these processes automatically update statistics and will produce a lot of activity of minimal value.

ANALYZING THE TRACE

Let's look at a typical trace of the Auto Stats event, shown in Figure 5-14:

EventClass	Duration	ObjectID	DatabaseName	EventSubClass	TextData	IndexID
Trace Start						
Auto Stats	1	1461580245	sqlstress	1	Created: CountryRegionCode	
Auto Stats	2	2133582639	sqlstress	1	Created: ProductDescriptionID	
Auto Stats	0	130099504	sqlstress	1	Created: ProductModelID	
Auto Stats	41	34	sqlstress	1	Updated: sys.sysschobjs.clst	1
Auto Stats	2	34	sqlstress	1	Updated: sys.sysschobjs.nc1	2
Auto Stats	40	34	sqlstress	1	Updated: sys.sysschobjs._WA...	11

Figure 5-14: The results of an Auto Stats trace.

Figure 5-14 shows six Auto Stats events. The first three are examples of where statistics are automatically created (for the first time). The last three show three system tables for which statistics were automatically updated. There appears to be nothing out of the ordinary in this trace. So what do you look for when analyzing a trace of Auto Stats events? Here are things you should be looking for.

- How often are Auto Stats events being fired? For example, do you see Auto Stats fired again and again for the same table, over a short time period?
- Are Auto Stats events occurring at inopportune times, for example during the busiest time of your production day? Does this negatively affect server performance?
- How long is it taking for each Auto Stats event to run? You should expect milliseconds. Long durations might indicate problems, especially if these events occur during busy times during the day.
- Which databases and objects are incurring the most Auto Stats events? If you export the trace data into a database table, you can

query the data to see if any particular tables produce more Auto Stats events than others.

- Which objects rarely, if ever, have Auto Stats events? This could indicate that a table just doesn't change much, or it may indicate a problem with Auto Stats not working as expected.

- What kind of Auto Stats events are occurring: synchronous or asynchronous? For any particular database, it will be one or the other. If you are using asynchronous Auto Stats, you can track if Auto Stats is queued, started, and completed.

- Are there any events that indicate a failure instead of a success? If so, you will need to find out why.

Based on the information you collect, you should be able to answer these questions:

- Are statistics being updated more often than you expect?
- Are statistics not being updated when you expect?
- Are statistics updates occurring at inopportune times of the day, and is this causing problems?
- Are statistics causing excessive utilization of server resources? To answer this, you will also need to monitor server resources and correlate the data.
- If you are using synchronous statistics, is this better or worse than using asynchronous? This will take careful profiling and correlation with how server resources are being used.

In most cases, SQL Server does a good job of managing statistics. If SQL Server appears to be having statistics issues of some sort, not only do you need to investigate with Profiler, you will also need to use other tools at the same time, in order to be able to draw appropriate conclusions.

HOW TO IDENTIFY EXCESSIVE STATEMENT COMPILATIONS

Whenever a query, batch file, stored procedure, or trigger is first submitted to the query optimizer, it creates an execution plan and stores it in the Plan Cache. The next time the code is submitted to SQL Server, the query optimizer will try to reuse the plan stored in the cache, preventing the need to recompile the code each time it is executed. This preserves resources and helps optimize the performance of SQL Server.

Under certain conditions, statements need to be recompiled, such as when statistics are updated for a table. A change in statistics may render the current execution plans "obsolete", and the only way for the query optimizer to know this is to recompile all the affected statements to ensure that the execution plan is based on the latest statistics. This is a normal process.

Nevertheless, in some cases statements are recompiled more often than necessary, wasting SQL Server resources and hurting SQL Server performance. Our goal, as a DBA or developer, is to identify situations where recompiles occur more often than we would normally expect.

THE SQL:STMTRECOMPILE EVENT

The good news, again, is that you only need a single event to identify and troubleshoot excessive statement compilations, and that is **SQL:StmtRecompile**. This event fires every time a statement-level recompilation occurs.

In fact, SQL Server 2005 has two events related to recompilations: SP:Recompile and SQL:StmtRecompile. However, SP:Recompile is discontinued and you should only use SQL:StmtRecompile. The reason for this is that, pre-SQL Server 2005, compilation was based on the batch or stored procedure level. In SQL Server 2005, compilation is now based on the statement level. This is a boon for DBAs and developers because SQL Server now only has to recompile those statements that need recompiling. In the past, if only a single statement inside a long stored procedure needed to be recompiled, all the code in the stored procedure was recompiled. This means that recompilations, when they are necessary, take fewer resources to complete.

While you only need to have a single event to diagnose most recompile problems, I like to include additional context events so that I better understand what is happening. So, the "core" events I suggest you collect are:

- SQL:StmtRecompile
- SQL:StmtStarting
- SQL:StmtCompleted

Events	EventSubClass	ObjectName	ObjectType	TextData	Duration	ApplicationName	DatabaseName
☐ **TSQL**							
☑ SQL:StmtCompleted				☑	☑	☑	☑
☑ SQL:StmtRecompile	☑	☑	☑	☑		☑	☑
☑ SQL:StmtStarting				☑		☑	☑

Figure 5-15: I like to include extra context events to help me better understand what is happening with the code.

Besides the main SQL:StmtRecompile event and the two context events listed above, you may also want to consider adding the following events if you want to see the relationship between statements and stored procedures, or recompiles within the context of statistics updates:

- RPC:Completed
- SP:Starting
- SP:Completed
- SP:StmtCompleted
- SQL:BatchStarting
- SQL:BatchStarting
- Auto Stats

I'm going to leave these seven events above out of this discussion, but you can add them if you find them useful.

SELECTING DATA COLUMNS

The SQL:StmtRecompile event offers a lot of data columns to choose from, but you don't need most of them. I generally select the following data columns, and order them as they are presented here:

- EventClass
- EventSubClass
- ObjectName
- ObjectType
- TextData
- Duration
- ApplicationName
- DatabaseName
- LoginName
- ServerName
- SPID
- EventSequence
- StartTime
- EndTime

We have covered most of these data columns previously, but there is one that acts a little differently from what we have seen before, and one that is new to us.

EVENTSUBCLASS

While we have talked about the **EventSubClass** data column several times already, you need to keep in mind that the contents of this data column vary from event to event. For this particular event, possible values are:

- 1 = Schema changed
- 2 = Statistics changed
- 3 = Deferred compile
- 4 = Set option changed
- 5 = Temp table changed
- 6 = Remote rowset changed
- 7 = For Browse permissions changed
- 8 = Query notification environment changed
- 9 = Partition view changed
- 10 = Cursor options changed
- 11 = Option (recompile) requested

Understanding these EventSubClass options is important when determining why a particular statement was recompiled by SQL Server. We will learn more about some of them when we analyze the results.

OBJECTTYPE

This data column specifies the type of object that has been recompiled, such as stored procedure (designated as "8272 – P"), and so on. To find a key for all the available codes, search on "ObjectType Trace Event Column" in Books Online.

SELECTING A COLUMN FILTER

I may or may not use column filters when I am tracing recompiles. If I do, I generally filter on the DatabaseName data column to restrict my analysis to one database at a time.

COLUMN ORGANIZATION

I like to group a recompile trace by the **EventClass data** column. This allows me to see the data grouped by recompiled events or, if I subsequently turn off grouping, then I can see recompiles in the context of the statement execution.

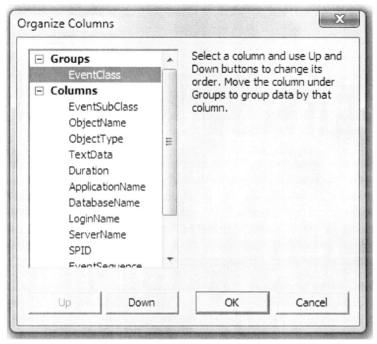

Figure 5-16: I prefer to group and aggregate by the EventClass data column.

RUNNING THE TRACE

On a busy server, recompiles could be occurring very frequently, resulting in a lot of data being captured in a trace file. This can hurt performance and use up a large amount of disk space. So I don't recommend doing a 24-hour trace for this analysis. Instead, I recommend instead that you identify busy times of the day for your server instance and then capture one hour's worth of data. However, the first time you do this, you will want to carefully watch the size of the log files. If they grow quickly, you may have to stop the trace before the end of an hour. In order to capture a representative number of recompiles, you may have to produce several short traces over the period of a typical production day and analyze each one separately. This will minimize data collected by the trace and the server resources used.

ANALYZING THE TRACE

Let's check out what our trace looks like, as shown in Figure 5-17:

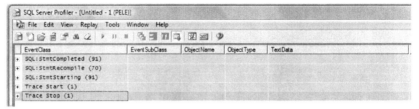

Figure 5-17: After running the trace, you will see the results groups aggregated by EventClass.

I chose to group and aggregate the results by the EventClass, so the trace results separate all the events into their event classes. We can see in figure 5-17 that during the time of the trace, 70 recompile events occurred. Is this a good or a bad number? Does this indicate an excessive number of recompiles? As noted in the introduction to this chapter, the only way to really answer these questions is to compare these numbers to those obtained for the baseline traces for your SQL Servers.

Another way to interpret the data is to look at the SQL:StmtStarting and SQL:StmtCompleted events. Each of these events was fired 91 times, so we can immediately see that of the 91 statements that executed, there were 70 recompiles. In other words, about 77 percent of the time, when a statement was executed, it was recompiled.

This appears to be a very high ratio. In theory, we want the percentage of recompiles to be a small fraction of the total number of statements that have run. In most cases, where you see the ratio of recompiles high compared to the number of statements, you should suspect a problem with excessive recompiles.

Let's drill down into the data and see what is happening. If you click on the + sign next to "SQL:StmtRecompile (70)", you'll see a screen such as that shown in Figure 5-18:

EventClass	Event SubClass	ObjectName	Object Type	TextData
SQL:StmtRecompile (70)				
SQL:StmtRecompile	3 - Deferred compile	DemoProc	8272 - P	SELECT * FR(
SQL:StmtRecompile	3 - Deferred compile	RowCountDemo	8272 - P	insert into #t1 v
SQL:StmtRecompile	3 - Deferred compile	RowCountDemo	8272 - P	select a
SQL:StmtRecompile	2 - Statistics changed	RowCountDemo	8272 - P	select a
SQL:StmtRecompile	3 - Deferred compile	CreateThenReference	8272 - P	insert into #t1 v
SQL:StmtRecompile	3 - Deferred compile	CreateThenReference	8272 - P	insert into #t1 v
SQL:StmtRecompile	3 - Deferred compile	CreateThenReference	8272 - P	insert into #t2 v
SQL:StmtRecompile	3 - Deferred compile	CreateThenReference	8272 - P	insert into #t2 v
SQL:StmtRecompile	3 - Deferred compile	CreateThenReference	8272 - P	select x.a, x.b,
SQL:StmtRecompile	3 - Deferred compile	CreateThenReference	8272 - P	select * fr
SQL:StmtRecompile	3 - Deferred compile	DemoProc	8272 - P	SELECT * FR(
SQL:StmtRecompile	3 - Deferred compile	RowCountDemo	8272 - P	insert into #t1 v
SQL:StmtRecompile	3 - Deferred compile	RowCountDemo	8272 - P	select a
SQL:StmtRecompile	2 - Statistics changed	RowCountDemo	8272 - P	select a

Figure 5-18: Drill down into the grouped and aggregated results and see exactly what kind of recompiles occurred.

From the EventSubClass data column, we can see that there are two main causes of the recompiles: a "Deferred compile" and a "Statistics changed." What do these mean?

A "Deferred compile" recompile event occurs because of deferred name resolution. In other words, an object referred to in the statement does not exist at compile time. Later, when the object does exist, it requires a recompile of the statement so that it can create an optimal execution plan. One example of when a deferred compile will occur is if a temporary table is used in a batch and does not exist when the first statements in the batch are compiled.

A "Statistics changed" recompile event occurs when the statistics for a table being referenced by the statement changes. A change in statistics can affect an execution plan, so every time a statistics update occurs for an index or column, all the related execution plans are thrown out and new ones have to be created.

Besides these two events, there are many more reasons why recompiles happen, and they are described in the EventSubClass data column.

It's also worth looking closely at what objects are the cause of the recompiles. Often, you will find that excessive recompiles are correlated with a small handful of objects. In this case, it is important to identify these objects and investigate why they are contributing to recompile problems.

In addition, you will probably want to identify the statements that are causing the recompiles. As with objects, you may discover that there is a relationship between specific Transact-SQL statements and recompiles.

Another way to view and analyze the data is to disaggregate it by removing the "Aggregated View" option from the Profiler window. This way, the events are displayed in the order they occurred and you can see not only the recompile events, but also the context events, giving you a better idea of what is happening. For example, in Figure 5-20, you can see that a new statement (from inside a stored procedure) is to be executed. However, before it can be executed, it goes through two "Deferred compiles" and one "Statistics changed" recompile, as shown in Figure 5-19:

EventClass	EventSubClass	ObjectName	ObjectType	TextData
SQL:StmtStarting				exec RowCountDemo
SQL:StmtRecompile	3 - Deferred compile	RowCountDemo	8272 - P	insert into #t1 valu
SQL:StmtRecompile	3 - Deferred compile	RowCountDemo	8272 - P	select a fr
SQL:StmtRecompile	2 - Statistics changed	RowCountDemo	8272 - P	select a fr
SQL:StmtCompleted				exec RowCountDemo

Figure 5-19: The events in blue above are all related to the same statement.

As well as running the above types of analysis, it is well worth importing the data into a database table and running Transact-SQL against it to identify trends in any of the above areas.

So, when you are analyzing your data, your goal is to identify why your code is experiencing recompiles, and then decide whether they can be prevented by following best coding and design practices. There follow are some tips for reducing or eliminating excessive recompiles:

- Transact-SQL statements within batches need to be identical so the query plan can be reused.
- Establish SET options at connection time and ensure that they do not change for the duration of the connection.
- Use qualified object names in your T-SQL code.
- "CREATE PROCEDURE ... WITH RECOMPILE" can be used to mark stored procedures that are called with widely varying parameters supplied during calls, but only use if necessary.
- Don't mix Data Definition Language and Data Manipulation Language statements within a single batch or stored procedure.
- Avoid schema changes on production databases.
- Avoid the RECONFIGURE command, which flushes the Plan Cache when it runs.
- Avoid excessive statistics updates.

HOW TO IDENTIFY EXCESSIVE DATABASE FILE GROWTH/SHRINKAGE

By default, whenever a new user database is created, its data and log files are set to Auto Grow. Auto Shrink is set to off. In almost all cases, these are the ideal settings. You want Auto Grow turned on in case the files aren't large enough and need to grow; otherwise the database would cease functioning when it ran out of room. Auto Shrink creates a lot of unnecessary overhead when it runs, which negates any of the benefits it might offer.

Now, with the above said, let's take a brief look at some best practices surrounding file growth and shrinkage. While Auto Grow should be left on for user databases, it is not a mechanism by which to *manage* the growth of your user databases. It is only there to cover you for unexpected events.

The DBA is responsible for managing the growth of user databases and should create database files and log files sized appropriately to cope with predicted growth rates. For example, if the DBA estimates that the data file will be about 250gb in size at the end of the first year of activity, then the initial database should be created at that size. The DBA then needs to monitor the used portion of the database and adjust the file sizes appropriately, if the predicted growth pattern proves inaccurate, not just leave it to the Auto Grow feature to grow the database.

One reason for this is that increasing the size of a database or log file uses server resources, so the DBA needs to control when (and often where) database growth should take place, avoiding times when file growth could hurt the production performance of the server. Another reason for avoid Auto Grow events is to reduce physical file fragmentation.

Occasionally, database files are larger than they need to be and should be shrunk to avoid wasting hard disk space. As noted above, the Auto Shrink option incurs a large resource overhead, and can also "over-shrink" your databases. It should be turned off and all file shrinkage manually controlled by the DBA. This way, the DBA can determine the final size of the database, and can schedule the shrinkage for when it will least affect server performance.

If you adopt these basic best practices, you should never encounter the problems that can arise from using Auto Grow and Auto Shrink, and therefore have no cause to run Profiler traces to investigate these issues. However, if you are using Auto Grow and/or Auto Shrink to manage file size, you can use Profiler to see how it is affecting your SQL Server. If your database sizes don't change much over time, you won't see any problems. However, if your databases sizes do change significantly, you may be surprised to see how much Auto Grow and Auto Shrink activity takes place on your server.

This section will demonstrate how to use Profiler to help identify and troubleshoot cases of excessive file Auto Grow or Auto Shrink.

DATA AND LOG FILE AUTO GROW/SHRINK EVENTS

Four Profiler events are used to monitor data and log file Auto Grow or Auto Shrink:

- Data File Auto Grow
- Data File Auto Shrink
- Log File Auto Grow
- Log File Auto Shrink

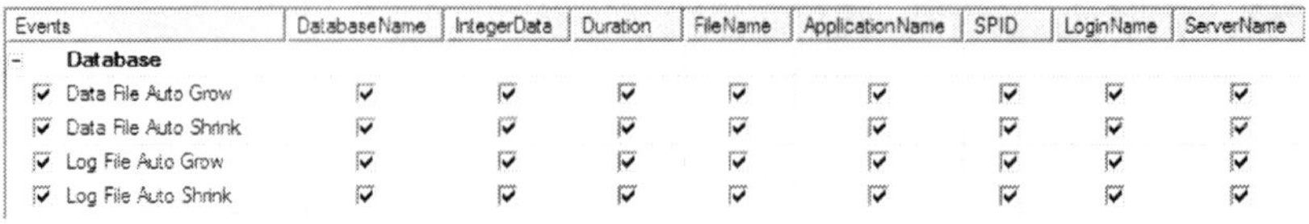

Events	DatabaseName	IntegerData	Duration	FileName	ApplicationName	SPID	LoginName	ServerName
- **Database**								
☑ Data File Auto Grow	☑	☑	☑	☑	☑	☑	☑	☑
☑ Data File Auto Shrink	☑	☑	☑	☑	☑	☑	☑	☑
☑ Log File Auto Grow	☑	☑	☑	☑	☑	☑	☑	☑
☑ Log File Auto Shrink	☑	☑	☑	☑	☑	☑	☑	☑

Figure 5-20: Four events are used to identify auto growth and auto shrinkage.

Each of these events is self-explanatory. The only thing that is not obvious is that they only fire when Auto Grow or Auto Shrink occur automatically. These events are not fired when the DBA manually grows or shrinks database or log files.

SELECTING DATA COLUMNS

I generally select the following data columns, ordered as shown below:

- DatabaseName
- EventClass
- IntegerData
- Duration
- FileName
- ApplicationName
- SPID
- LoginName
- ServerName
- StartTime
- EndTime

We have covered most of these data columns previously, but there are a couple of new ones.

INTEGERDATA

This value is the number of 8K pages that were either added or removed by the Auto Grow or Auto Shrink process.

FILENAME

This is the logical name of the file that experienced Auto Grow or Auto Shrink.

SELECTING A COLUMN FILTER

I may or may not use column filters when I am tracing recompiles. If I do, I generally filter on the DatabaseName data column to focus my analysis on one database at a time.

SELECTING COLUMN ORGANIZATION

I like to group an Auto Grow/Auto Shrink trace by the **EventClass** data column, as shown in figure 5-21. This allows me to see the data grouped by the type of event or, if I turn off grouping, then I can see the events in chronological order:

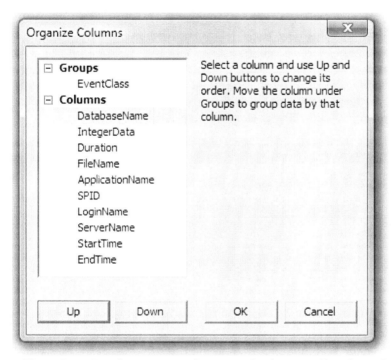

Figure 5-21: I prefer to group and aggregate by the EventClass data column.

RUNNING THE TRACE

This is a very lightweight trace and there is no problem running it for a 24-hour period if you want to see what is happening throughout the day, which I recommend.

ANALYZING THE TRACE

Let's check out our trace, shown in Figure 5-22:

EventClass	DatabaseName	IntegerData	Duration	FileName	ApplicationName
+ Data File Auto Grow (389)					
+ Data File Auto Shrink (1)					
+ Log File Auto Grow (45)					
+ Trace Start (1)					

Figure 5-22: The results are grouped and aggregated by EventClass.

This trace is grouped and aggregated on the EventClass data column, which is a great way to start analyzing the data. Right away, we see a huge number of Data File Auto Grow events, plus quite a few Log File Auto Grow events, and a single Data File Auto Shrink event.

Given that this trace lasted less than 5 minutes, it would be safe to say that these numbers are excessive. You may be thinking that I had to create some unusual Transact-SQL code to create a trace with this many events in such a short amount of time. Not at all. What I did was something many DBAs do every day, and that is to import a large quantity of data (20 million rows) into a table.

Hopefully this dramatic, but quite common, example demonstrates that using Auto Grow to manage your database file sizes is not a great idea.

Let's drill down more and see what happened:

EventClass	DatabaseName	IntegerData	Duration	FileName	ApplicationName
Data File Auto Grow (389)					
Data File Auto Grow	sqlstress	128	153	sqlst...	Microsoft SQ...
Data File Auto Grow	sqlstress	128	170	sqlst...	Microsoft SQ...
Data File Auto Grow	sqlstress	128	126	sqlst...	Microsoft SQ...
Data File Auto Grow	sqlstress	128	106	sqlst...	Microsoft SQ...
Data File Auto Grow	sqlstress	128	93	sqlst...	Microsoft SQ...
Data File Auto Grow	sqlstress	128	106	sqlst...	Microsoft SQ...
Data File Auto Grow	sqlstress	128	156	sqlst...	Microsoft SQ...
Data File Auto Grow	sqlstress	128	203	sqlst...	Microsoft SQ...
Data File Auto Grow	sqlstress	128	60	sqlst...	Microsoft SQ...

Figure 5-23: As you can see in this example, Auto Grow required a lot of disk I/O and time as the data file was automatically expanded.

Expanding the Data File Auto Grow EventClass, I see each individual event. As you can see, each one increased the size of the database by 128 x 8K pages, and the duration of each Auto Grow event varied from 60 to 203 milliseconds. In fact, when I total all 389 events, the database grew by just under 400mb, with a total duration of about 45 seconds.

If this had happened during a busy time of the day, the server's performance would have been affected, due to the memory, disk I/O, and CPU resources required to expand the data file. If this growth was managed manually, it could have been done as a single event at a time of the day when activity was slower, so that it had less effect on users. Moreover, this doesn't even consider the resources used to grow the log file.

If this is not enough proof of excessive file growth, we can ungroup and disaggregate the results by clicking View | Aggregated View, as shown in Figure 5-24:

EventClass	DatabaseName	IntegerData	Duration	FileName	ApplicationName
Trace Start					
Data File Auto Shrink	sqlstress	50944	186	sqlstress	
Data File Auto Grow	sqlstress	128	153	sqlstress	Microsoft SQ...
Data File Auto Grow	sqlstress	128	170	sqlstress	Microsoft SQ...
Data File Auto Grow	sqlstress	128	126	sqlstress	Microsoft SQ...
Log File Auto Grow	sqlstress	96	186	sqlstres...	Microsoft SQ...
Data File Auto Grow	sqlstress	128	106	sqlstress	Microsoft SQ...

Figure 5-24: The data is not disaggregated, showing the events in the order they occurred.

In its ungrouped and disaggregated view, we see each event as it happened. Notice that, by coincidence, a Data File Auto Shrink event occurred, reducing the database by 50,944 8K pages. This event was followed by four Data File Auto Grow events, then a Log File Auto Grow event. While we can't see the StartTime in the figure above, these events occurred less than one second apart. Obviously, you don't want your server expanding a database or log file that often. The overhead is unnecessary and easily prevented.

With most of the problems we have identified with Profiler up to this point, Profiler provides us with good data about a problem, but it doesn't always provide us with easy solutions. In this particular case, the solution is simple. Follow the best practices already described and proactively manage the size of your database files. This way, you will never see an example as bad as the one shown here.

HOW TO IDENTIFY EXCESSIVE TABLE/INDEX SCANS

Table or index scans can be a good thing or a bad thing for SQL Server performance. If a table is small, then a scan is often the fastest way to return rows. On the other hand, if the table is large and you only need to return a few rows from it, then a table scan will be very inefficient. As DBAs or developers, we only want to see table or index scans used where they are most efficient, so our goal is to try to identify inefficient scan activity.

While there is no single event that will do all this for us, there are a series of events we can use to help us identify tables or indexes that are subject to a lot of scans; we can then investigate those to see whether or not the scans are appropriate.

THE SCAN:STARTED EVENT

The **Scan:Started** event fires whenever a table or an index scan occurs within a SQL Server instance and is the primary event that will help you to identify excessive scanning. In addition, I like to capture the following context events:

- RPC:Completed
- SP:StmtCompleted
- SQL:BatchStarting
- SQL:BatchCompleted
- Showplan XML

SELECTING THE DATA COLUMNS

Selecting the ideal combination of data columns for this trace is not particularly easy. The problem is that the Scan:Started event lacks a lot of useful data columns, and its data columns don't overlap well with the data columns for the context events. This requires collecting more data columns that I would prefer, incurring greater overhead. Generally, I like to select the following data columns:

- ObjectID
- ObjectName
- Duration
- EventClass
- TextData
- CPU
- Reads
- Writes
- IntegerData
- DatabaseName
- ApplicationName
- StartTime
- EndTime
- SPID
- LoginName
- EventSequence
- BinaryData

We have seen all of these data columns before, so they don't need another introduction. What you might be asking is: why am I collecting both the ObjectID and the ObjectName data columns?

Isn't one or the other of these columns redundant? No. The ObjectID is collected for the Scan:Started event only, and it is used to group and aggregate scans by object (table or index) ID. Unfortunately, ObjectName is not available for the Scan:Started event. For the context events, ObjectName is available, but it does not refer to the same object referred to in the Scan:Started event. Instead, ObjectName, in the context events, refers to the stored procedure (assuming there is one) that was executed.

SELECTING A COLUMN FILTER

I generally filter on the DatabaseName data column in order to reduce the amount of events that are displayed, so I can focus on one database at a time.

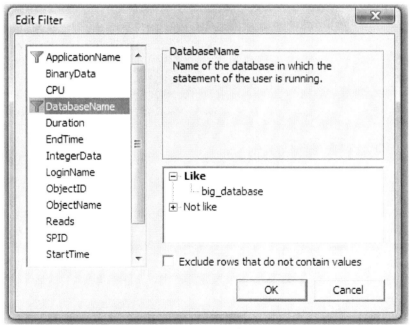

Figure 5-25: Filter on DatabaseName to focus on one database at a time.

COLUMN ORGANIZATION

I group by the **Object ID** data column. This makes it much easier to identify those objects that incur large numbers of table or index scans. In addition, I can remove the grouping later in order to see the scan events in context with the code that created the scans. You can order the data columns any way that works best for you.

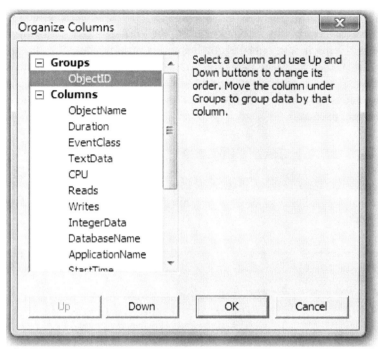

Figure 5-26: I prefer to group and aggregate by the ObjectID data column.

RUNNING THE TRACE

If you have a busy production server, this trace will capture many events, so I don't recommend that you run this trace for more than one hour at a time. As usual, you will want to select a time period to conduct the trace that is representative of a typical production load. If your workload varies a lot over time, you may need to conduct multiple traces in order to capture a representative workload. If you have a very busy server, then you may have to trace for a period shorter than one hour.

ANALYZING THE TRACE

Let's check out what our trace looks like, shown in Figure 5-27:

ObjectID	ObjectName	Duration	EventClass
+	1142399239 (56)		
+	1250207604 (6)		
+	1292023834 (15)		
+	1321771766 (6)		
+	1385928159 (6)		
+	1625824904 (27)		
+	1657825018 (41)		
+	1769825417 (27)		
+	1770489386 (84)		
+	1785825474 (32)		
+	1801825531 (17)		
+	1836025772 (155)		
+	1874209827 (18)		
+	2072446507 (9)		

Figure 5-27: Use this trace to identify those objects that are subject to lot of scans.

After performing a scan trace, our first goal is to identify those objects (tables or indexes) that incur the greatest number of scans. For example, in figure 5-27, one particular object experienced 155 scans. At this point we don't know if this is good or bad, so we need to conduct some further investigation.

One of the first things I want to know is the name of the object that corresponds to the offending Object ID, and I find this out using the following code:

```
SELECT  name
FROM    sys.objects
WHERE   object_id = 1836025772
```

Upon running this query, I find out that the name of the object is "ship_tbl," which is a table in the database. Next, I like to know how many rows the table has so I can determine if the table is small or large. Using Management Studio (or the appropriate T-SQL code), I find out that the table has 70,831 rows. This is not a small table.

Next, I like to check out the indexes on the table in order to better understand what is going on. Using Management Studio (or the appropriate T-SQL code), I find that the table has a single index, which is a clustered, composite index based on the first four columns of the table. In addition, I notice that the first column of the clustered index is not selective enough to be useful if the WHERE clause filters on this column alone. The index is only useful if the WHERE clause uses multiple columns of the index.

At this point, I am thinking that this particular table may not be well indexed because it has a single composite index. To prove this, I need to see this object in the context of the code that runs against it. To do this,

I ungroup and disaggregate the data by selecting View|Aggregated View in order to view the events in chronological order. Then, I use the Profiler Find option to locate the first occurrence in the trace of ObjectID 1836025772.

Figure 5-28 shows me that this object is scanned several times during the execution of a stored procedure:

ObjectID	ObjectName	Duration	EventClass	TextData
			SQL:BatchStarting	exec dbo.ADGSP_SO_LOADNOTSHIP
	ADGSP_SO_LOADNOTSHIP	0	SP:StmtCompleted	SET NOCOUNT ON
	ADGSP_SO_LOADNOTSHIP		Showplan XML	<ShowPlanXML xmlns="http://schemas....
1292023834			Scan:Started	
1292023834			Scan:Started	
1292023834			Scan:Started	
1836025772			Scan:Started	
1836025772			Scan:Started	
1836025772			Scan:Started	
1836025772			Scan:Started	
1836025772			Scan:Started	
1836025772			Scan:Started	
1836025772			Scan:Started	
1836025772			Scan:Started	
1836025772			Scan:Started	

Figure 5-28: The screen shot shows the top of the stored procedure dbo.ADGSP_SO_LOADNOTSHIP.

There are so many scan events for this stored procedure that I can't show all of them on a single screen. However, at the top of figure 5-28, we see that the stored procedure dbo.ADGSP_SO_LOADNOTSHIP begins executing. Next comes a SET NOCOUNT ON statement. In the third line we see the Showplan XML event. This is the graphical execution plan for the dbo.ADGSP_SO_LOADNOTSHIP stored procedure. After that we see many Scan:Started events relating to our ship_tbl table (ObjectID 1836025772).

Further down the trace, in Figure 5-29, we see more scan events, including three that relate to a different object:

ObjectID	ObjectName	Duration	EventClass	TextData	CPU	Reads	Write
1836025772			Scan:Started				
1836025772			Scan:Started				
1836025772			Scan:Started				
1836025772			Scan:Started				
1836025772			Scan:Started				
1836025772			Scan:Started				
1836025772			Scan:Started				
1836025772			Scan:Started				
683917558			Scan:Started				
683917558			Scan:Started				
683917558			Scan:Started				
	ADGSP_SO_LOADNOTSHIP	10679	SP:StmtCompleted	SELECT DISTINCT so_hdr_tbl.g...	4931	158328	
		10679	SQL:BatchCompleted	exec dbo.ADGSP_SO_LOADNOTSHIP	4931	158334	

Figure 5-29: The screen shot shows the bottom of the stored procedure dbo.ADGSP_SO_LOADNOTSHIP.

Toward the end of the trace, we see the SP:StmtCompleted event, indicating that the code inside the stored procedure has been fired. Finally, we see the SQL:BatchCompleted event. Associated with these final two events, we can also see the Duration, CPU, and Reads. These values are all suspiciously high.

At this point, I like to look at the graphical execution plan of the code. As this plan is much too large to show here, trust me when I say that it contains multiple Clustered Index Scans of the ship_tbl table, among many other problems. At this point, I would need to drill down even further to identify why the scans are occurring and see if there is any benefit from modifying or adding indexes to the table, to turn the scans into index seeks.

You may be thinking that the process I described here is a lot like the process for identifying slow queries, and involves just as much work. You'd be right on both counts. Essentially, what we are doing in this trace is finding slow-performing queries, albeit by a slightly different route. However, whereas the process in Chapter 4 focused only on Duration, this one examines scans and the objects that are affected by the scans.

HOW TO IDENTIFY MEMORY PROBLEMS

Traditionally, identifying memory problems has been done using Performance Monitor, system-stored procedures and, in SQL Server 2005 onwards, Dynamic Management Views (DMVs). Although SQL Server 2005 Profiler is not one of the primary tools for investigating memory issues, it does offer three events that can provide insight into these issues that we can't get from other tools.

MEMORY PROFILING EVENTS

The three Profiler events that can help us understand different types of memory pressures in SQL Server 2005 are:

- Execution Warnings
- Sort Warnings
- Server Memory Change

When I conduct an initial trace using the above events, I use them by themselves to see if they cause problems. If I see any problems, then I conduct follow-up traces that include additional context events, such as:

- RPC:Completed
- SP:StmtCompleted

- SQL:BatchStarting
- SQL:BatchCompleted
- Showplan XML

Since we've encountered all the above context events previously, let's focus on the three key memory events, as shown in Figure 5-30:

Events	EventSubClass	TextData	Duration	IntegerData	ApplicationName	DatabaseName
Errors and Warnings						
Execution Warnings	☑	☑	☑		☑	☑
Sort Warnings	☑				☑	☑
Server						
Server Memory Change	☑			☑		

Figure 5-30: Use these three events for your initial traces.

In previous traces, all the events were clearly related. This trace is different. While all three events are memory-related, they each represent a different way of measuring memory pressure on a SQL Server.

EXECUTION WARNINGS

Before a query can be executed, it must first be granted enough memory to execute. Most of the time there is enough memory available and the memory is granted immediately. However, if the server is under intensive memory pressure, queries may have to wait their turn in order to get the amount of memory they need to execute. The Execution Warnings event fires whenever a query has to wait one second or more before it is allocated the memory it needs.

SORT WARNINGS

When SQL Server is asked to perform an ORDER BY operation, it tries to perform the sort in memory in order to provide the best performance. However, if the amount of data to be ordered is large, the data might instead have to be written to the tempdb database as part of the sorting process. Because disk I/O is now involved, sort performance can suffer.

SERVER MEMORY CHANGE

This event fires when the memory of a SQL Server instance increases or decreases by either 1mb, or by 5% of the maximum server memory allocated to it, whichever is greater. If you start up a SQL Server instance, you would expect to see this event fire as its memory is being allocated. On the other hand, once a server has been running for a while, you would not expect to see this event fire very often. If the event is fired frequently over a short time period, this might indicate that SQL

Server is fighting the operating system, or another application, for memory.

SELECTING THE DATA COLUMNS

Fortunately, few data columns are needed to capture the required information from these three events. These are the data columns I normally select for this trace:

- EventClass
- EventSubClass
- TextData
- Duration
- IntegerData
- ApplicationName
- DatabaseName
- LoginName
- ServerName
- SPID
- StartTime

We've encountered each of these data columns before, but the data returned by EventSubClass and IntegerData varies from event to event.

EVENTSUBCLASS

If the event type is Execution Warnings, you see either of these two values:

- **"1=Query wait"** – indicates that a particular query had to wait at least one second before it could be allocated enough memory to run
- **"2=Query timeout"** – indicates that SQL Server killed the query instead of running it because it was never allocated enough memory to run.

If the event type is Sort Warnings, you see either of these two values:

- **"1=Single pass"** – SQL Server only had to perform a single pass to sort the data in tempdb
- **"2=Multiple pass"** – two or more passes were required to sort the data in tempdb. The more passes taken, the more resources SQL Server must use to sort the data.

If the event type is Server Memory Change, you see either of these two values: **"1=Memory Increase"** or **"2=Memory Decrease"**, indicating whether SQL Server is asking for more memory, or giving up memory.

INTEGERDATA

If the event type is Server Memory Change, the value in this data column represents the new memory size, in megabytes, that is being used by SQL Server at the time the event is fired.

SELECTING A COLUMN FILTER

When I perform the initial trace, I don't use any filters at all. This is because memory tends to be a server-wide problem and it's necessary to collect all these events in order to get a broad view of how these memory events are affecting the server. If I decide to drill down later for more detailed traces, I tend to filter at the **DatabaseName** level.

COLUMN ORGANIZATION

I group by the **EventClass** data column. This separates the three types of memory events and aggregates the number of times they occurred during the trace. You can order the data columns any way that works best for you.

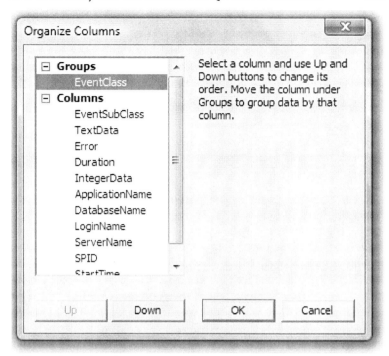

Figure 5-31: I prefer to group and aggregate by the EventClass data column.

RUNNING THE TRACE

If you are only tracing the three memory events, the trace will be lightweight and you should be able to run it for a 24-hour period in order to get a representative look at how memory is behaving in your server.

ANALYZING THE TRACE

Depending on the memory problems your server has, if any, it may take some time to see any of these events occur on your server. Figure 5-32 shows a trace that captured one Execution Warnings event, five Server Memory Change events, and 105 Sort Warnings events:

EventClass	EventSubClass	TextData	Error	Duration
+ Execution Warnings (1)				
+ Server Memory Change (5)				
+ Sort Warnings (105)				
+ Trace Start (1)				
+ Trace Stop (1)				

Figure 5-32: This trace is simple and easy to read.

If this was a trace collected over a 24-hour period, I would assume that there are no memory problems with this server, at least in regard to these three memory events. On the other hand, if this was a 5-minute trace, then I might begin to worry. Once again, however, it would largely depend on how this trace compares to my baseline trace.

Let's drill down into the details of each event, starting with Execution Warnings, as shown in Figure 5-33:

EventClass	EventSubClass	TextData	Duration	IntegerData	ApplicationName	DatabaseName
Execution Warnings (1)						
Execution Warnings	1 - Query Wait		15000		stress utility	Big_Database

Figure 5-33: You want as few Execution Warnings as possible on your server.

The **EventSubClass** data column indicates that the query was executed, but that it was delayed before it could get enough memory to execute. The **Duration** data column shows that the query waited 15 seconds before it could run. Seeing a few of these events is normal, but if you see them happening often, your server needs more memory. If memory does not become available within a reasonable amount of time, the query can time out and you would see a time-out error in the EventSubClass. Obviously you want to avoid having any queries timed out due to a lack of available memory.

Figure 5-34 shows the five Server Memory Change events:

EventClass	EventSubClass	TextData	Duration	IntegerData	ApplicationName
Server Memory Change (5)					
Server Memory Change	1 - Increase			111	
Server Memory Change	1 - Increase			222	
Server Memory Change	1 - Increase			343	
Server Memory Change	1 - Increase			497	
Server Memory Change	2 - Decrease			384	

Figure 5-34: SQL Server can ask for more memory, or it can give it up.

To create the above example, I stopped and then restarted the SQL Server instance, to free up memory. Then I began running a load on the server. As noted earlier, for the Server Memory Change event to fire, memory (RAM) use must increase or decrease by either 1mb or 5% of the maximum server memory allocated to SQL Server, whichever is greater. In the first four events, we see increases in memory, from 111mb to 497mb. So, as SQL Server started processing requests after restart, it started requesting RAM.

Later, SQL Server decided to give up some RAM and its use went down to 384mb. While the numbers are small here, because it was done on a test server, you should see similar increases of memory of your SQL

Server after it is turned on and it begins production. At some point the amount of memory should stabilize, with some minor changes here and there as SQL Server's activity increases or decreases. What you do not want to see, once the server is in production, is a lot of memory increases and decreases over a short period of time, which would indicate that SQL Server and the OS, or some other application on the physical server, are fighting for memory. If this is the case, you should either add more RAM to the server, or decide which applications need the memory most and allocate it accordingly.

Finally, Figure 5-35 shows some of the Sort Warnings, including many "Single pass" warnings and two "Multiple pass" warnings:

EventClass	EventSubClass		ApplicationName	DatabaseName	LoginName	ServerName
Sort Warnings (105)						
Sort warnings	1 - Single pass		stress utility	Big_Database	pele\Brad	PELE
Sort warnings	1 - Single pass		stress utility	Big_Database	pele\Brad	PELE
Sort warnings	1 - Single pass		stress utility	Big_Database	pele\Brad	PELE
Sort warnings	1 - Single pass		stress utility	Big_Database	pele\Brad	PELE
Sort warnings	1 - Single pass		stress utility	Big_Database	pele\Brad	PELE
Sort warnings	1 - Single pass		stress utility	Big_Database	pele\Brad	PELE
Sort warnings	2 - Multiple pass		stress utility	Big_Database	pele\Brad	PELE
Sort warnings	2 - Multiple pass		stress utility	Big_Database	pele\Brad	PELE
Sort warnings	1 - Single pass		stress utility	Big_Database	pele\Brad	PELE

Figure 5-35: More than likely, Sort Warnings will have the greatest number if events.

Ideally, all sorts would occur in RAM, but this not practical. If you see many sort warnings, you may want to consider creating a follow-up trace that includes the statements and execution plan of the event, so you can see what code is causing the Sort Warnings. In some cases, adding more memory might reduce the Sort Warnings, or you may be able to rewrite queries so that less data is returned and so less sorting has to occur. As a last resort, you can try to optimize the performance of tempdb.

SUMMARY

At this point, you should be very familiar with the key events and data columns offered by SQL Server Profiler, and also know how to apply many of them to deal with real-world problems. Although we have covered a lot of what Profiler has to offer, we still have not even outlined half its total capability. As you practice using Profiler with your own servers and environment, you will eventually learn what works best for you..

Chapter 6
USING PROFILER TO AUDIT DATABASE ACTIVITY

DBAs are entrusted with an organization's confidential data. It is their job to secure that data and ensure that no one has improper access to it. In recent years, owing to new laws and regulations, company security has meant the involvement of lawyers and auditors, who not only want to ensure that DBAs are doing their job in keeping the data secure, but also track what they are doing and ensure that they are honest.

While many DBAs see this as in intrusion into their territory, they have no choice but to comply. Not only has this increased their workload, it has also required new tools that allow the DBA – and the lawyers and auditors – to verify that security is working as it should be.

In SQL Server 2005, Microsoft added many new auditing events to Profiler that allow fine-grained monitoring of most SQL Server-related activity. Activating these events is a bit like switching on SQL Server's internal security cameras, and keeping an eye on who is doing what, and when.

Having said this, using Profiler to perform 24/7 auditing is not practical. Over 40 different audit specific events can be captured, and capturing all these events would place an unacceptable resource burden on most production databases. In addition, while the data can be collected, Profiler doesn't offer any easy way to store or analyze the data, which makes management of the data and extraction of reports difficult. If an organization needs this level of database auditing, it should seek a third-party tool that is designed specifically for this purpose, or move to SQL Server 2008, which includes new auditing functionality.

Profiler's auditing capabilities are better used for short-term auditing – for investigating a specific problem, such as who is accessing a particular table, who updated a specific record, or who accidently deleted a row or a table. In other words, Profiler is a very effective tool when the audit expectations are clearly defined. It is not designed to be a general-purpose auditing tool.

In this chapter we will focus on the following topics:

- What Audit events you can capture
- Selecting data columns

- Selecting column filters
- Organizing columns
- How to conduct an Audit Trace

CAPTURING AUDIT EVENTS

Profiler offers a total of 46 audit events, grouped into two Event Categories: **Objects** and **Security Audit**. There are three Objects events:

- Object:Created
- Object:Altered
- Object:Deleted

And there are 43 **Security Audit** events:

- Audit Add DB User Event Class
- Audit Add Login to Server Role Event
- Audit Add Member to DB Role Event
- Audit Add Role Event
- Audit Addlogin Event
- Audit App Role Change Password Event
- Audit Backup/Restore Event
- Audit Broker Conversation
- Audit Broker Login
- Audit Change Audit Event
- Audit Change Database Owner
- Audit Database Management Event
- Audit Database Mirroring Login Event
- Audit Database Object Access Event
- Audit Database Object GDR Event
- Audit Database Object Management Event
- Audit Database Object Take Ownership Event
- Audit Database Operation Event
- Audit Database Principal Impersonation Event
- Audit Database Principal Management Event
- Audit Database Scope GDR Event
- Audit DBCC Event
- Audit Login Change Password Event
- Audit Login Change Property Event
- Audit Login
- Audit Login Failed Event
- Audit Login GDR Event

- Audit Logout
- Audit Object Derived Permission Event
- Audit Schema Object Access Event
- Audit Schema Object GDR Event
- Audit Schema Object Management Event
- Audit Schema Object Take Ownership Event
- Audit Server Alter Trace Event
- Audit Server Object GDR Event
- Audit Server Object Management Event
- Audit Server Object Take Ownership Event
- Audit Server Operation Event
- Audit Server Principal Impersonation Event
- Audit Server Principal Management Event
- Audit Server Scope GDR Event
- Audit Server Starts and Stops
- Audit Statement Permission Event

For the most part, the purpose of each event is self-evident from its name. For example, if you want to find out who is modifying objects, such as stored procedures, you can use the **Object:Altered** event. If you want to find out who added a user to a database, use the **Audit Add DB User** event. If you can't figure out what a particular event does from its name, you can use the help available from the Events Selection screen. Just move the cursor over the audit event, and a description of the event appears at the bottom of the screen (see Figure 6-1):

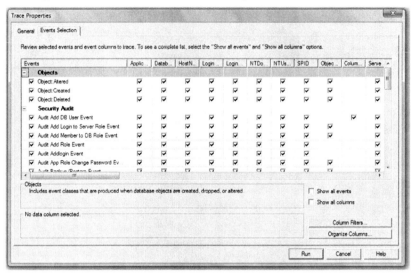

Figure 6-1: Profiler offers 46 events just for auditing. Each has a description of the event that appears at the bottom of the screen when you hover the cursor over the event.

So what events should you use when auditing? First, you need to be focused, and know what your goal is; then you need to select the minimum number of events that help you accomplish this goal.

Earlier I said that almost any SQL Server event can be audited. However, if you looked closely at the 46 events listed above, you may have noticed some events seem to be missing. For example, there don't appear to be any events to monitor SELECT, INSERT, UPDATE, or DELETE activity on a given table. How do you audit this kind of activity? In fact, besides the 46 audit-specific events, you can also use any of the available Profiler events to audit activity because most Profiler events include a data column for the user responsible for causing the event.

So, for example, if you want to identify every user who SELECTs, INSERTS, UPDATES, or DELETES data from a table, you could use the following events and track the LoginName, LoginSID, NTUserName data columns to see who was doing what:

- RPC:Completed
- SP:StmtCompleted
- SQL:BatchCompleted

By now, you may be beginning to appreciate why using Profiler for general auditing is not a good idea. In effect, if you sought to audit every user activity, you would end up wanting to capture almost all the Profiler events all of the time, which is just not practical.

When using Profiler for auditing, keep the scope of the audit small by using as few events as possible.

SELECTING DATA COLUMNS

Just as you want to minimize the number of events you capture, you also want to minimize the number of data columns: you should only select those that meet the specific goals of the audit.

There are many different reasons for performing an audit, so it's impossible to list all the different combinations of data columns you might want to select. However, I would like to list those data columns that you may want to consider when conducting a targeted Profiler audit trace. They include:

- ApplicationName
- ColumnPermissions
- DatabaseName or DatabaseID (you don't need both)
- EndTime
- Event
- HostName
- LoginName
- LoginSID
- NTDomainName
- NTUserName
- ObjectName or ObjectID (you don't need both)
- OwnerName
- Permissions
- RoleName
- StartTime
- ServerName
- SessionLoginName
- SPID
- Success
- TargetLoginName
- TargetLoginSID
- TargetUserName
- TextData

Some of the above data columns should be familiar to you, but there are a many new ones that we haven't covered yet. These include:

ColumnPermissions: This data column is available for audit events only and is used to help you track column permission activity.

LoginName: Most events include the LoginName data column. It stores the login of the user who caused the event. Depending on the type of login used, this column can contain either the SQL Server login ID or the Windows Login ID (domain\username). This very useful data column helps you to identify who is causing potential problems. It is also is a good column to filter on. This way, you can limit trace results to those of a specific user.

LoginSid: This commonly-used data column contains the security identify (SID) of the user who caused the event. In most cases you will probably not need it, as the LoginName data column provides essentially the same data and is easier to read. If you need to find out the login name of a SID, you can do so by querying the sys.server_principals view in the master database.

NTDomainName: This data column contains the name of the domain the user responsible for the event resides in.

NTUserName: This data column contains the Windows user name of the user responsible for the event. In many cases, this data duplicates the data found in the LoginName column.

OwnerName: This data column, which is used for some Audit events, lists the database user name of the object owner.

Permissions: This data column is only available for selected Audit events. It contains values representing the type of permissions affected by the event.

RoleName: If the event is caused by a client running under a SQL Server database role, the role name is located in this data column.

SessionLoginName: This data column contains the login name of the account that started the session that produced the event. This can be useful to know if the event was fired using an account other than the one originally logged-in under.

Success: Many events indicate whether or not they were successful. A value of 1 means success, and a value of 0 means failure.

TargetLoginName: Used for Audit events that target a login, this data column contains the name of the targeted login. For example, if a T-SQL statement is creating a new login name, then this value would be the name of the newly created login name.

TargetLoginSid: Used for Audit events that target a login, this data column contains the SID of the targeted login. For example, if a T-SQL statement is creating a new login name, then this value would be the SID of the newly created login name.

TargetUserName: Used for Audit events that target a database user, this data column contains the name of the targeted user. For example, if a T-SQL statement grants permission to a user, then this value would be the name of that user who was granted that permission.

When you first begin using the above data columns, you will probably need to experiment with different ones until you find the "best" combination of data columns that collect the data you need, but time don't collect more data than you need.

SELECTING COLUMN FILTERS

For audit traces, I am a big fan of using column filters. This is because the number of audit events that occur in a busy production database can very easily run into thousands per minute. By using a restrictive Column Filter, you can reduce the number of events that are captured and keep the amount of data to a manageable level.

I recommend that you select as narrow a filter as you can. For example, perform the audit on a specific database, specific application, specific object, specific user, or some combination of these, as shown in Figure 6-2:

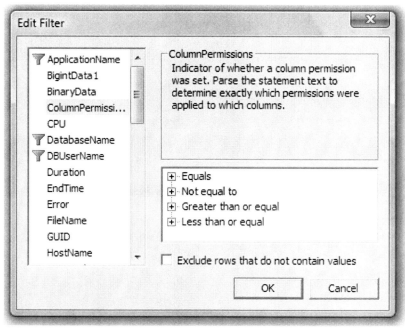

Figure 6-2: Be sure your Column Filters are very specific.

ORGANIZING COLUMNS

I suggest that you group and aggregate events on the **EventClass**. This way you will be able to more easily see what events are occurring and how often. Then you can choose to drill down for the details. This also gives you the option of removing the grouping and of viewing the data in the order the events occurred. Order the data columns in any order that works well for you.

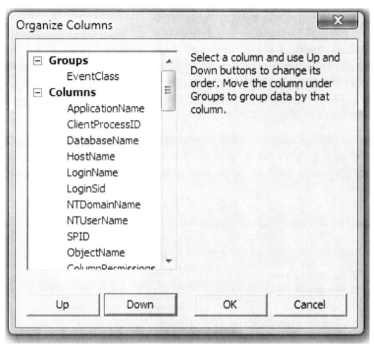

Figure 7-3: Grouping and aggregating by Event Class is a good way to present your data for later analysis.

HOW TO CONDUCT AN AUDIT TRACE

Once you have selected the appropriate events, data columns, column filters and column organization that meet your targeted auditing goals, it is time to start the trace. Before you begin, though, you have a hard decision to make: how long to run it?

Often, a problem with audit traces is that you don't know when a particular event will occur. It is obviously very hard to predict when a user might try to access a particular table, or delete an object. As such, audit traces may have to run a long time in order to be able to capture the desired activities.

As you might expect, long traces can produce a lot of data and impose a resource burden on SQL Server. The trick is to balance the amount of data collected against the length of the data collection period. For example, if you think you know that a particular event will occur within a limited time period, then you can collect more events and data columns. On the other hand, if you have no idea when an event might occur, you may have to run your trace for longer periods, but with a very limited set of events and data columns, and with a restrictive column filter.

NOTE:

See chapter 10, *How to Capture Profiler Traces Programmatically*, in order to learn additional ways of running a trace that minimize the impact it makes on a server's resources.

Figure 7-4 shows an example Profiler auditing trace, grouped on the EventClass data column:

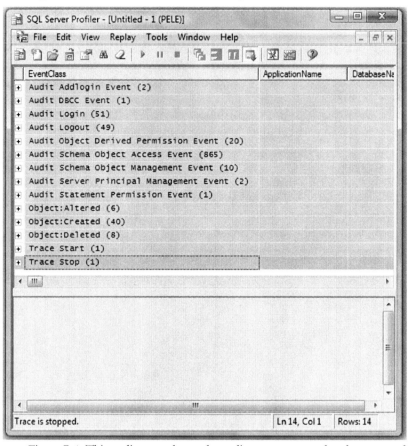

Figure 7-4: This audit trace shows the audit events grouped and aggregated.

I ran this trace for just under two minutes on a relatively underused test server. As you can see, a large number of events were captured in this time, including 865 "Schema Object Access" events. Figure 7-5 shows an ungrouped view of the same data:

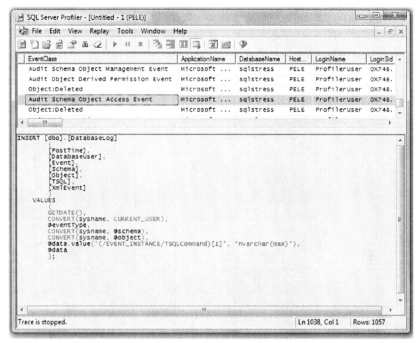

Figure 7-5: This is an ungrouped view of the data. Notice that 1,057 audit events were captured.

In Figure 7-5, I've highlighted one of the Schema Object Access events, in this case a table insert. The other data columns collected with the event show us the login of the user who made the insert, the database on which it was executed, and so on.

If you have no choice but to run a long audit, keep a close eye on the size of the trace file, together with how the trace is affecting your production server's performance. If the server is not too busy, then the impact of the trace should be negligible. If you do see a negative impact on performance, you will then have to decide if this particular audit trace is justified in terms of the value of the data you are collecting. In some cases you may have to accept less server performance for a given time period in order to collect the data you need. In other cases, the overhead used by a Profiler audit trace may be an unacceptable option, and you may have to find another way to collect the audit data you are seeking.

SUMMARY

You can see why I don't recommend using Profiler for heavy auditing tasks. If you really need this level of auditing capability, especially 24/7 auditing, you need a third-party auditing application that can not only produce a lightweight audit, but can also store, manage, and report on the audit data collected.

However, if you have a very limited and specific auditing objective, then Profiler can be a very powerful tool for the DBA.

Chapter 7

USING PROFILER WITH THE DATABASE ENGINE TUNING ADVISOR

Besides Profiler, probably the most underused and misunderstood tool that comes with SQL Server 2005 is the Database Engine Tuning Advisor (DTA). Many people think that the DTA is just a reheated version of the old Index Tuning Wizard. This is not the case. The DTA is a powerful tool that will help you better tune your SQL Server databases.

I could easily write an entire book on the many benefits and features of DTA, but since our focus is on Profiler, this chapter will content itself with showing how to create and capture a Profiler trace that can be used to feed the DTA with the information it needs to make optimized tuning recommendations.

It will also describe how to run a DTA analysis of your Profiler trace and how to interpret the results. If you are new to using DTA, this will be a good introduction. Here's how the chapter is structured:

- Features and Benefits of Using the DTA
- How to Create a Trace for Use by the DTA
- Running the Trace
- How to Perform a Simple Missing Index Analysis Using the DTA
- Understanding the Results of the DTA Analysis

FEATURES AND BENEFITS OF USING THE DTA

If you are familiar with the older Index Tuning Wizard, but have not sat down to learn the features of the DTA, you may think that the DTA is only for novice DBAs who don't know enough about SQL Server to tune their indexes manually. That would be wrong. The DTA provides features designed for both the novice and experienced DBA. In fact, I would bet that the DTA can do a better job of tuning indexes than most DBAs who perform the same task manually.

The DTA works by analyzing the **execution plans** behind all the statements that are included in the **workload** that you supply to it. This workload can take the form of a single query or, more commonly, a

Profiler trace. Based on this workload, the DTA can perform a lot of useful analysis. For example:

- The DTA supports the analysis of heaps, clustered and non-clustered indexes, indexed views, and partitions. In other words, it can take any of these physical structures and identify ways they can be modified in order to boost the performance of the workload submitted to it. It does this by analyzing the statements running against these physical structures, then determining the optimal indexing scheme necessary to optimize their performance.

- The DTA can analyze a single statement, batches of statements, Profiler traces stored in native format, Profiler Traces stored in a database table, and XML input files. It can also work with statements which have user-defined functions, reference temp tables, and which are inside triggers. In other words, the DTA can help tune database physical structures using statements found at any level, all the way from a single query to an entire server.

- The DTA can determine what physical design structures are no longer needed in a database and should be dropped. For example, it can identify indexes that are never used.

- If you are using SQL Server 2005 Enterprise Edition, you can ask the DTA for a recommendation on online index creation options, which can help to minimize the load on a busy production server.

- Integrated tuning allows the DTA to consider tradeoffs between different physical design structures, such as clustered and non-clustered indexes, indexed views, and partitions. In addition, INSERT, UPDATE, and DELETE statements are considered, along with SELECT statements, when selecting the ideal combination of indexes. In other words, the overhead associated with INSERTs, UPDATEs, and DELETEs and indexes is considered as a part of the recommended indexing scheme. The DTA also considers the order in which columns should be arranged for composite and included indexes.

- What-if analysis can be performed to test hypothetical configurations against current configuration, in order to identify ideal configurations. For example, the DBA can test to see if a particular index should be clustered or not, for optimum performance.

- The DTA produces many analysis reports, allowing the DBA to delve further into how the database is working internally.

There is also a lot of flexibility in the tool. For example, the DBA can:

- Choose exactly which physical design features to analyze.

- Select to tune physical structures for a single database, or multiple databases at the same time.

- Select exactly how long to run an analysis, by setting a maximum analysis time. For example, if a particular trace might normally take three hours to complete, but you only have one hour to devote to the analysis, you can tell the DTA to limit itself to one hour. While the results of the analysis might not be as ideal if you had allowed the full three hours, you will still get back information useful for tuning your database.

- Use the DTA via the standard GUI interface or from the command prompt. The command prompt option uses somewhat less overhead, helping to reduce the impact of the analysis on your SQL Server.

- Save tuning sessions and reexamine them at any time, helping DBAs to compare tuning results over different time periods.

- Offload the overhead of tuning onto a test server, even if the test server is not identical to the production server.

It should be obvious by now just how powerful the DTA is – and this is not even an exhaustive list of every DTA feature and benefit.

HOW TO CREATE A TRACE FOR USE BY THE DTA

As noted earlier, in order for the DTA to perform an analysis, it must be given a workload. This workload can be as simple as a single query, but a more powerful way to use the tool is to provide a workload via a Profiler Trace, containing statements that are representative of your server's typical activity.

The DTA will then analyze the trace to find out which statements are run, how often they are run, and what indexes are currently being used to run them. Based on this analysis, it will determine how the current indexing scheme might be changed in order to improve statement execution times. It presents its findings as a series of recommendations, which can include adding, dropping or modifying indexes, index views, and partitions. Note carefully, though: the DTA's recommendations are based on the workload it is given. If you provide a non-representative workload, then you may well receive non-optimal recommendations.

When creating a Profiler trace to act as our workload for the DTA, our goal is to create a workload trace that is as lightweight as possible, while still providing the essential data that the DTA needs to perform its analysis. Fortunately, SQL Server Profiler includes a trace template, called **Tuning**, which is (almost) ideal for collecting events and data columns for DTA analysis. In the following sections, not only will we examine the default Tuning template, we'll also implement a variation of this template that is even more lightweight, and just as effective.

USING THE PROFILER DEFAULT TUNING TEMPLATE

The built-in Tuning template is shown in figure 7-1:

Events		TextData	Duration	SPID	DatabaseID	DatabaseName	ObjectType	LoginName
−	**Stored Procedures**							
☑	RPC.Completed	☑	☑	☑	☑	☑		☑
☑	SP:StmtCompleted	☑	☑	☑	☑	☑	☑	☑
−	**TSQL**							
☑	SQL.BatchCompleted	☑	☑	☑	☑	☑		☑

Figure 7-1: The events and data columns for the Tuning template.

As you can see, this template is already very lightweight. It only includes three events and seven data columns. It also uses no filters or column organization. We have discussed all these events and data columns previously, so we won't talk about them again here. However, it is possible to create an even more lightweight trace.

A SLIM-LINE TUNING TEMPLATE

The DTA requires that a Profiler trace include the following three events:

- RPC:Completed
- SP:StmtCompleted
- SQL:BatchCompleted

In fact, if you include any other events in the trace, the DTA will just ignore them. While we can't remove any events from the default Tuning template, there is scope to trim out some of the data columns. The difference is not large, but every little bit helps when you are creating a DTA trace on a busy production server and you want to minimize its impact.

There follows a description of how the DTA uses the selected data columns in its analysis:

- **TextData** – This data column is mandatory. It is used by the DTA to identify what code is running in each statement.
- **Duration** – Although not mandatory, the DTA can use this data column to more effectively tune the workload, as it can give higher priority to those statements that take the longest to run
- **SPID** – Not mandatory for the DTA, but it is mandatory when collecting the Profiler trace. In the absence of the DatabaseID or

DatabaseName columns, the DTA will use the SPID to identify the database on which the event took place.

- **DatabaseID** and **DatabaseName** – Neither of these data columns are mandatory, but if you include at least one of them as part of the trace, then the DTA will use it to identify the database on which the event was executed. If you include neither, then the DTA will resort to the SPID, LoginName, or TextData columns (for example, it can examine the USE command to find out the correct database) to identify the database. If the DTA can't identify the database a statement has been executed in, then it will be unable to analyze the statement.

- **ObjectType** – Not required by the DTA, according to any documentation I could find.

- **LoginName**: – Not mandatory, but the DTA can use LoginName to impersonate the user who ran the code. However, if that user does not have the SHOWPLAN permission, which enables the user to create execution plans for the statements contained in the trace, then the DTA will not tune those statements. If the LoginName is not included in the workload trace, then the DTA will instead run the statements by impersonating the user who started the DTA tuning session.

As you can see, you can leave out most of the data columns if you want to. Personally, I have made a compromise by dropping the DatabaseID and ObjectType data columns, which are either redundant or of no use to the DTA, leaving in those that are useful, even if not mandatory, as shown in Figure 7-2:

Events	TextData	Duration	SPID	DatabaseName	LoginName
− **Stored Procedures**					
☑ RPC:Completed	☑	☑	☑	☑	☑
☑ SP:StmtCompleted	☑	☑	☑	☑	☑
− **TSQL**					
☑ SQL:BatchCompleted	☑	☑	☑	☑	☑

Figure 7-2: This is a lighter weight version of a DTA trace.

I also don't add any filters or arrange the columns in any special order. This allows my trace to be just a little more lightweight than the default Tuning trace included with the SQL Server Profiler.

You can choose to use the default Tuning template, or mine, or create your own template and it is not compatible with DTA, then the DTA will provide you with error message feedback.

RUNNING THE WORKLOAD TRACE

Creating a Profiler trace for DTA analysis is no different from creating any other Profiler trace, but there are a few points that need making:

- If you decide to create your own custom workload trace, define it as a template called "DTA trace" or similar. This way, you won't have to recreate the trace each time you want to run it.

- Save the Profiler trace results to a file and enable file rollover. The default 5mb size is fine. Do not save the trace results directly to a database table, as this will only increase overhead.

- Check the "Server Processes Trace Data" checkbox. This will ensure that all trace events are captured. We don't want to skip any trace events when trying to capture a representative sample of statements.

- Pick a time of the day that is representative of your typical server load and run the trace for as long as possible – say 8 hours, for example. If you can't run the trace for this long, due to its negative impact on server resources, or because of disk space limitations, then consider taking multiple, smaller traces – say 15, 30, 60 minute traces – over a period of a day, or several days. Each DTA analysis will have to be separate, but you may not have any choice.

- If you have no choice but to collect multiple, smaller traces, instead of one large trace, there are two different workarounds you might want to consider that allow you to take multiple traces and combine them into a single workload file so that it can be analyzed by the DTA as a single unit. By performing the DTA analysis on a single, larger file, the DTA will be able to have more data to work with and should produce better results than from having to analyze multiple, smaller files, one at a time. In addition, you will be presented with a single set of recommendations, instead of a different DTA recommendation for each individual workload file. This makes analyzing the results easier.

  o The first workaround is to use the pause option, instead of starting and stopping the trace multiple times over a day or several days. If you pause a Profiler trace, it will stay paused until you restart the trace. When you restart the trace, Profiler will display a dialog box asking you "Trace data saving options have been reset. Do you want to proceed without saving the output?" Click the "No" button, and then the "Trace Properties" dialog box appears. Click the "Run" button, and the trace will resume, saving the trace data in the same file you specified when you created the trace. Once you have collected several different "snapshots" of representative workload trace data over one or more days, stop the trace, and then you can use the resulting trace file (or rollover files if you choose that option) as the input for your DTA analysis.

o The second workaround is similar to the first one, but it assumes that instead of pausing the trace, you stop it instead. When you stop a trace, there is no way to resume it and continue to save trace data in the same trace files. To get around this design flaw in Profiler, what you can do instead is to collect all the workload trace file you have made over one or more days. Next, import each of the trace files into a different SQL Server table. Unfortunately, you can't import them into the same table. Once you have imported all the data into multiple tables, then write some T-SQL code to extract all the data from all the separate tables into a single, large table. Now you have all the data located in a single location. To analyze the workload that is now stored in a single, large table, use this table as the source of your workload when you run the DTA analysis. This way, the DTA has access to all the data in a single location and only one DTA analysis has to be performed.

- On busy production servers, the trace file (or rollover files, if you choose this option) can grow big very quickly. You will want to keep a close eye on the amount of disk space used by the trace so that you don't accidently run out of room.

- To further minimize the workload on a production server when collecting Profiler trace data for DTA analysis, consider using SQL Trace to capture the data. This is discussed in the chapter, "How to Capture Profiler Traces Programmatically."

PERFORMING A MISSING INDEX ANALYSIS USING THE DTA

Once you have captured the Profiler workload trace, you are ready to analyze it with the DTA. Let's now use the DTA to look for missing indexes, based on a Profiler trace I took from a very poorly performing SQL Server. The following are the step-by-step instructions to perform the analysis.

STARTING THE DTA

You can start the DTA from either:

- SQL Server Profiler (Tools | Database Engine Tuning Advisor)

- Management Studio (Tools | Database Engine Tuning Advisor)
- The Start menu

When the DTA starts, you will be asked to log onto the server that includes the database(s) you want to analyze, as shown in Figure 7-3. You must login with Sysadmin or dbo_owner rights to analyze a database with DTA.

Figure 7-3: You must login with Sysadmin or dbo_owner rights to analyze a database with DTA.

Once you are logged in, you'll see the main screen of the DTA, shown in Figure 7-4:

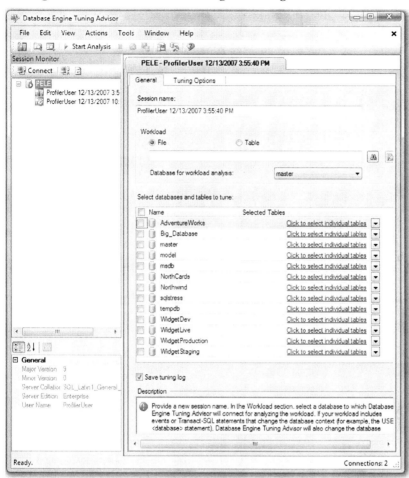

Figure 7-4: The main screen of the DTA.

At the left-hand side of the screen you see a server with the name of PELE. Under this are two different DTA sessions. The green icon indicates a previously created DTA session, while the blue icon indicates your current session. DTA maintains a history of DTA sessions so you can compare one session to another. You can delete previous sessions if you want.

Starting at the top, on the right side of the screen, you'll see the default name of the current DTA session. You can rename it if you like.

In the section below that, you must specify where the workload for the DTA analysis is located. A workload can be a Profiler trace file or a table in a database. In our example, our workload is a Profiler trace file.

Next, you will see the option "Database for workload analysis" This option specifies the first database to which the DTA connects when first tuning a workload. Select the database you will be analyzing with the DTA. If you will be analyzing more than one database, then select the first of the multiple databases you will be analyzing.

Finally, you will see a list of all the databases on the server. You can analyze a single database, multiple databases, or all the non-system databases at the same time. In our example, we will be analyzing a single database.

DEFINING THE WORKLOAD AND SPECIFYING THE DATABASE

To specify the workload file, in this case, select the "File" radio button, and click on the browse icon, to the right of the text box. The "Select Workload File" screen appears, as shown in Figure 7-5:

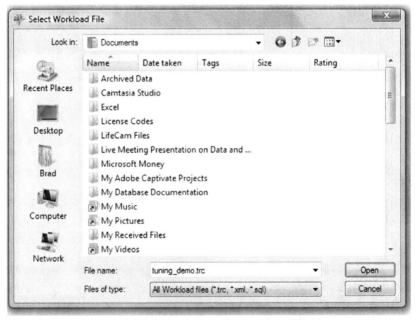

Figure 7-5: Select the workload file to be used by DTA.

Next, select the name of the database you want to analyze, next to the "Database for workload analysis" option.

Then select the database against which you want to run the workload, simply by checking the appropriate check box, see figure 7-7. You can limit the analysis to certain tables in that database by clicking on the down-arrow icon the right of the database name. However, we want all tables in the database to be analyzed, so we don't have to do any further steps.

Figure 7-7: The first page of the screen is filled out and we are now ready to go to the next screen.

RUNNING THE DTA ANALYSIS

Click on the "Tuning Options "tab, shown in Figure 7-8:

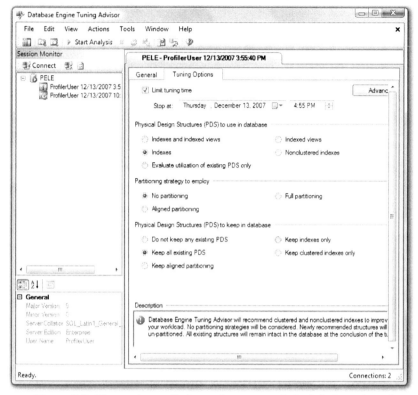

Figure 7-8: We can leave all the options set to their default settings for our analysis.

This screen allows us to choose the type of analysis to perform. Since we are only focusing on indexing, we want to use the Indexes option, which is already selected on the screen by default. The rest of the screen can be left alone.

To begin running the DTA analysis, click on the "Start Analysis" button at the top of the screen. Once you do, a screen appears showing you the progress of the analysis, shown in Figure 7-9.

A DTA analysis can take from a few minutes to many hours, depending on the workload used, the type of analysis you selected, and the current load of the production server it is using to analyze the execution plans of each of the statements captured in your workload trace.

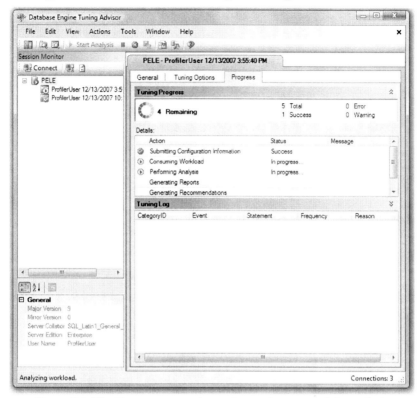

Figure 7-9: The Progress screen lets us know the status of the analysis.

When the analysis is complete, the Recommendations screen will appear which will display all the DTA's recommendations for increasing the performance of our SQL Server, based on the workload it analyzed.

ANALYZING THE RESULTS

The "Recommendations" screen for the analysis I performed is shown in Figure 7-10 (this is a partial screen shot as the entire screen too large to fit here):

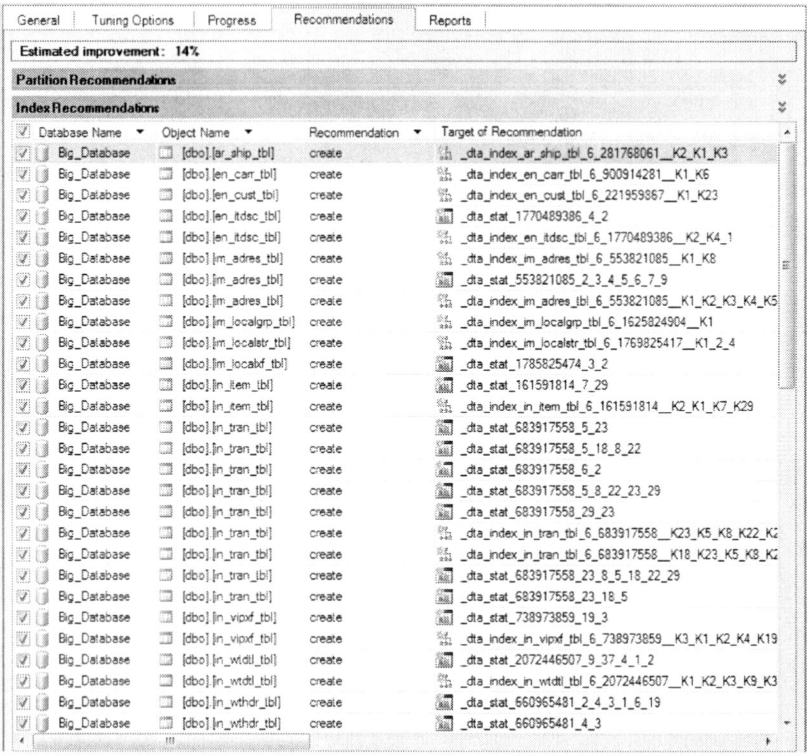

Figure 7-10: Apparently, the DTA found a lot to fix in this analysis.

At the top of the screen, DTA estimates the percentage improvement in performance that should result from implementing all its recommendations – in this case 14%. However, keep in mind that this estimated boost is based on the workload given, and the actual boost in performance will probably be different (generally smaller). The more representative the workload that was analyzed by the DTA, the more accurate the estimate will be.

The rest of the screen displays the DTA's "Index Recommendations". This title is a little deceiving. A more accurate title would be "Index and Column Statistics Recommendations" since not every item in this long list refers to the creation of a new index. The list also includes recommendations for the creation of new column statistics, which can be used by the query optimizer to devise better execution plans. A quick glance at the "Target of Recommendation" column in figure 7-10 will tell you which is which. You will see the word _index _ as part of the name if the object to be created is an index, or _stat_ if it is a column statistic.

Now, let's jump to the Reports tab and examine the Tuning Summary screen, shown in Figure 7-11:

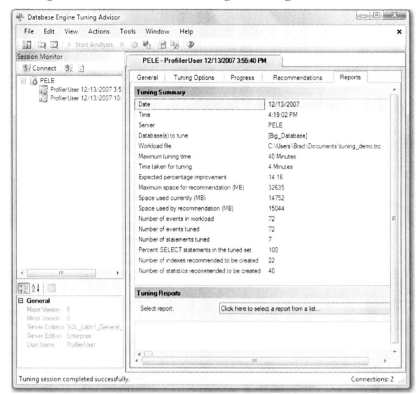

Figure 7-11: DTA offers a large number of reports to help you fully understand how the workload interacts with a database's physical objects.

The Tuning Summary screen provides a lot of useful information. For example:

- The trace took only 4 minutes to analyze.
- There were 72 events in the workload, of which 72 were tuned. Don't be surprised if every event is not tuned, as not every event captured by a Profiler trace is a query that runs against a table.
- The DTA recommends 22 new indexes and 40 column statistics be added. This is a lot of new indexes, considering that the trace included only 72 different statements.

If you want, you can click on the drop-down box in the "Tuning Reports" section at the bottom of the screen and run additional reports, as shown in Figure 7-12:

Figure 7-12: This is a list of the available reports you can run.

IMPLEMENTING THE DTA'S RECOMMENDATIONS

Of the 22 new indexes and 40 column statistics that the DTA recommends, your choices are to:

1. Accept all the recommendations and have the DTA automatically implement them for you

2. Review each individual recommendation and only implement those you agree with.

This is a tough call, but here is my advice:

- Assuming that you are confident the workload is representative of the actual statements being run on your production server, and assuming that you don't have either the time or experience to individually evaluate each recommendation, then I would accept all the recommendations and have DTA create the recommended indexes and column statistics.

- If you are confident the workload is representative of the actual statements being run by your production server, and you have the time and experience to be able to evaluate each index recommendation, then I would recommend that you review each one, and only take it if makes sense based on your knowledge of the overall workings of the database. This advice is for indexes only. There is no way a DBA can easily evaluate if a column statistics recommendation is good or not, so I would accept the DTA's recommendations on all column statistics.

- If you are not confident that the workload is a representative of the statements running on your production server, then you need to run the analysis several times and compare the results to see if you get similar recommendations. If you do, then you can either accept them all, or be selective, depending on your time and experience.

How do you check out the code that the DTA will use to implement each index or column statistic? Click back to the "Recommendations" screen and scroll all the way to the right. The very last column is called "Definition" and if you click on the blue hyperlink (see Figure 7-13) a box will appear with the code that the DTA suggests you use to create the index or column statistic:

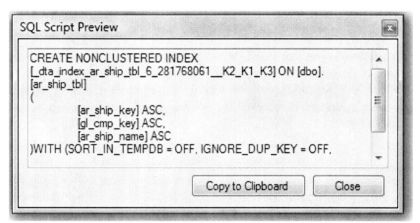

Figure 7-13: Hard to see, but the furthest right column shows a blue hyperlink.

The box looks as shown in Figure 7-14:

```
SQL Script Preview

CREATE NONCLUSTERED INDEX
[_dta_index_ar_ship_tbl_6_281768061__K2_K1_K3] ON [dbo].
[ar_ship_tbl]
(
        [ar_ship_key] ASC,
        [gl_cmp_key] ASC,
        [ar_ship_name] ASC
)WITH (SORT_IN_TEMPDB = OFF, IGNORE_DUP_KEY = OFF,
```

Copy to Clipboard   Close

Figure 7-14: This is the code DTA recommends you implement for a single new index or column statistic.

As the DBA, it's your job to evaluate this code and decide whether or not it is right for your database. If it is, then you have the option to copy this code to the Clipboard and paste it into Management Studio to execute.

Of course, if you have dozens of indexes or column statistics to add, you probably don't want to have to add them one at a time, manually. DTA gives you the additional options of either adding some or all of them at the same time.

Assuming you want to implement all or most of the recommendations, you need to ensure the checkbox is checked next to each recommendation you want to implement (you can see this checkbox at the very left of figure 7-13). If you remove a check, then that recommendation will not be implemented.

Then, from the Main Menu, select "Actions | Apply Recommendations" and you will see the screen shown in Figure 7-15:

Figure 7-15: You can decide to run the code now, or schedule it to run later.

At this point you can decide to implement all of the recommendations now, or schedule them to execute at a future time. Ideally, you will want to run the recommendations when the server is not very busy, as database users can be blocked for the duration of the process of creating new indexes.

You have now implemented your DTA recommendations. But you are not done yet. Once I implement DTA recommendations, I like to go back (if I can), and see if the indexes are really helping. One thing I like to do is to compare Performance Monitor and/or Profiler traces taken before and after the DTA recommendations were implemented. In addition, I like to run another DTA trace and analysis after the recommendations have been put into place, just to catch anything that the first recommendations missed.

SUMMARY

By now, you will see the benefit of creating Profiler traces and running DTA analyses. Ideally, you should be performing this type of analysis on all your SQL Server instances at regular time intervals. Data and queries changes over time, and so do indexing needs.

Chapter 8
CORRELATING PROFILER WITH PERFORMANCE MONITOR

In the past, when watching the % Processor Time counter in Performance Monitor on my live production SQL Servers, I would occasionally see sudden spikes in CPU utilization, to 50, 70 or even 80%. These spikes might last several minutes or more, then disappear. In some extreme cases I would see spikes that lasted 30, or even 60 minutes. I always wanted to know which SQL Server activity was causing the spike, but the problem was that I had no way of correlating a specific statement running in SQL Server to a specific resource usage spike.

With SQL Server 2005 Profiler, I now have the tools to identify the causes of such spikes. I can import Performance Monitor log data and compare it directly with Profiler activity. If I see a spike in CPU utilization, I can identify which statement or statements were running at the same time, and diagnose potential problems.

This chapter will describe how to perform a correlation analysis using Profiler and Performance Monitor, covering:

- How to collect Profiler data for correlation analysis
- How to collect Performance Monitor data for correlation analysis
- How to capture Profiler traces and Performance Monitor logs
- How to correlate SQL Server 2005 Profiler data with Performance Monitor data
- How to analyze correlated data

I assume you have a basic working knowledge of Performance Monitor (sometimes called System Monitor) as well as Profiler, in order to focus on how to use the two tools together. If you need further information on the basics of using Performance Monitor, check out Books Online.

HOW TO COLLECT PROFILER DATA FOR CORRELATION ANALYSIS

While it is possible to correlate most Profiler events to most Performance Monitor counters, the area of greatest correlation is between Profiler Transact-SQL events and Performance Monitor counters that indicate resource bottlenecks.

This is where I focus my efforts, and the following sections describe how I collect Profiler data for correlation with Performance Monitor. As always, feel free to modify my suggestions to suit your own needs. The key, as always when using Profiler, is to capture only those events and data columns you really need in order to minimize the workload on your production server when the trace is running.

EVENTS AND DATA COLUMNS

My favorite Profiler template, when correlating Profiler trace data with Performance Monitor counter data, is the one I outlined in Chapter 4, on *How to Identify Slow Running Queries*. This template collects data on the following events:

- RPC:Completed
- SP:StmtCompleted
- SQL:BatchStarting
- SQL:BatchCompleted
- Showplan XML

In addition, I include these data columns:

- Duration
- ObjectName
- TextData
- CPU
- Reads
- Writes
- IntegerData
- DatabaseName
- ApplicationName
- StartTime
- EndTime
- SPID
- LoginName
- EventSequence
- BinaryData

Note that in order to perform an accurate correlation between Profiler and Performance Monitor data, you need to capture both the StartTime and EndTime data columns as part of your trace.

FILTERS

The only filter I create is based on **Duration**, because I want to focus my efforts on those SQL Statements that are causing the most problems. Selecting the ideal Duration for the filter is not always easy. Generally, I might initially capture only those events that are longer than 1000 milliseconds in duration. If I find that there are just too many events to easily work with, I might "raise the bar" to 5000 or 10000 milliseconds. You will need to experiment with different durations to see what works best for you.

In the example for this chapter, I use 1000 milliseconds. I don't filter on DatabaseName, or any other data column, because I want to see every statement for the entire SQL Server instance. Performance Monitor counters measure the load on an instance as a whole, not just the load on a single database.

ORDERING AND GROUPING COLUMNS

I don't do any grouping, but I generally order the data columns in an order that works well for me. You can perform any grouping or aggregation you want, but it won't affect the correlation analysis, and so I generally omit it.

HOW TO COLLECT PERFORMANCE MONITOR DATA FOR CORRELATION ANALYSIS

I assume you know the basics of using Performance Monitor, but in case you don't know how to create logs, I will describe in this section how to set up a Performance Monitor log to capture counter activity, which can then be correlated with Profiler trace events.

NOTE:

Performance Monitor comes in different versions, depending on the operating system, and the way logs are created differs from version to version. In this example, I am using the version of Performance Monitor that is included with Windows Vista and Windows 2008.

The activity data collected by Performance Monitor can be displayed "live" on a graph, or you can store it in a log file, using what is called a *user defined data collector set*. In order to correlate Performance Monitor data with Profiler trace data, you must store the activity data in a log file. This log file can then be imported into Profiler for the correlation analysis.

Performance monitor provides a wizard to help you do this, which entails three main steps:

- Creating a new Log file definition
- Selecting Performance Counters
- Creating and saving the Log file

DEFINING A NEW PERFORMANCE MONITOR LOG FILE

On starting Performance Monitor, you will see a screen similar to the one shown in Figure 8-1. By default, Performance Monitor operates in "live graphing" mode, which shows the graph being created on the screen in real time.

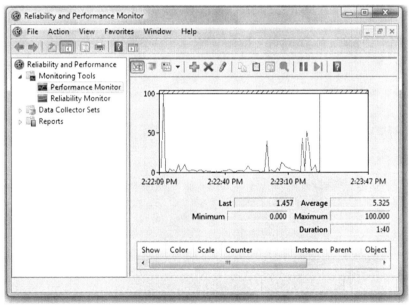

Figure 8-1: Start Performance Monitor. The appearance of the screen will vary somewhat from OS to OS.

In Vista and SQL Server 2008, a Performance Monitor log is referred to as a **Data Collector Set**. To set up a new data collector set (i.e. log file), double-click on **"Data Collector Sets"** then right-click on **"User Defined"** and select **"New | Data Collector Set"**, as shown in Figure 8-2.

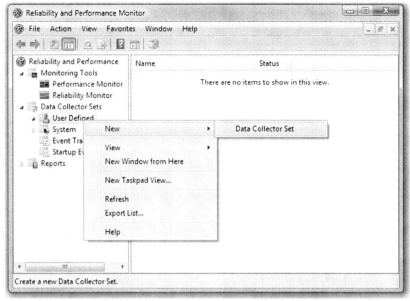

Figure 8-2: You need to create a new "Data Collector Set."

You will be presented with the "Create a new Data Collector Set" screen, as shown in Figure 8-3:

Figure 8-3: Give the Data Collector Set its own name.

Assign the Data Collector Set a name, such as "System Correlation". At the bottom of the screen, select "Create Manually" and click "Next". I recommend that you use the manual option over the template option because you have more flexibility when selecting the events you want to collect. The screen shown in Figure 8-4 appears.

To create our Performance Monitor log, check the box next to "Performance Counter" and click "Next". The other events that can be collected are of no use to us when performing our correlation analysis.

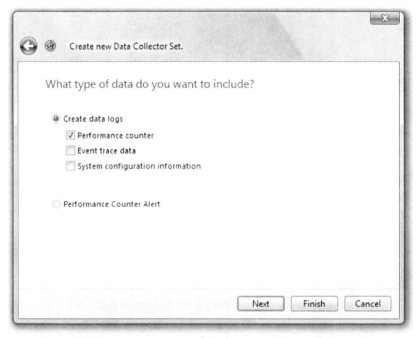

Figure 8-4: You want to create a "Performance Counter" data collector set.

SELECTING PERFORMANCE COUNTERS FOR THE LOG FILE

The next screen in the wizard, shown in Figure 8-5, allows you to select the counters you'd like to record and save in the log file.

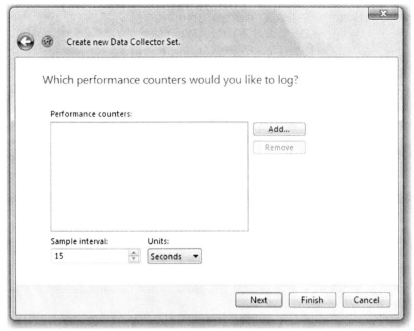

Figure 8-5: You now need to select the Performance Monitor counters you want to capture as part of your log file.

- **LogicalDisk: % Disk Time** – Indicates the activity level of a particular logical disk. The higher the number, the more likely there is an I/O bottleneck. Be sure to select those counters for the logical drives that contain your mdf and ldf files. If you have these separated on different logical disks, then you will need to add this counter for each logical disk.

- **LogicalDisk: Avg. Disk Queue Length** – If a logical disk gets very busy, then I/O requests have to be queued. The longer the queue, the more likely there is an I/O bottleneck. Again, be sure to select those counters for each logical drive that contains your mdf and ldf files.

- **Memory: Available Mbytes** – Measures how much RAM is currently unused, and so available for use by SQL Server and the OS. Generally speaking, if this drops below 5mb, this is a possible indication of a memory bottleneck.

- **Memory: Pages/sec** – Measures how much paging the OS is performing. A high number may indicate a potential memory bottleneck.

- **Processor: % Processor Time: Total** – Measures the percentage of available CPUs in the computer that are busy. Generally speaking, if this number exceeds 80% for long periods of time, this may be an indication of a CPU bottleneck.

- **<u>System: Processor Queue Length</u>** – If the CPUs get very busy, then CPU requests have to be queued, waiting their turn to execute. The longer the queue, the more likely there is a CPU bottleneck.

The first two are for LogicalDisk, the second two are for Memory, and the last two (although they have different instance names) are for the Processor. I find that using two counters per area, rather than one, provides just enough information to identify the cause of most bottlenecks. You will probably want to modify the above list to suit your own needs and environment, but it's a good starting point.

Having selected your performance counters, the screen will look similar to Figure 8-6:

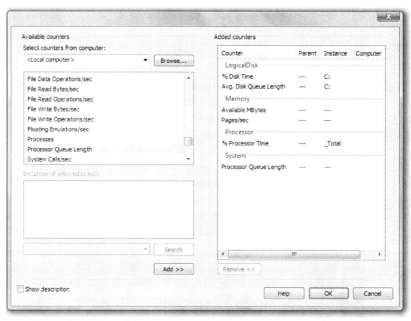

Figure 8-6: Select those counters that best meet your needs.

Click "OK" to proceed, and the screen shown in Figure 8-7 returns:

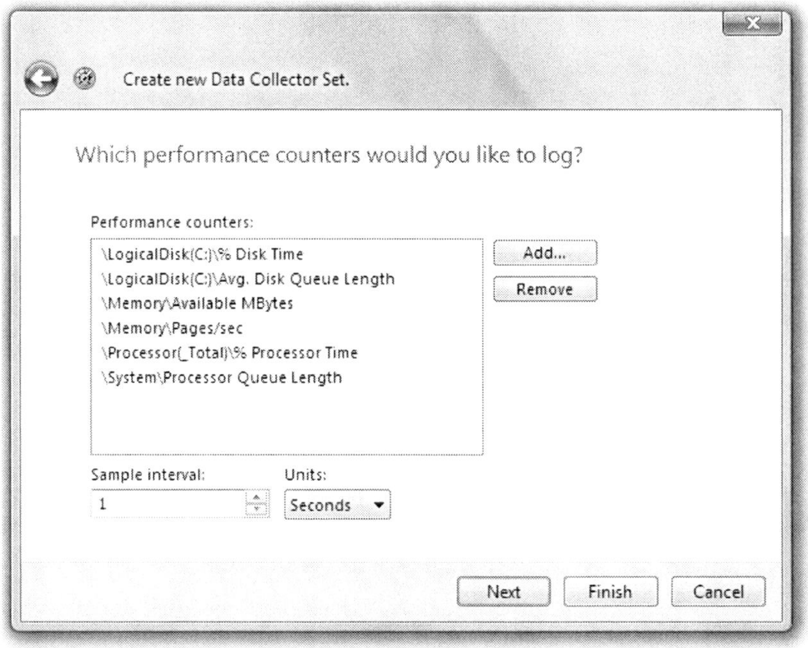

Figure 8-7: Set the "Sample Interval."

The next step is to choose how often Performance Monitor counter data is to be collected. The default value is once every 15 seconds. However, when it comes to performing a Profiler and Performance Monitor correlation analysis, accurate timing is important, so I highly recommend that you select a sample interval of 1 second.

The upside to this is that a 1-second interval will help you to better see the correlation between Profiler events and Performance Monitor counters. The downside is that you will collect a lot of data very quickly. Generally, this is not a problem if you capture a minimum number of counters and don't run your trace for hours at a time.

My test w/ these 6 counters and a /sec interval creates 1.5mb/hour

CREATING AND SAVING THE LOG FILE

Once you have entered the sample interval, click "Next", and the screen shown in Figure 8-8 appears:

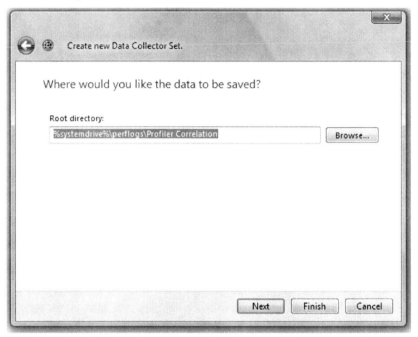

Figure 8-8: Specify where you want Performance Monitor logs to be stored.

Specify where you would like to store the Performance Monitor log. Any place will work, but you don't want to forget this location as you will need to be able to retrieve the log file for importing into Profiler later. Once you have specified the log location, click "Next" to continue and the screen shown in Figure 8-9 appears.

If this is the only data collector set you have, then it will be set to the default data collector set. If you have other data collector sets, you can choose one of those to be the default. From the perspective of this analysis, the default setting is irrelevant. Either way, make sure that "Save and Close" is selected, and then click "Finish" to save your work. The wizard will close, returning you to the Performance Monitor.

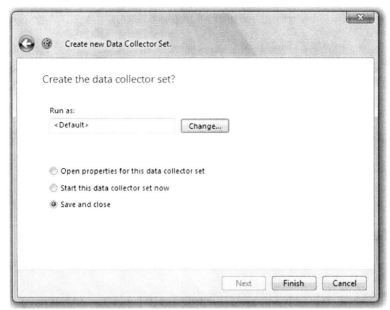

Figure 8-9: You can specify if this data collector set is to be the default set or not.

You will see your new Log file, Profiler Correlation, listed under Data Collector sets, as shown in Figure 8-10:

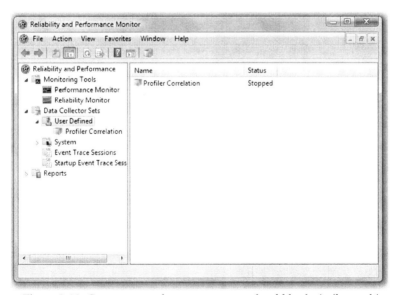

Figure 8-10: Once you are done, your screen should look similar to this.

COLLECTING PERFORMANCE MONITOR DATA

We are now done with the hard work. The only thing left to do is to start collecting the "Profiler Correlation" data. To do this, right-click on the "Profiler Correlation" data collection set and select "Start", as shown in Figure 8-11:

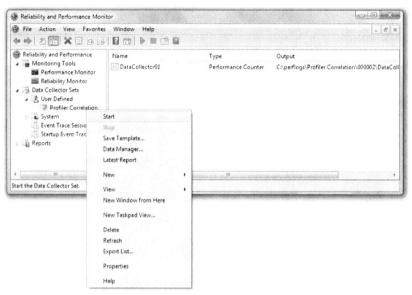

Figure 8-11: Right-click on the name of the Data Collector Set to start and stop it.

To stop collecting activity data, right-click on the "Profiler Correlation" data collection set and click "Stop". You can also schedule Data Collection Sets to start and stop automatically, using the Vista-based Performance Monitor main menu.

In the next section, we will look at the best ways to start and stop both Profiler traces and Performance Monitor data collection sets.

HOW TO CAPTURE PROFILER TRACES AND PERFORMANCE MONITOR LOGS

Now that we've created both a Profiler trace and a Performance Monitor Data Collector Set, we are ready to start both the tools and begin collecting the data that we will later correlate. Here are some points to keep in mind when running these tools to capture data:

- Run your copy of Profiler and Performance Monitor on a computer other than the SQL Server you are monitoring.

- Both the Profiler trace and the Performance Monitor logs should be started and stopped at about the same time. For example, if you decide to run an analysis for a two-hour period, start both tools at the 8:00 AM and end them at 10:00 AM. If the traces don't occur at the same time, they cannot be correlated.

- Be sure that the SQL Server instance that you are monitoring, and the computer on which you are running Profiler and Performance Monitor, are in the same time zones. If they are not, the data cannot be correlated correctly.

- Make sure that the physical server running your SQL Server instance is not doing other work that could interfere with the analysis, such as running a different program or performing a backup. The only way to perform an accurate correlation analysis is to ensure the SQL Server is performing only regular production activity.

- As I have said many times, be sure that you only collect the minimum necessary number of events, data columns, and counters that you need for your analysis, especially when collecting data every second. We want to minimize the impact that Profiler and Performance Monitor have on the system.

- Run your trace and log files at a "representative" time of day. For example, if you find that your server's resources are peaking almost every morning between 9:00 AM and 11:00 AM, then this is the best time to capture your data.

- Monitor the size of the Profiler trace file and Performance Monitor log file during the capture, to ensure that not too much data is being collected. If the file sizes get too big, you may have to stop your data capture sooner than you planned.

Once you have completed capturing the data for both tools, you are ready to perform the correlation analysis.

HOW TO CORRELATE SQL SERVER 2005 PROFILER DATA WITH PERFORMANCE MONITOR DATA

Correlating Performance Monitor and Profiler data is a straightforward process that simply involves importing both sets of data into Profiler. Start Profiler and load the trace file you want to correlate. It should be displayed on the screen, as shown in Figure 8-12, just as for any other trace:

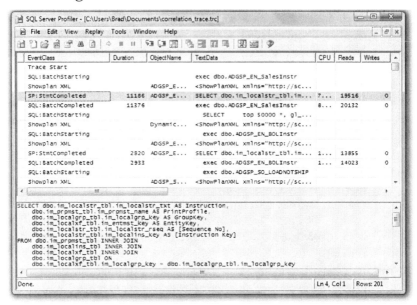

Figure 8-12: Start Profiler and load the trace file.

From the main menu of Profiler, select **File | Import Performance Data**, as shown in Figure 8-13:

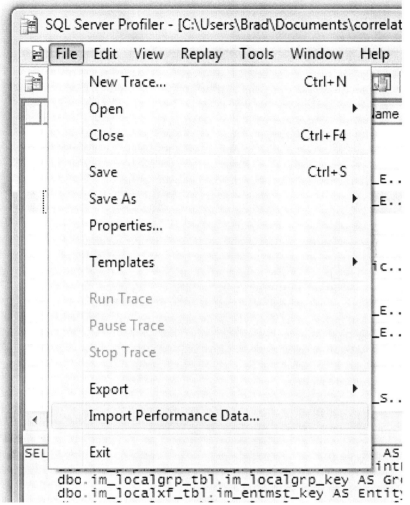

Figure 8-13: Select File | Import Performance Data

NOTE:

If the "Import Performance Data" option is grayed out, exit Profiler, then restart it, reload the trace data, and try again.

The screen shown in Figure 8-14 appears:

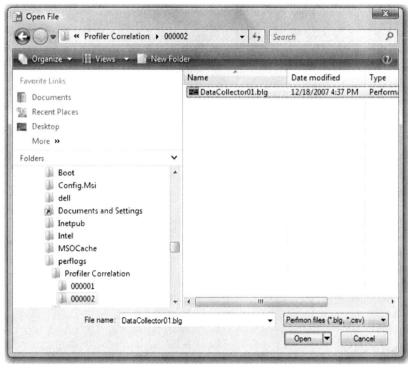

Figure 8-14: Select the Performance Monitor log you want to correlate with your Profiler data.

Locate your Performance Monitor log file and then click "Open".

The screen shown in Figure 8-15 allows you to select which counters to display as part of the correlation analysis. Ideally, you should include no more than about six, or the analysis screen (shown in Figure 8-17) will get too busy and be hard to read.

In this example, only six counters were collected, so import them all by clicking on the checkbox next to the server's name, as shown in Figure 8-16:

Figure 8-15: You must select the counters you want to correlate with your Profiler data.

Figure 8-16: This is what the screen looks like if you select all the counters.

Once you have selected the counters you want to include, click on "OK." The correlation analysis screen appears, as shown in Figure 8-17:

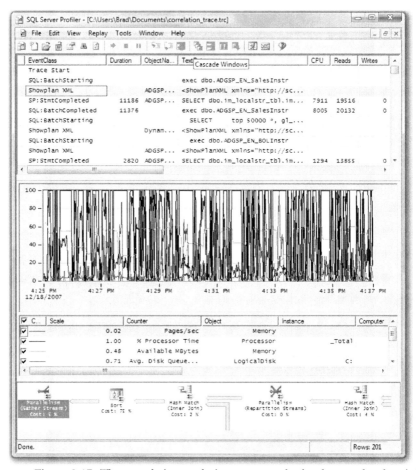

Figure 8-17: The correlation analysis screen can be hard to read unless it is displayed on a big screen.

As you can see, despite the fact that we limited ourselves to six performance counters, the screen is still very busy (although I did have to shrink the screen to fit this page). The next section discusses how to read and analyze this correlated data.

HOW TO ANALYZE CORRELATED DATA

Before we analyze the data, let's take a closer look at the screen in Figure 8-17. It's divided into four sections. The top section of the screen (see figure 8-18) is one that we are already very familiar with. It lists all the captured Profiler events in the order they occurred, and data columns are ordered the way you specified when you created the trace:

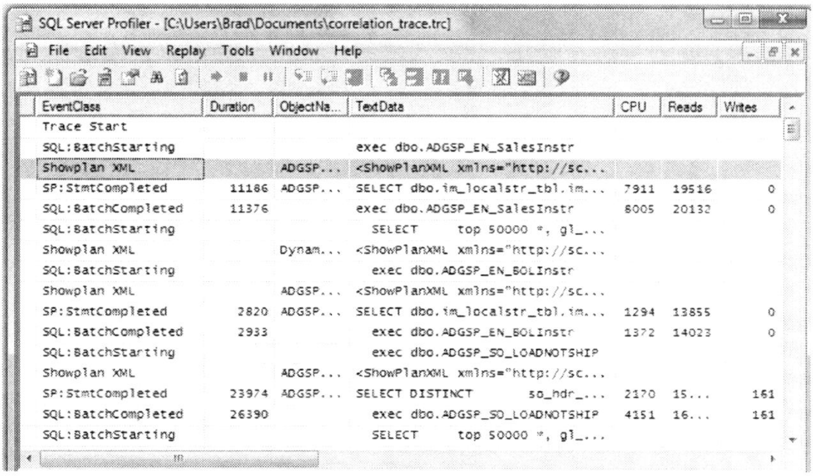

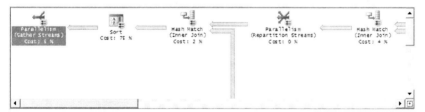

Figure 8-18: We have seen this Profiler screen many times before.

You should also be familiar with the bottom section of the screen (figure 8-19). It displays the contents of the TextData column for the event selected in Figure 8-18. In this case, a ShowPlan XML event was selected, so we see a graphical execution plan for the query following this event:

Figure 8-19: The bottom screen displays the value of the TextData data column of the event selected in the top screen.

So far, so good. Now let's examine the middle section of the screen, shown in Figure 8-20:

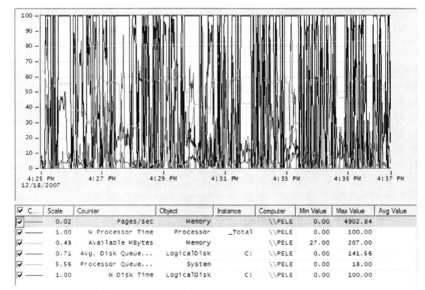

☑	C...	Scale	Counter	Object	Instance	Computer	Min Value	Max Value	Avg Value
☑		0.02	Pages/sec	Memory		\\PELE	0.00	4902.84	
☑		1.00	% Processor Time	Processor	_Total	\\PELE	0.00	100.00	
☑		0.48	Available MBytes	Memory		\\PELE	27.00	207.00	
☑		0.71	Avg. Disk Queue...	LogicalDisk	C:	\\PELE	0.00	141.56	
☑		5.56	Processor Queue...	System		\\PELE	0.00	18.00	
☑		1.00	% Disk Time	LogicalDisk	C:	\\PELE	0.00	100.00	

Figure 8-20: The second and third screens are show above.

It shows a line graph of all the counter activity for the duration of the trace, below which is a table showing each of the counters used in the graph. This table includes lots of valuable information, such as minimum, maximum, and average values for each counter.

If the line graph becomes too busy, you can deselect some of the counters, making the screen easier to read. For example, if I remove all the counters except for % Processor Time, the screen looks as shown in Figure 8-21.

It is much easier to view the graph one counter at a time, but bear in mind that you may then miss out some valuable information, such as how one counter relates to another.

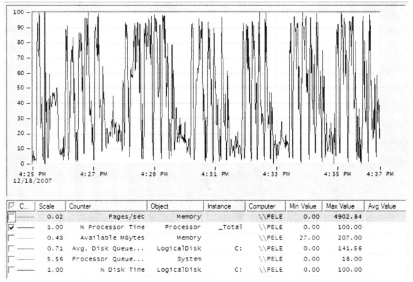

C..	Scale	Counter	Object	Instance	Computer	Min Value	Max Value	Avg Value
	0.02	Pages/sec	Memory		\\PELE	0.00	4902.84	
✓	1.00	% Processor Time	Processor	_Total	\\PELE	0.00	100.00	
	0.48	Available MBytes	Memory		\\PELE	27.00	207.00	
	0.71	Avg. Disk Queue...	LogicalDisk	C:	\\PELE	0.00	141.56	
	5.56	Processor Queue...	System		\\PELE	0.00	18.00	
	1.00	% Disk Time	LogicalDisk	C:	\\PELE	0.00	100.00	

Figure 8-21: It is much easier to view only one counter at a time.

Another way to make it easier to view the line graph activity is to zoom in on the data, using a hidden zoom option. For example, consider the original graph, shown again in Figure 8-23, which is very difficult to read:

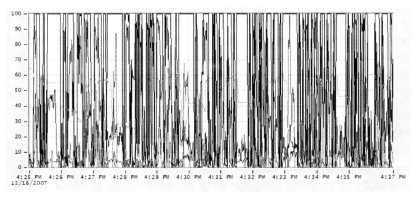

Figure 8-22: This screen is impossible to read.

If we zoom in on a particular time range, it becomes much easier to see what is going on. To zoom in, click on the graph at a start point, say 4:29 PM. Holding down the left mouse button, drag the mouse pointer to an end point, such as 4:30 PM and then release the mouse button. The screen will zoom in, displaying the time range you specified and making the screen much more readable, as you can see in Figure 8-23:

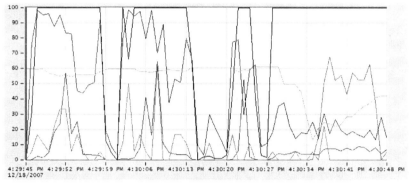

Figure 8-23: This line graph is much easier to read.

If you want to zoom back out again, right-click on the line graph and choose "Zoom Out". As you can probably tell, correlation analysis is a manual process. There is nothing automated about it.

There are two different ways to approach a correlation analysis:

1. **Start from Performance Monitor** – identify time periods where a certain resource has become a bottleneck, and then look for corresponding Profiler events in that period.

2. **Start from Profiler** – identify a long running event and then examine the performance counter data to see if this event has caused a resource issue

We'll examine each technique in turn.

CORRELATION ANALYSIS PART ONE: STARTING FROM PERFORMANCE MONITOR

Of the different ways you can correlate data, I find the simplest is to identify long period of excess resource activity and then drill down until you identify the statement or statements that are causing the problem.

So, let's say we want to start out reviewing Performance Monitor data, looking for areas where one or more server resources have became a bottleneck for an extended time period. Having done this, we can then identify those Profiler events that occurred during the same time period, and so try to locate the cause of the stress on those server resources.

The first step I take is to maximize the screen size, in order to view the data in a much more readable fashion. Next, I select a single performance counter at a time and look for periods of time where that resource is maxed out (or close). In this example, I am going to focus on % Disk Time because I want to identify statements that have a significant impact on disk I/O. Having deselected all counters other than %Disk Time, and zoomed in to a short, 2-minute time period, the line graph looks as shown in Figure 8-24:

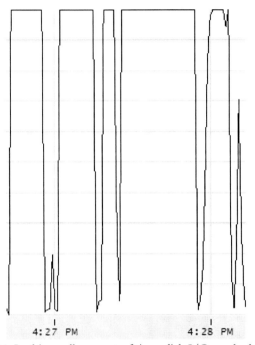

Figure 8-24: In this small amount of time, disk I/O reached 100% six times.

As you can see, there is a period of about a minute and a half where % Disk Time reached 100%. Obviously, whenever a disk is operating at 100% of capacity, this is a very strong indication of a disk I/O bottleneck. Of the six times the line chart reaches 100% disk activity, the fourth has the longest duration.

Our next job is to find out what Profiler events were running during this time period. To do this, click on the line at the left of the fourth spike. A red line should appear where you clicked, and the event that was executing at the time indicated by the red line should be highlighted, as shown in Figure 8-25:

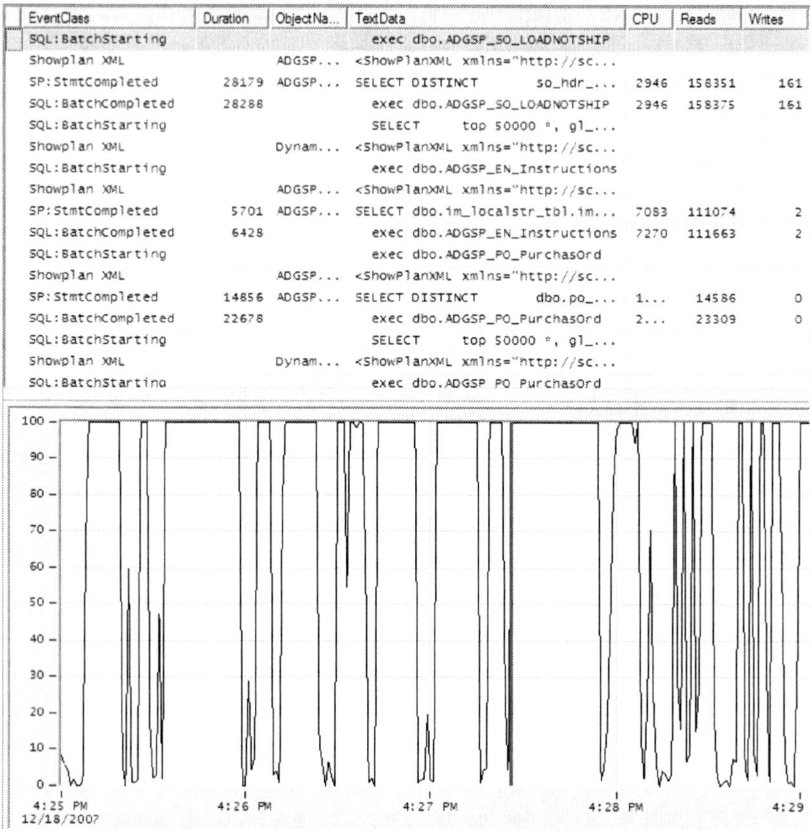

EventClass	Duration	ObjectNa...	TextData	CPU	Reads	Writes
SQL:BatchStarting			exec dbo.ADGSP_SO_LOADNOTSHIP			
Showplan XML		ADGSP...	<ShowPlanXML xmlns="http://sc...			
SP:StmtCompleted	28179	ADGSP...	SELECT DISTINCT so_hdr_...	2946	158351	161
SQL:BatchCompleted	28288		exec dbo.ADGSP_SO_LOADNOTSHIP	2946	158375	161
SQL:BatchStarting			SELECT top 50000 *, gl_...			
Showplan XML		Dynam...	<ShowPlanXML xmlns="http://sc...			
SQL:BatchStarting			exec dbo.ADGSP_EN_Instructions			
Showplan XML		ADGSP...	<ShowPlanXML xmlns="http://sc...			
SP:StmtCompleted	5701	ADGSP...	SELECT dbo.im_localstr_tbl.im...	7083	111074	2
SQL:BatchCompleted	6428		exec dbo.ADGSP_EN_Instructions	7270	111663	2
SQL:BatchStarting			exec dbo.ADGSP_PO_PurchasOrd			
Showplan XML		ADGSP...	<ShowPlanXML xmlns="http://sc...			
SP:StmtCompleted	14856	ADGSP...	SELECT DISTINCT dbo.po_...	1...	14586	0
SQL:BatchCompleted	22678		exec dbo.ADGSP_PO_PurchasOrd	2...	23309	0
SQL:BatchStarting			SELECT top 50000 *, gl_...			
Showplan XML		Dynam...	<ShowPlanXML xmlns="http://sc...			
SQL:BatchStarting			exec dbo.ADGSP PO PurchasOrd			

Figure 8-25: When I click on the left hand side of the line graph, it turns red and also highlights the Profiler event in the top of the screen.

Now click on the right side of the spike, and a red line should appear, indicating when the resource spike ended, as shown in Figure 8-26:

EventClass	Duration	ObjectNa...	TextData	CPU	Reads	Writes
SQL:BatchStarting			exec dbo.ADGSP_SO_LOADNOTSHIP			
ShowPlan XML		ADGSP...	<ShowPlanXML xmlns="http://sc...			
SP:StmtCompleted	28179	ADGSP...	SELECT DISTINCT so_hdr_...	2946	158351	161
SQL:BatchCompleted	28288		exec dbo.ADGSP_SO_LOADNOTSHIP	2946	158375	161
SQL:BatchStarting			SELECT top 50000 *, gl_...			
ShowPlan XML		Dynam...	<ShowPlanXML xmlns="http://sc...			
SQL:BatchStarting			exec dbo.ADGSP_EN_Instructions			
ShowPlan XML		ADGSP...	<ShowPlanXML xmlns="http://sc...			
SP:StmtCompleted	5701	ADGSP...	SELECT dbo.im_localstr_tbl.im...	7083	111074	2
SQL:BatchCompleted	6428		exec dbo.ADGSP_EN_Instructions	7270	111663	2
SQL:BatchStarting			exec dbo.ADGSP_PO_PurchasOrd			
ShowPlan XML		ADGSP...	<ShowPlanXML xmlns="http://sc...			
SP:StmtCompleted	14856	ADGSP...	SELECT DISTINCT dbo.po_...	1...	14586	0
SQL:BatchCompleted	22678		exec dbo.ADGSP_PO_PurchasOrd	2...	23309	0
SQL:BatchStarting			SELECT top 50000 *, gl_...			
ShowPlan XML		Dynam...	<ShowPlanXML xmlns="http://sc...			
SOL:BatchStarting			exec dbo.ADGSP PO PurchasOrd			

Figure 8-26: The red line is now at the right side, or the end of, the peak.

Notice also that the highlighted line at the top of the screen is now reflecting a different event (or row) on the Profiler screen. This indicates the event that was running when the spike ended. To make this clearer, Figure 8-27 shows an expanded section of the Profiler trace, with the events that mark the start and end of the resource spike highlighted in blue:

EventClass	Duration	ObjectNa...	TextData	CPU	Reads	Writes	IntegerData
SQL:BatchStarting			exec dbo.ADGSP_SO_LOADNOTSHIP				
ShowPlan XML		ADGSP...	<ShowPlanXML xmlns="http://sc...				127
SP:StmtCompleted	28179	ADGSP...	SELECT DISTINCT so_hdr_...	2946	158351	161	85
SQL:BatchCompleted	28288		exec dbo.ADGSP_SO_LOADNOTSHIP	2946	158375	161	

Figure 8-27: The two rows highlighted in blue indicate the top and bottom boundaries of the events that were running during the spike in % Disk Time. Using Profiler, you can only see one blue line at a time. I have cheated here to make my point more obvious.

By selecting the beginning and ending points of our resource spike on the line graph, we have identified the events that occurred during this time period. Hopefully these events will look familiar to you, as we have seen them before in this book. Essentially, we see four events that represent the execution of a single statement within a stored procedure:

- Row one is a **SQL:BatchStarting** event and indicates that a stored procedure is about to execute
- Row two shows the execution plan for the statement within the stored procedure.
- Row three is the execution of the statement within the stored procedure. This is where the actual work takes place.
- Row four, while shown to be outside the time line, is actually a part of this single query. The **SQL:BatchCompleted** event indicates that the stored procedure has completed.

As you can see with this example, the timing correlation may not always be 100% perfect, but it will be close.

So what did this exercise tell us? Essentially, we now know why the %Disk Time spiked as it did. Not only can we see that the statement within the stored procedure was the cause of the spike, we can also see from the Profiler data that the statement had to read a total of 158,375 pages total and make 161 page writes, in order to return 85 rows of data. In addition, we can look at the graphical execution plan for the statement, and consider ways to rewrite the query so that it is more efficient.

Although this is not a dramatic example, it shows you how you can correlate a spike in server resource activity in the line graph, with specific events running inside SQL Server.

CORRELATION ANALYSIS PART TWO: STARTING FROM PROFILER

For this analysis, we'll start from the Profiler data then drill down into the Performance Monitor activity. For example, let's say that you are reviewing the Profiler trace data and find an event that takes 11190 milliseconds to run. Eleven seconds is a long time for a query to run, so you want to find out if running this particular query harms Server performance.

The first step is to identify the beginning and ending events that comprise the statement. In this example, the events are shown in Figure 8-28:

EventClass	Duration	ObjectName	TextData	CPU	Reads	Writes	IntegerData
SQL:BatchStarting			exec dbo.ADGSP_PO_PurchasOrd				
ShowPlan XML		ADGSP_P...	<ShowPlanXML xmlns="http://schemas....				48977
SP:StmtCompleted	11167	ADGSP_P...	SELECT DISTINCT dbo.po_hdr_tb...	9438	14610	0	72023
SQL:BatchCompleted	11190		exec dbo.ADGSP_PO_PurchasOrd	9438	14623	0	

Figure 8-28: To begin this analysis, first identify all the events that comprise a single statement.

We see that a stored procedure has executed a single statement and that this is encapsulated within four events. We can also see that the statement executed within the stored procedure took 14,623 page reads to return 72,023 rows of data. Now let's see how this particular statement affected server resource usage, as indicated by our Performance Monitor counters.

The process is simply the "reverse" of that described in the previous section. When you click on the first event, SQL:batchStarting, a red line will appear on the line graph, indicating the point in time where that event occurred, as shown in Figure 8-29.

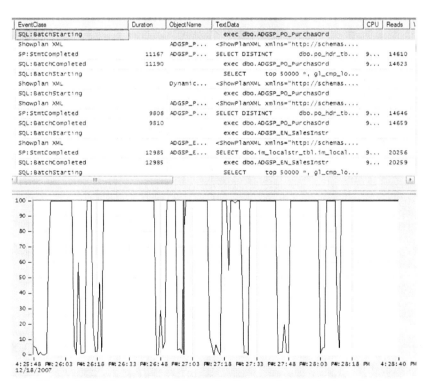

Figure 8-29: I have zoomed in on the line graph to make it easier for you to see where the statement starts.

You can immediately see that this Profiler event preceded a spike in disk I/O activity. When you click of the fourth of the four events,

SQL:BatchCompleted, a red line appears at the point in time this event occurred (i.e. when the statement completed executing), as shown in Figure 8-30.

You can see that the completion of execution of the statement marks the end of the 100% spike in disk activity. This is strong evidence that this statement is having an impact on server resources. Now it is up to you to decide if the impact is big enough to merit action and, if so, what steps you will take to fix the query so that is runs more efficiently in the future.

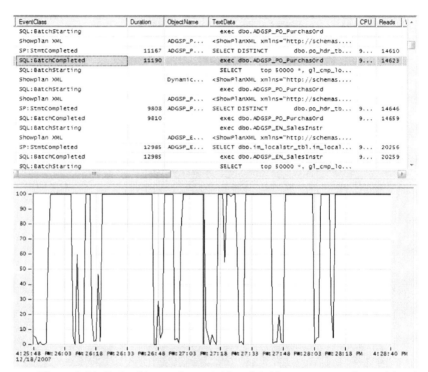

Figure 8-30: By looking at figure 8-29 and 8-30, you can see the activity that occurred when the statement executed.

SUMMARY

In this chapter, you learned how to correlate Profiler events with Performance Monitor activity. This gives you the ability to find out what statement might be causing a spike in server resource usage, or to examine a single statement and find out how running it affects resource utilization.

Correlation analysis is a manual process, so it can be time-consuming and needs practice. However, once you master it, you will find it an invaluable tool for identifying relationships between Profiler events and actual physical server activity.

Chapter 9
HOW TO CAPTURE PROFILER TRACES PROGRAMMATICALLY

So far in this book we have used the Profiler GUI, exclusively, to create and capture traces. However, SQL Server also offers the ability to create and capture Profiler traces programmatically, using Transact-SQL.

In most cases, the Profiler GUI and Profiler system stored procedures offer the same features, but there are a number of pros and cons to consider when choosing which tool to use. The advantages of using the GUI are the ones we've enjoyed throughout the book:

- It's easy to use, with a shallow learning curve.
- You don't have to write any Transact-SQL code to create or run traces.
- All events and data columns are displayed on the screen, making it easy to pick and choose the ones you need.
- You can select column order, and perform grouping and aggregation of data, directly from the Profiler screen.

In many cases, especially if you are a novice DBA, you will probably want to use the GUI to create and collect your traces. However, that method does have a few drawbacks. It adds additional resource overhead when collecting traces and it doesn't offer any programmatic control over when the trace data is collected. You can schedule an end time, and that's about it.

So, if there are occasions when you really need to minimize overhead, or need an extra level of control over how a trace is captured, then using Transact-SQL is an option. This chapter will demonstrate how to create and capture Profiler traces using Transact-SQL and system-stored procedures, specifically covering these topics:

- Pros and cons of capturing traces programmatically.
- An overview of how to capture trace data programmatically.
- The system-stored procedures used for capturing traces.
- Putting the pieces together: writing your own trace capture scripts.
- How to use the Profiler GUI to create Transact-SQL trace scripts.
- How to use a trace function to perform SELECT queries directly against a physical trace file.

PRO AND CONS OF CAPTURING TRACES PROGRAMMATICALLY

As noted in the introduction, there are a couple of advantages of collecting trace data using Transact-SQL rather than the Profiler GUI, namely:

- It uses less overhead than the Profiler GUI.
- You can programmatically start and stop Profiler traces.
- You can create, modify, and analyze traces from programs you write yourself.

However, there are also a few limitations to be aware of – for example:

- You will need to write Transact-SQL code to create and control traces, which incurs a steeper learning curve than using the Profiler GUI. However, you can get round much of this by creating trace definitions in the Profiler GUI and then exporting them as Transact-SQL.
- You can't perform grouping and aggregation for display by the Profiler GUI.

With all this in mind, let's take an overview of how you capture traces programmatically.

CAPTURING TRACE DATA PROGRAMMATICALLY: AN OVERVIEW

There are several steps involved in capturing traces using system-stored procedures, so before we jump into the details, it's useful to look at an overview of the process.

When creating and running a Profiler trace using Transact-SQL, you will need two separate scripts: one to create and start the trace (let's call it *start_trace*), and one to stop it (*stop_trace*).

In the *start_trace* script, you will use four different system-stored procedures to create and start the trace. The script will perform the following steps:

- Create a New Trace, using **sp_trace_create**. This signifies that a new trace is being created.
- Select the trace events and data columns for the new trace, using **sp_trace_setevent.**
- Select the filters (if any) to be used by the new trace, using **sp_trace_setfilter.**

- Start the trace, using **sp_trace_setstatus.**

At this point, the trace is started and is running in the background on your SQL Server instance (this is sometimes referred to as a server-side trace). It will continue to run until stopped. When you are ready to stop the trace, you run the second script, **stop_trace**. By executing a single system stored procedure (**sp_trace_setstatus**) twice, with a different parameter each time, this script will:

1. Stop the trace.

2. Close the trace.

At this point, the trace is ended. The result is a trace file, which you can load into the Profiler GUI for analysis, view directly using a Transact-SQL trace function, or import into a SQL Server database. You can also use the trace as the source for the Database Engine Tuning Advisor (DTA).

REQUIRED SYSTEM STORED PROCEDURES

As discussed in the previous section, four system stored procedures are used to create and run Profiler traces programmatically:

- sp_trace_create
- sp_trace_setevent
- sp_trace_setfilter
- sp_trace_setstatus

All four of them are used when you create and start the trace in the **start_trace** script, and when **sp_trace_setstatus** is used to stop and close the trace in the **stop_trace** script. The following sections describe the syntax for each stored procedure, and explain how each works.

SP_TRACE_CREATE

The **sp_trace_create** system-stored procedure creates the trace definition. The syntax for the command is as follows:

```
sp_trace_create [ @traceid = ] trace_id OUTPUT
          , [ @options = ] option_value
          , [ @tracefile = ] 'trace_file'
      [ , [ @maxfilesize = ] max_file_size ]
      [ , [ @stoptime = ] 'stop_time' ]
      [ , [ @filecount = ] 'max_rollover_files' ]
```

where:

TraceID is a number assigned by SQL Server to uniquely identify the trace being created. You don't have to enter any value, as this is done for you automatically. The TraceID created by this stored procedure is used by the other three stored procedures, as we shall soon see.

Options allows you to specify certain behaviors, while collecting the trace, according to the value you assign:

- Option Value 2 – **TRACE_FILE_ROLLOVER**: Specifies that when the **max_file_size** of the trace file is reached, it will be closed and a new file created. This is identical to the Profiler GUI setting used to specify whether or not you want file rollover.
- Option Value 4 – **SHUTDOWN_ON_ERROR**: Instructs the SQL Server instance to shut down if the trace cannot be written to a file. In other words, if anything prevents the trace from being written, the SQL Server service will shut down, turning your instance off.
- Option Value 8 – **TRACE_PRODUCE_BLACKBOX**: Specifies that the trace file maintain a maximum size of 5MB, and if more events occur than can be stored in the 5mb file, then old events will be discarded to make room for newer events. In other words, the last 5mb of trace events are always stored, while older events are removed.

In some cases you may want to leave **Options** set to 0, which means that none of the above behaviors are invoked.

TraceFile is the physical path and filename of the trace file. Generally, you will want to store this on the same physical box as the SQL Server instance being traced, although it should be saved on a separate drive from the one used to store SQL Server data or log files.

MaxFileSize specifies the maximum size to which a trace file can grow. The default value is 5mb. This option can be used with or without use of the TRACE_FILE_ROLLOVER option.

StopTime specifies the time at which the trace is to stop. A value of NULL indicates no stop time. If you decide to turn traces on and off programmatically, then you won't need this option.

Filecount specifies the maximum number of trace files to be kept with the same base filename, and is used in combination with the TRACE_FILE_ROLLOVER option, assuming you use it.

SP_TRACE_SETEVENT

Once the trace definition is created, we need to specify which events and data columns we want to capture, using **sp_trace_setevent**. What may not be immediately obvious is that this stored procedure must be executed once for *every event-data column combination* that you want to trace. For example, if you want capture one event with 15 data columns, you must execute the stored procedure 15 times. If you want to capture 10 events, each with 15 data columns, you must run the stored procedure 150 times. We will see an example of this a little later in the chapter.

The syntax for the command is:

```
sp_trace_setevent [ @traceid = ] trace_id
          , [ @eventid = ] event_id
          , [ @columnid = ] column_id
          , [ @on = ] on
```

where:

TraceID is the trace identifier created by the **sp_trace_create** stored procedure. The TraceID value, generated by sp_create_trace, can be stored in a variable and then automatically assigned here, when the **sp_trace_setevent** stored procedure is executed.

EventID is a code that represents the event you want to capture. You must look up this value from a table listed in Books Online.

ColumnID is a code that represents the data column for the event you want to capture. You must look up this value from a table listed in Books Online.

On specifies whether to turn an event on (1) or off (0). A value of 1 also turns the column on for this event (assuming **ColumnID** has a non-null value). Likewise, a value of 0 turns both the column and the event off.

SP_TRACE_SETFILTER

Execution of the **sp_trace_setfilter** stored procedure is optional and only required if you want to create a filter for your trace. If you do use this stored procedure, it must run after the first two above.

You can only create one filter per stored procedure execution. Therefore, if you want to add multiple filters to the trace, you must execute the **sp_trace_setfilter** command once for each filter.

The syntax for the command is:

```
sp_trace_setfilter [ @traceid = ] trace_id
            , [ @columnid = ] column_id
            , [ @logical_operator = ] logical_operator
            , [ @comparison_operator = ]
comparison_operator
```

```
, [ @value = ] value
```

where:

TraceID is the trace identifier created by the **sp trace create** stored procedure. Again, using variables, you can automatically assign the TraceID value for this stored procedure.

ColumnID is the ColumnID, used in the **sp trace setevent** stored procedure, of the column on which you wish to set the filter.

LogicalOperator specifies an AND (value 0) or an OR (value 1) relationship between this filter and any others created in the trace.

ComparisonOperator specifies the type of comparison to be undertaken in the filter. Again, you must use a special code to represent a given operator:

- 0 – = (Equal)
- 1 – <> (Not Equal)
- 2 – > (Greater Than)
- 3 – < (Less Than)
- 4 – >= (Greater Than Or Equal)
- 5 – <= (Less Than Or Equal)
- 6 – LIKE
- 7 – NOT LIKE

Value is the value on which you want to filter. You may have to specify the value's data type as part of this stored procedure, as parameters are strongly typed.

SP_TRACE_SETSTATUS

The **sp_trace_setstatus** stored procedure performs three different functions: to start, stop, and close a trace. The syntax for the command is:

```
sp_trace_setstatus [ @traceid = ] trace_id , [
@status = ] status
```

where:

TraceID is the trace identifier created by the **sp_trace_create** stored procedure. Again, using variables, you can automatically assign the TraceID value for this stored procedure.

Status is used to specify the required action on the trace. The three options are:

- 0 – Stops the specified trace.
- 1 – Starts the specified trace.
- 2 – Closes the specified trace and deletes its definition from the server.

Now that we have a basic understanding of the four system-stored procedures used to create Profiler traces programmatically, let's put it all together into two working scripts.

PUTTING THE PIECES TOGETHER: WRITING YOUR OWN TRACE CAPTURE SCRIPTS

Before we can write a trace capture script, we first need to decide what kind of trace we want to perform. Any of the traces we have talked about up until this point in this book can be captured using a script. For this example, we'll reproduce programmatically (as closely as possible) the trace we used in Chapter 4, to identify slow running queries.

To save you referring back, this trace captured five events:

- RPC:Completed
- SP:StmtCompleted
- SQL:BatchStarting
- SQL:BatchCompleted
- Showplan XML

With these events, we recorded data for fifteen data columns:

- Duration
- ObjectName
- TextData
- CPU
- Reads
- Writes
- IntegerData
- DatabaseName
- ApplicationName
- StartTime
- EndTime
- SPID
- LoginName
- EventSequence

- BinaryData

We created one trace filter:

- DatabaseID = "AdventureWorks"

We also performed some grouping and aggregation for this trace, when we used the Profiler GUI, but those options are not available when creating traces using Transact-SQL.

A frustrating aspect of creating a trace using stored procedures is that their parameter values are strongly typed. For example, **MaxFileSize** has to be a 'bigint' and the **TraceID** has to be an 'int'. If you don't use these stored procedures often, it is hard to remember the datatypes used by each parameter.

Another issue we have to deal with is handling the TraceID. The value of TraceID is output by the **sp_trace_create** stored procedure, and used as an input by the other three stored procedures. We need to create a variable to store the TraceID value produced by **sp_trace_create** and feed it to the other stored procedures. Lastly, we need to consider the issue of adding some error-trapping code, to help us identify possible problems.

With all this in mind, let's start creating the *start_trace* script, which will create, define and start the Profiler trace.

THE START_TRACE SCRIPT: CREATING, DEFINING AND STARTING THE TRACE

To make this discussion easier to follow, I will break this script into several parts. In this example I try not to over-elaborate. I keep the code to a minimum so that we don't get distracted by side issues or waste a lot of time discussing topics that are outside the scope of this book.

DECLARING VARIABLES

The first thing we do is declare a number of variables, which will allow us to:

- Define our strongly typed parameters in a single location.
- Store values to some of the parameters, so we only have one place to go in our script to make a change to them.
- Store values that we need to pass along from one part of the script to another (such as the TraceID or error codes).

Here are the variables that need to be declared for the *start_trace* script:

```
Declare Variables
DECLARE @em INT ;
DECLARE @TraceID INT ;
DECLARE @maxFileSize BIGINT ;
DECLARE @fileName NVARCHAR(128) ;
DECLARE @on BIT ;
```

where:

- **@em** is used to capture error codes produced by the **sp_trace_create** stored procedure. We will use this variable several times in the script, for the error-handling code.
- **@TraceID** is used to capture the TraceID assigned by SQL Server to the trace being created. This value is created by the **sp_trace_create** and then passed to the other stored procedures as needed.
- **@maxFileSize** is used to assign the maximum file size of the trace file.
- **@fileName** is used to assign the physical path and filename of the captured trace.
- **@on** is used by the **sp_trace_setevent** stored procedure to turn on the event and its data column.

The first two variables are used to pass information from one part of the script to another. The last three variables are used to represent three of the parameters used by the stored procedures. They have been declared here to make it easier to manage their data type. If you create your own script and use different parameters than I have used, you may want to define some additional variables to deal with their unique data types.

ASSIGNING VALUES TO PARAMETERS

The next section of the *start_trace* script assigns values to the @maxFileSize, @fileName and @on parameters, stored in our variables:

```
-- Set Trace Values
SET @maxFileSize = 5 ;
SET @fileName = N'C:\ProfilerTrace' ;
SET @on = 1 ;
```

Where:

@maxFileSize has been assigned a value of "5", which also happens to be the default value for this parameter. In this example, I am not using the **TRACE_FILE_ROLLOVER** option, so the trace would end when the trace file reaches 5mb in size. In reality, you would either want to make this value much greater, or activate the

TRACE_FILE_ROLLOVER option so that when the file reaches 5mb it would be close and a new file created.

@fileName is the path and filename for the saved trace file. Notice that you do not need to append an extension to the filename. This is done for you automatically. In this example I use: **'C:\ProfilerTrace'**.

@on has been set to 1, which means that the event, and its data column, are turned on for the trace.

Creating parameters as variables makes your scripts much more flexible than if you had "hard-coded" these values in the stored procedures themselves.

CREATING THE TRACE

With the variables declared and the parameters set, it's time to implement the first of the four system-stored procedures, **sp_trace_create**:

```
-- Create Trace
EXEC @em = sp_trace_create @TraceID OUTPUT,
0,
@fileName,
@maxFileSize,
NULL ;
```

We start with the standard EXEC (execute) command:

```
EXEC @em = sp_trace_create @TraceID OUTPUT,
```

As part of this command, we assign to the **@em** variable the return value generated by the execution of the **sp_trace_create** stored procedure. If an error is encountered during execution of this stored procedure, an integer value will be returned, indicating the nature of the error. Any value not equal to 0 indicates an error. The **@em** variable is used later in the script for error-trapping.

In the same line of code, we also assign to the **@TraceID** variable the output value of the stored procedure: **@TraceID OUTPUT**, the unique identifier for the trace. This value is used later in the script for the other three stored procedures.

The remainder of the code sets the parameters for the stored procedure, as follows:

- **0** – no options are being used
- **@fileName** – the physical path and filename of the trace file, as defined in the previous section

- **@maxFileSize** – the maximum file size of the trace file, as defined in the previous section
- **NULL** – we are not setting a stop time for the execution of the stored procedure

ERROR HANDLING

If the execution of the **sp_trace_create** returns any error code, this statement traps it and sends it to the error-handling code found later in the script. This code is optional, but useful.

```
-- Error Handling
IF ( @em != 0 )
    GOTO error
```

SPECIFYING THE TRACE EVENTS AND DATA COLUMNS

Having created the trace definition, it's time to assign the events to be traced, together with the data columns to be collected for each one. This section of code is long, as it essentially repeats the same line of code for every event-data column combination. Since we have 5 events and 15 data columns, we have to run the **sp_trace_setevent** stored procedure a total of 75 times:

```
-- Set the Trace Events and Data Columns to Collect

--Collect RPC:Completed Event and Selected Data
Columns
EXEC sp_trace_setevent @TraceID, 10, 13, @on ;
EXEC sp_trace_setevent @TraceID, 10, 34, @on ;
EXEC sp_trace_setevent @TraceID, 10, 1,  @on ;
EXEC sp_trace_setevent @TraceID, 10, 18, @on ;
EXEC sp_trace_setevent @TraceID, 10, 16, @on ;
EXEC sp_trace_setevent @TraceID, 10, 17, @on ;
EXEC sp_trace_setevent @TraceID, 10, 25, @on ;
EXEC sp_trace_setevent @TraceID, 10, 35, @on ;
EXEC sp_trace_setevent @TraceID, 10, 10, @on ;
EXEC sp_trace_setevent @TraceID, 10, 14, @on ;
EXEC sp_trace_setevent @TraceID, 10, 15, @on ;
EXEC sp_trace_setevent @TraceID, 10, 12, @on ;
EXEC sp_trace_setevent @TraceID, 10, 11, @on ;
EXEC sp_trace_setevent @TraceID, 10, 51, @on ;
EXEC sp_trace_setevent @TraceID, 10, 2,  @on ;

--Collect SP:StmtCompleted Event and Selected Data
Columns
EXEC sp_trace_setevent @TraceID, 43, 13, @on ;
EXEC sp_trace_setevent @TraceID, 43, 34, @on ;
EXEC sp_trace_setevent @TraceID, 43, 1,  @on ;
EXEC sp_trace_setevent @TraceID, 43, 18, @on ;
EXEC sp_trace_setevent @TraceID, 43, 16, @on ;
```

```
EXEC sp_trace_setevent @TraceID, 43, 17, @on ;
EXEC sp_trace_setevent @TraceID, 43, 25, @on ;
EXEC sp_trace_setevent @TraceID, 43, 35, @on ;
EXEC sp_trace_setevent @TraceID, 43, 10, @on ;
EXEC sp_trace_setevent @TraceID, 43, 14, @on ;
EXEC sp_trace_setevent @TraceID, 43, 15, @on ;
EXEC sp_trace_setevent @TraceID, 43, 12, @on ;
EXEC sp_trace_setevent @TraceID, 43, 11, @on ;
EXEC sp_trace_setevent @TraceID, 43, 51, @on ;
EXEC sp_trace_setevent @TraceID, 43, 2,  @on ;

--Collect SQL:BatchStarting Event and Selected Data
Columns
EXEC sp_trace_setevent @TraceID, 13, 13, @on ;
EXEC sp_trace_setevent @TraceID, 13, 34, @on ;
EXEC sp_trace_setevent @TraceID, 13, 1,  @on ;
EXEC sp_trace_setevent @TraceID, 13, 18, @on ;
EXEC sp_trace_setevent @TraceID, 13, 16, @on ;
EXEC sp_trace_setevent @TraceID, 13, 17, @on ;
EXEC sp_trace_setevent @TraceID, 13, 25, @on ;
EXEC sp_trace_setevent @TraceID, 13, 35, @on ;
EXEC sp_trace_setevent @TraceID, 13, 10, @on ;
EXEC sp_trace_setevent @TraceID, 13, 14, @on ;
EXEC sp_trace_setevent @TraceID, 13, 15, @on ;
EXEC sp_trace_setevent @TraceID, 13, 12, @on ;
EXEC sp_trace_setevent @TraceID, 13, 11, @on ;
EXEC sp_trace_setevent @TraceID, 13, 51, @on ;
EXEC sp_trace_setevent @TraceID, 13, 2,  @on ;

--Collect SQL:BatchCompleted Event and Selected Data
Columns
EXEC sp_trace_setevent @TraceID, 12, 13, @on ;
EXEC sp_trace_setevent @TraceID, 12, 34, @on ;
EXEC sp_trace_setevent @TraceID, 12, 1,  @on ;
EXEC sp_trace_setevent @TraceID, 12, 18, @on ;
EXEC sp_trace_setevent @TraceID, 12, 16, @on ;
EXEC sp_trace_setevent @TraceID, 12, 17, @on ;
EXEC sp_trace_setevent @TraceID, 12, 25, @on ;
EXEC sp_trace_setevent @TraceID, 12, 35, @on ;
EXEC sp_trace_setevent @TraceID, 12, 10, @on ;
EXEC sp_trace_setevent @TraceID, 12, 14, @on ;
EXEC sp_trace_setevent @TraceID, 12, 15, @on ;
EXEC sp_trace_setevent @TraceID, 12, 12, @on ;
EXEC sp_trace_setevent @TraceID, 12, 11, @on ;
EXEC sp_trace_setevent @TraceID, 12, 51, @on ;
EXEC sp_trace_setevent @TraceID, 12, 2,  @on ;

--Collect Showplan XML Event and Selected Data
Columns
EXEC sp_trace_setevent @TraceID, 122, 13, @on ;
EXEC sp_trace_setevent @TraceID, 122, 34, @on ;
EXEC sp_trace_setevent @TraceID, 122, 1,  @on ;
EXEC sp_trace_setevent @TraceID, 122, 18, @on ;
EXEC sp_trace_setevent @TraceID, 122, 16, @on ;
EXEC sp_trace_setevent @TraceID, 122, 17, @on ;
EXEC sp_trace_setevent @TraceID, 122, 25, @on ;
EXEC sp_trace_setevent @TraceID, 122, 35, @on ;
EXEC sp_trace_setevent @TraceID, 122, 10, @on ;
EXEC sp_trace_setevent @TraceID, 122, 15, @on ;
EXEC sp_trace_setevent @TraceID, 122, 12, @on ;
```

```
EXEC sp_trace_setevent @TraceID, 122, 11, @on ;
EXEC sp_trace_setevent @TraceID, 122, 51, @on ;
EXEC sp_trace_setevent @TraceID, 122, 2,  @on ;
```

Let's consider just one of these stored procedure executions and examine its component parts:

```
--Collect RPC:Completed Event and Selected Data
Columns
EXEC sp_trace_setevent @TraceID, 10, 13, @on ;
```

The **sp_trace_setevent** stored procedure takes four input parameters:

- **TraceID** – the unique identifier for the trace to which the selected events and data columns belong. As discussed, we assign to this parameter the value of the output parameter generated by sp_trace create, which we stored in our @TraceID variable
- **EventID** – in which we define the event to be captured. As noted earlier, rather than use the name of the event (RPC:Completed), we need to refer to this event via an integer code, in this case "10".
- **ColumnID** – this is the integer code that represents the data column to be captured for this EventID. In this case, "13" refers to the Duration data column.
- **On** – we assign this parameter the value stored in the @on variable, which is "1", indicating that we wish to turn this event and data column combination on for this trace definition.

If you want to collect many events or data columns, be prepared to look up a lot of codes, and write a lot of repetitive T-SQL code. As you might guess, this procedure is tedious and error-prone, so be careful.

SETTING FILTERS

You will need to run the **sp_trace_setfilter** stored procedure once for each filter you want to add to your trace. The next line of code in the script creates a single filter on DatabaseID.

```
-- Set Filters
EXEC sp_trace_setfilter @TraceID, 3, 0, 0, 6 ;
```

The **sp_strace_setfilter** stored procedure has five input parameters:

- **TraceID** – again, we associate the filter with a specific trace by assigning to this parameter the value of the output parameter generated by sp_trace create, stored in our @TraceID variable

- **Column id** – "3" is the ID of the column on which the filter is applied, referring to the DatabaseID data column.
- **Logical operator** – the value "1" denotes that this filter has an "OR" relation to any other filters defined in the trace.
- **Comparison operator** – "0" represents the "equals" comparison operator and defines the comparison to be made between **Column id** and **Value**.
- **Value** – we only wish an event to be recorded if it originates from the database with a DatabaseID of "6", the database ID of AdventureWorks database on my SQL Server instance.

As you can see, you must look up many codes for the parameters. None of this is intuitive, and it can be tedious to set up.

STARTING THE TRACE

Having created the trace definition, added events and data columns, and defined any necessary filters, we are ready to start the trace. Once the trace is started, it will remain running until either:

- You stop it.
- A preset stopping point is reached (such as file size).
- You run out of disk space.

The code to start the trace is as follows:

```
-- Start the Trace
EXEC sp_trace_setstatus @TraceID, 1 ;
```

We simply execute the **sp_trace_setstatus** stored procedure, providing values for the two input parameters: the **TraceID**, as described previously, and the **Status** parameter, to which we assign the value "1", in order to start the trace.

FINISHING THE SCRIPT

To finish out the *start_trace* script, we need to include the following code.

```
-- Display trace id for later use
SELECT TraceID=@TraceID ;
GOTO finish ;

-- Error Trap
error:
SELECT  ErrorCode = @em ;
```

```
-- Exit
finish: ;
GO
```

This code returns any error code, and ends the script. In addition, the TraceID code is displayed. You will need to include this code in the *stop_trace* script, which is used to stop and close the trace.

THE STOP_TRACE SCRIPT: STOPPING AND CLOSING THE TRACE

The trace is now running. In most cases, you will want to manually stop and close the trace using a second script. The *stop_trace* script contains two simple steps: stopping the trace and closing the trace. Both steps are accomplished by using the **sp_trace_setstatus** stored procedure. Stopping and closing are two separate steps because that gives you the flexibility to stop and start a trace repeatedly without have to close and recreate it each time.

The code to stop and close the trace is simple and straightforward:

```
-- Stop the trace
EXEC sp_trace_setstatus 2, 0 ;

-- Close the trace */
EXEC sp_trace_setstatus 2, 2 ;
```

As before, the **sp trace setstatus** stored procedure accepts two input parameters, **TraceID** and **Status**. Since we have already completed running the *start_trace* script, the @TraceID variable we defined there is out of scope. This means that we have to manually enter the **TraceID** for the *stop_trace* script, and is the reason we displayed the value of the @TraceID variable at the end of the *start_trace* script. The value of the variable @TraceID in our example is "2".

In the first execution of the procedure we assign **Status** a value of "0" to stop the trace, and in the second execution a value of "2" to close it.

Once we have run this code, the trace is gone, but our trace file is ready for use. At this point, we can load the trace file into the Profiler GUI, import it into a database table, view it directly using a trace function, or use it to feed the DTA.

NOTE:

Many DBAs schedule the start and stop scripts as SQL Server Agent jobs. This way, they can easily schedule when a trace begins and ends.

CREATING T-SQL TRACES FROM THE PROFILER GUI

In the previous section I explained how to use Transact-SQL to create a trace programmatically. I also described how much effort it is to create such code. Well, I have been saving a surprise for you, and here it is: most of the coding above doesn't have to be written by hand. In other words, you can use the Profiler GUI to generate most of the code for you.

"Why didn't you tell us about this feature sooner?" Well, if you had known about this earlier, you may have never taken the opportunity to fully understand how the code works! It's never a good idea to generate code blindly, without knowing exactly what it is doing. However, now you fully understand the code, it's safe to move on and find out how to auto-generate it.

First, you must create a Profiler trace from within the Profiler GUI, just as we've done throughout the book. Alternatively, you can use a pre-defined trace template. For this example, I am going to use the template I created in chapter 4 to identify long-running queries.

Next, load the trace into the Profiler GUI, and then select: **File | Export | Script Trace Definition | For SQL Server 2005**. You will be prompted to enter a path and filename for the Transact-SQL file that will be created, containing the code needed to create and run the trace programmatically. Once you have entered a path and filename, click on the "Save" button and you should get a message telling you that the Transact-SQL script file was saved successfully.

Open up the script file in SSMS and view the code. In this example, it looks like this:

```
/**********************************************************
/
/* Created by: SQL Server 2005 Profiler
*/
/* Date: 12/15/2008  02:28:55 PM          */
/**********************************************************
/

-- Create a Queue
declare @rc int
declare @TraceID int
declare @maxfilesize bigint
set @maxfilesize = 5
```

```
-- Please replace the text InsertFileNameHere, with
an appropriate
-- filename prefixed by a path, e.g.,
c:\MyFolder\MyTrace. The .trc extension

-- will be appended to the filename automatically. If
you are writing from

-- remote server to local drive, please use UNC path
and make sure server has
-- write access to your network share

exec @rc = sp_trace_create @TraceID output, 0,
N'InsertFileNameHere', @maxfilesize, NULL
if (@rc != 0) goto error

-- Client side File and Table cannot be scripted

-- Set the events
declare @on bit
set @on = 1
exec sp_trace_setevent @TraceID, 122, 1, @on
exec sp_trace_setevent @TraceID, 122, 25, @on
exec sp_trace_setevent @TraceID, 122, 2, @on
exec sp_trace_setevent @TraceID, 122, 10, @on
exec sp_trace_setevent @TraceID, 122, 14, @on
exec sp_trace_setevent @TraceID, 122, 26, @on
exec sp_trace_setevent @TraceID, 122, 34, @on
exec sp_trace_setevent @TraceID, 122, 11, @on
exec sp_trace_setevent @TraceID, 122, 35, @on
exec sp_trace_setevent @TraceID, 122, 12, @on
exec sp_trace_setevent @TraceID, 10, 15, @on
exec sp_trace_setevent @TraceID, 10, 16, @on
exec sp_trace_setevent @TraceID, 10, 1, @on
exec sp_trace_setevent @TraceID, 10, 17, @on
exec sp_trace_setevent @TraceID, 10, 25, @on
exec sp_trace_setevent @TraceID, 10, 2, @on
exec sp_trace_setevent @TraceID, 10, 10, @on
exec sp_trace_setevent @TraceID, 10, 18, @on
exec sp_trace_setevent @TraceID, 10, 26, @on
exec sp_trace_setevent @TraceID, 10, 34, @on
exec sp_trace_setevent @TraceID, 10, 11, @on
exec sp_trace_setevent @TraceID, 10, 35, @on
exec sp_trace_setevent @TraceID, 10, 12, @on
exec sp_trace_setevent @TraceID, 10, 13, @on
exec sp_trace_setevent @TraceID, 10, 14, @on
exec sp_trace_setevent @TraceID, 45, 16, @on
exec sp_trace_setevent @TraceID, 45, 1, @on
exec sp_trace_setevent @TraceID, 45, 17, @on
exec sp_trace_setevent @TraceID, 45, 25, @on
exec sp_trace_setevent @TraceID, 45, 10, @on
exec sp_trace_setevent @TraceID, 45, 18, @on
exec sp_trace_setevent @TraceID, 45, 26, @on
exec sp_trace_setevent @TraceID, 45, 34, @on
exec sp_trace_setevent @TraceID, 45, 11, @on
exec sp_trace_setevent @TraceID, 45, 35, @on
exec sp_trace_setevent @TraceID, 45, 12, @on
exec sp_trace_setevent @TraceID, 45, 13, @on
exec sp_trace_setevent @TraceID, 45, 14, @on
exec sp_trace_setevent @TraceID, 45, 15, @on
exec sp_trace_setevent @TraceID, 12, 15, @on
```

```
exec sp_trace_setevent @TraceID, 12, 16, @on
exec sp_trace_setevent @TraceID, 12, 1, @on
exec sp_trace_setevent @TraceID, 12, 17, @on
exec sp_trace_setevent @TraceID, 12, 10, @on
exec sp_trace_setevent @TraceID, 12, 14, @on

exec sp_trace_setevent @TraceID, 12, 18, @on

exec sp_trace_setevent @TraceID, 12, 26, @on
exec sp_trace_setevent @TraceID, 12, 11, @on
exec sp_trace_setevent @TraceID, 12, 35, @on
exec sp_trace_setevent @TraceID, 12, 12, @on
exec sp_trace_setevent @TraceID, 12, 13, @on
exec sp_trace_setevent @TraceID, 13, 1, @on
exec sp_trace_setevent @TraceID, 13, 10, @on
exec sp_trace_setevent @TraceID, 13, 14, @on
exec sp_trace_setevent @TraceID, 13, 26, @on
exec sp_trace_setevent @TraceID, 13, 11, @on
exec sp_trace_setevent @TraceID, 13, 35, @on
exec sp_trace_setevent @TraceID, 13, 12, @on

-- Set the Filters
declare @intfilter int
declare @bigintfilter bigint

exec sp_trace_setfilter @TraceID, 10, 0, 7, N'SQL
Server Profiler - 3d71b363-c360-491f-a308-
1966ab502dad'
set @bigintfilter = 1000000
exec sp_trace_setfilter @TraceID, 13, 0, 4,
@bigintfilter

exec sp_trace_setfilter @TraceID, 35, 0, 6,
N'Big_Database'
-- Set the trace status to start
exec sp_trace_setstatus @TraceID, 1

-- display trace id for future references
select TraceID=@TraceID
goto finish

error:
select ErrorCode=@rc

finish:
go
```

As you can see, it looks a lot like the code we wrote manually. All you need to do is modify the code so that it includes the physical location where you want the trace results to be written, and then you can run it as is, or you can modify it to suit your needs. In any event, having the Profiler GUI create the Transact-SQL code for you can save you a lot of time.

However, note that this code is only for creating and starting the trace. You will still need to create the appropriate Transact-SQL code to turn it off, as that is not generated for you.

USING A TRACE FUNCTION TO QUERY A TRACE FILE

A couple of times in this chapter I have referred to something called a **trace function**. SQL Server offers a function you can use to extract trace data directly from a physical trace file, using Transact-SQL, without having to import the data into a SQL Server table. The function is called **fn_trace_gettable**, and its syntax is as follows:

```
fn_trace_gettable (filename, number_of_files)
```

where:

- **filename** is the path and filename of the physical trace file you want to query.
- **number_of_files** is the number of rollover files you want to be read (assuming you have any). For example, if you want to read all rollover files, you can enter "default" as your value. If you only want to read a single file, then enter "1", and so on.

Now, let's see this command in action. Let's say we want to return all the events (rows) in a trace file. To perform this task, you can run the following Transact-SQL from SSMS:

```
SELECT  *
FROM    FN_TRACE_GETTABLE('c:\profiler_trace.trc',
DEFAULT)
```

Or, if you want to return only those events that have a databaseid of "4", you could run this Transact-SQL code:

```
SELECT  *
FROM    FN_TRACE_GETTABLE('c:\profiler_trace.trc',
DEFAULT)
WHERE   databaseid = '4'
```

In other words, you can treat any physical trace file as if it were a database table, and you can run virtually any Transact-SQL SELECT statements against the file. This way, you don't have to worry about first importing the trace file into a real database table before you run any Transact-SQL against it.

Of course, it is also easy, if you prefer, to load everything into a central database repository and build your reports from there. You can then either load the trace into a new database table:

```
-- Specify Location of Database
USE ProfilerDatabase
GO
-- Load Trace into a New Database Table
SELECT * INTO sqlTraceTable

FROM ::fn_trace_gettable('c:\ProfilerTrace.trc',
DEFAULT) ;
```

or you can load the trace file into an existing table:

```
-- Specify Location of Database
USE ProfilerDatabase
GO
-- Load Trace into an Existing Database Table
INSERT INTO sqlTraceTable
SELECT * FROM
::fn_trace_gettable('c:\ProfilerTrace.trc', DEFAULT)
;
```

SUMMARY

While creating traces programmatically has many benefits, it is a much more time-consuming and complicated procedure than using the Profiler GUI. If you are new to Profiler, I suggest you use the Profiler GUI until you become comfortable with it. Once you have gained experience using the Profiler GUI, then you can decide if the extra effort required to create traces using Transact-SQL is justified by the benefits it provides.

Chapter 10
PROFILER BEST PRACTICES

In this chapter we will explore some of the best and most effective ways to use the Profiler. While some of the suggestions simply reinforce important points already made in the book, others are new. Consider this chapter a knowledgebase for using SQL Server Profiler. We cover these topics:

- General Profiler Best Practices
- Creating Traces
- Running Traces
- Analyzing Traces
- Performance Monitor
- Database Engine Tuning Advisor

Once you master the best practices in this chapter, you will be well on your way to becoming a Profiler Master.

GENERAL PROFILER BEST PRACTICES

This section deals with best practices that apply to Profiler usage in almost any scenario.

PROFILER IS NOT JUST FOR DBAS

This book has focused on how Administrative/Production DBAs can use Profiler in their day-to-day tasks. However, Profiler is not just for DBAs. Developers, database designers, business intelligence specialists, IT professionals – even accountants – can all make valuable use of the tool. If you are a DBA who knows how to use Profiler, share this knowledge with others in your organization. By sharing your knowledge and helping others, you can become a valued team member, instead of that cranky DBA everybody blames for the slowness of their applications.

PROFILER MAY NOT BE THE BEST CHOICE TO ANALYZE A PARTICULAR PROBLEM

Although I have spent a lot of time in this book recommending that you use Profiler to help you identify and troubleshoot many different kinds of SQL Server problems, sometimes Profiler is not the best tool for the job. One example we have already discussed is using Profiler to perform auditing. While Profiler can certainly do auditing, it is an inefficient and resource-hogging way to perform it. In other cases, System monitor counters (some of which overlap Profiler events) are better than using the corresponding Profiler events. So, while Profiler is a great tool for many tasks, it is not the only tool available to DBAs. Some times another tool will offer you a more efficient and less resource-intensive way to perform the same task.

USE PROFILER TO LEARN HOW APPLICATIONS WORK

Many DBAs use Profiler to perform detective work. In other words, Profiler allows you to see what commands are being sent from a client to SQL Server. This can provide useful information, especially if you are trying to figure out why a particular third-party application is performing a task the way it does. This also applies to applications written in-house, but with which you are not familiar. In other cases, I know DBAs who use Profiler to observe how SQL Server client tools, such as SSMS, communicate with SQL Server, so they can better learn how SQL Server works. Reviewing Profiler traces can often be a very educational experience.

USE PROFILER FOR TRANSACT-SQL, SSIS, AND ANALYSIS SERVICES

While the focus of this book has been on how to use Profiler to capture traces of any code that is sent from a client to the SQL Server Engine, it is not the only way Profiler can be used with SQL Server. Profiler also has the ability to capture traces of SSIS activity (using the same events and data columns as when tracing Transact-SQL code) and Analysis Services activity (using a different set of events and data columns, not covered in this book). As you become more proficient using Profiler, keep all its capabilities in mind. There is nothing more frustrating than troubleshooting a problem the hard way, only remembering later that you could have resolved the problem much faster if you had used Profiler.

USE PROFILER TO MONITOR LIVE ACTIVITY

The most common way to use Profiler is run time-limited traces to troubleshoot a specific problem, and so the examples in this book have reflected this. Another way to use Profiler is to monitor live, production activity on a 24/7 basis. Wait just a moment. Did I just recommend using Profiler 24/7? Isn't this contrary to the advice you've read throughout this book, recommending you do everything you can to minimize the tracing overhead on your servers?

Well, as with every rule, there are exceptions. Generally speaking, if your production server does not show any signs of performance bottlenecks, and you configure a lightweight trace with judicious use of filters to minimize the number of events returned, Profiler can be a very useful real-time monitoring tool.

Here's why. Many SQL Server-related problems occur unexpectedly, or appear to be random. Often, it is not until a problem has recurred numerous times that you notice that it even exists. Once you've identified an issue, you'd like to run a trace and get to the bottom of the problem. However, if the problem occurs randomly, how do you decide when to run the trace? This is not always an easy task.

If you configure Profiler to perform on-going, real-time monitoring of your server, you can catch and identify problems when they first occur, gathering the data you need to resolve the problem quickly, instead of chasing them after the fact. For example, you might have an on-going trace that looks for any query that takes longer than 60 seconds, or a trace to identify blocking and deadlocking, and so on. As long as you keep the trace lightweight, and the server is not over-burdened, then the impact of the Profiler trace will not noticeable to your users.

If you decide to use Profiler for 24/7 monitoring, remember that you will need to make time to review the data, looking for problems. If you don't have that time, then don't waste your effort – and server resources – creating Profiler traces you will never look at or use.

CREATE PROFILER BASELINES

Many times, when analyzing Profiler data, it is useful to compare current activity with past activity, so that you can more easily determine what is "normal" and what is not. The only way to do this is to create Profiler baseline traces and save them for later analysis.

Unfortunately, SQL Server Profiler does not make it easy to compare trace files; it is essentially a manual process and involves quite a bit of work. As such, many DBAs don't bother. However, having taken the time to create baseline trace files of your production servers, and saved the results to a SQL Server database, you have information that can help you make better decisions today and potentially save you a lot of time.

For example, you might decide to collect baseline Profiler traces for the four most critical production SQL Servers. This might entail performing an 8-hour trace on each server once each month, during a typical production day. The trace would capture key events and data columns and be stored in a SQL Server database. You can then write T-SQL scripts to analyze this data, identifying which queries run the most often, their average duration, and how often they run. By comparing this data from baseline to baseline, you can plot the variation in activity on your servers, over time.

WHEN (AND WHEN NOT) TO TRACE DATA

The time at which you capture a particular trace will vary depending on the purpose of the trace. If you are performing a baseline trace, then you will want to run it over a typical production day to ensure that it reflects normal production activity. If you are tracing audit activity to see who is accessing what, you may have to audit for long periods of time, if not 24/7. If you want to perform real-time monitoring, then you may be tracing 24/7. If you are troubleshooting a specific problem, you will want to run the trace when the problem is occurring, or most likely to occur. The point here is obvious: you only want to run traces when the activity you are seeking to capture is occurring. Capturing trace data any other time is a waste of resources.

Conversely, there are times when you *won't* want to capture a Profiler trace. For example, when:

- The server is not performing as it normally does.
- The server is very busy and the use of Profiler might impact user performance.
- Scheduled jobs are running (such as imports or backups), unless you are trying to capture a trace of the scheduled job.

HOW OFTEN TO TRACE DATA

Again, the frequency with which you collect a certain type of trace data will depend on its purpose. For example, you may want to run monthly baseline traces. On the other hand, you may want to run monthly or quarterly traces for the purposes of feeding the DTA in order to ensure that your indexes are up to date. There are many reasons why you might want to conduct traces on a periodic basis. Plan these traces and schedule them into your work schedule so they won't be forgotten.

WHERE TO STORE TRACE DATA

This is actually a two-part question. First, you must decide where you will store the original trace file as it is being captured. Second, you must decide where to store historical traces, assuming you want to keep them.

When I perform a Profiler trace using the GUI, I prefer to run the trace from a computer other than the SQL Server being traced. This helps to reduce the load on the production server as the trace is being run. As such, trace files are stored on the local computer, not on the SQL Server being profiled.

If I am performing a Profiler trace programmatically (a server-side trace), I store the data locally, ideally on a disk drive that does not store the mdf or ldf files.

Once I am done with a trace file, I delete it. There is no point on keeping data that won't be reused. On the other hand, if I decide to keep the trace file for historical or baselining purposes, I prefer to move the data from the original trace file format into SQL Server tables, stored in a database designated for this specific purpose. Once the data has been imported into SQL Server tables, I then delete the original files, as there is no point in keeping two copies of the same data.

PROFILER GUI VS. PROFILER SYSTEM STORED PROCEDURES

In chapter 9, we discussed the pros and cons of using the Profiler GUI versus Transact-SQL for collecting Profiler traces. If you have not read this chapter, or have read it but still can't make up your mind which approach to take, here are my recommendations, distilled into two simple points:

- If the SQL Server instance you want to trace is not regularly exceeding its resource capacity, then using the Profiler GUI to capture well-designed traces should not affect the server's performance at a level noticeable to users.
- If the SQL Server instance you want to trace is at, or exceeding, its capacity most of the time, then you should capture your well-designed trace programmatically, in order to minimize any further impact on Server performance.

A well-designed trace is defined as a trace that only includes the minimum number of events and data columns required to gather the data needed to troubleshoot the problem at hand.

ENSURING ADEQUATE DISK SPACE FOR A TRACE

Before you start a trace, check to ensure you have enough disk space to store the events you capture. Ensure that the drive on which you intend to store the trace file has adequate capacity. If space is tight, and it is hard for you to predict how much disk space the trace will need, consider limiting the size of the trace file. Alternatively, you will have to manually monitor the trace file size to ensure that you don't run out of disk space.

If you are using the Profiler GUI, you need to ensure that the amount of free space available to the **temp** directory, on the machine where the Profiler is running, has at least 10mb of available disk space. While a trace is running, the Profiler GUI uses the temp directory to temporarily store trace data. Depending on the nature of the trace, the size of the temp file can become large. If the drive housing the temp directory has less than 10mb of free space, Profiler will stop working.

PRACTICE MAKES PERFECT

Profiler can sometimes seem like quite a complex tool to use but, as with all things, practice makes perfect. The more you use and experiment with Profiler, the more proficient you become. As I mentioned in Chapter 1 of this book, Profiler is one of the most useful tools available to the DBA, for troubleshooting SQL Server problems. Time invested in mastering Profiler is time well spent. I've met very few exceptional DBAs who were not very proficient at using this tool.

CREATING TRACES

This section reviews the optimum ways to create traces.

USE TEMPLATES OR SCRIPTS

To save time, create a series of your own GUI-based Profiler templates that you can use over and over. If you prefer to use Transact-SQL to perform traces, then create a collection of reusable scripts. Not only will you save time, you will also reduce the potential for introducing errors into your traces. Don't forget that these scripts and templates are not set in stone – you can modify them anytime you want.

COLLECT ONLY RELEVANT DATA

Throughout this book I have recommended that you collect only the minimal number of events and data columns required to perform the task at hand. Admittedly, this is a very general statement. Here are some specific recommendations to help you follow this general guideline:

- **Keep the focus of each trace as narrow as possible.** For example, create a trace that only looks for blocking locks, or deadlocks, or long running queries. Don't create traces that attempt to look for more than one problem at a time. There are some exceptions to this rule, such as when you collect baseline traces, where your goal is to identify typical activity, not to troubleshoot specific problems.

- **Don't collect duplicate events or data columns.** Some activities have both a starting and a completed event. While it can often be useful to include both, it is not always necessary. You may have to experiment a little to determine if you need only the starting event, the completed event, or both events. Similarly, certain data columns – for example DatabaseID and DatabaseName – provide redundant data. You should collect one or the other, not both.

- **Avoid selecting events that occur frequently.** Some events, such as the Statistics Update event, occur rarely. Others, such as many of the Lock events, occur very frequently. Unfortunately, there is no general rule that can tell you which events are common or uncommon in your particular environment, so you may have to experiment to find out how often particular events are captured. Try to avoid selecting events that occur frequently, unless you can limit the trace to a very short duration.

The more experience you gain working with Profiler, the easier it will be for you to pick only those events and data columns that you need.

USE FILTERS TO REDUCE THE NUMBER OF EVENTS COLLECTED

Filters can help reduce the number of events that are collected and stored as part of a trace file. In many cases, this will reduce the load on the server being traced. Below are listed some specific filters you may want to include in your traces:

- **Duration** – this will help you focus on long-running events, ignoring fast-running events that may not be relevant to your troubleshooting.

- **LoginName** – if you know that the problem is limited to a single user.

- **DatabaseName** or **DatabaseID** – if you know that the problem is limited to a single database.

- **SPID** – if you know the application is limited to a specific SPID.
- **ApplicationName** – to collect only events from a specific application. Or, you can filter on the application name to exclude events from applications you don't want to trace. For example, you might want to create a filter to exclude any events from SQL Profiler or Management Studio.

This list could continue until every data column available was discussed. However, I think you get the idea. Only return those events that are relevant to resolving the problem at hand.

RUNNING TRACES

This section reviews how to minimize the performance impact of capturing Profiler data.

RUN ONLY ONE TRACE AT A TIME

It is not generally recommended – and so we haven't discussed it in this book – but it is possible to run multiple traces at the same time. As you can imagine, each instance of a trace uses up a finite amount of resources and running multiple traces simultaneously exacerbates the problem. If you need to run multiple traces, generally it is better to combine them into a single trace, or to run the traces one at a time.

THE SQL SERVER 2005 DEFAULT TRACE

Did you know that SQL Server 2005 is always running a default trace? Yes, by default, SQL Server 2005 runs a default trace of 32 mostly lightweight events, and each event captures every available data column. DBAs can directly access the default trace file by going to \Program Files\Microsoft SQL Server\MSSQL.1\MSSQL\LOG\ folder and opening up the most recent *.trc file. SQL Server keeps this log file to a minimal size and it rolls over frequently.

This default trace file can sometimes be useful. For example, if the SQL Server instance crashes, the default trace might contain data useful for determining the cause of the crash. In addition, SSMS uses these trace events for some of its management reports.

The question you may be asking is: does this default trace produce much overhead, and should it be turned off? The overhead associated with the default trace is minimal and can generally be ignored. However, if you want, the default trace can be turned off (or on) by using this command:

```
sp_configure 'default trace enabled', 0
```

where:

- 0 = turn default trace off
- 1 = turn default trace on

If you do turn the default trace off, you won't be able to see the events that occurred preceding a SQL Server crash, should one occur, and you won't be able to run some SSMS reports.

DON'T RUN PROFILER WHEN OTHER ACTIVITY IS HAPPENING

It is recommended that you don't run Profiler when any non-standard activity on the SQL Server is occurring. For example, if you are performing a backup job, or reindexing indexes, or importing data, don't run a Profiler trace until the event is over. This helps to reduce the overall load of the server and ensures that Profiler results you do receive aren't skewed by the abnormal activity. The exception to this recommendation would be if it is your goal to Profile the abnormal activity.

STORE TRACE FILES ON DISK, THEN IMPORT INTO A SQL SERVER TABLE

While the Profiler GUI allows you to save trace events directly into a SQL Server database table, it is not a good idea. Doing so causes a lot of unnecessary overhead. It is much more efficient from a resource perspective to capture a trace to a trace file, and then import it into a database table once the trace is complete.

TURN TRACES OFF AND ON AUTOMATICALLY

Take advantage of the ability to turn traces off and on automatically. Not only can this save you time, it might prevent you from leaving a trace running much longer than necessary, wasting disk space and server resources.

If you are using the Profiler GUI, you must start a trace manually, but you can set the trace to end automatically. If you are using Transact-SQL to capture a trace, you can use SQL Server Agent to start and stop traces automatically.

ANALYZING TRACES

This section describes some ways to make analyzing Profiler trace data a little easier.

LIMIT DATA COLLECTED

By now, you may be getting a sense of déjà vu. Didn't I just talk about the importance of limiting events and data columns a few pages ago? Yes, but here is another good reason to limit how much trace data you collect. The more data you collect, the harder it is to analyze. Analyzing trace data is not easy, given the tools available with SQL Server 2005, so any way in which you can reduce the amount of data there is to analyze is worth pursuing.

USE GROUPING AND AGGREGATION

If you are using the Profiler GUI, you can group and aggregate results from the Profiler window. If you have not investigated this option carefully, please do so. While the grouping and aggregation function is not very sophisticated, it can be very useful, such as when you want to order long-running queries from the longest running to the shortest running.

ANALYZE TRACE DATA USING TRANSACT-SQL

As just noted, the tools provided by SQL Server 2005 aren't great for analysis, so you may want to become creative and create your own queries, or Reporting Services reports, to analyze trace results.

PERFORMANCE MONITOR

This section sets out some ways in which to better integrate the use of Performance Monitor with Profiler.

DON'T PERFORM A CORRELATION ANALYSIS WHEN THE SERVER IS BUSY

It is important that there are no external events or services running that might disrupt the correlation analysis between a Profiler trace file and a Performance Monitor counter log file. For example, if you are running IIS on the same server as SQL Server, then it will be hard to show any accurate correlation between Profiler traces and Performance counter logs because you won't know how IIS activity is affecting the Performance Monitor counters. In addition, if you are backing up or restoring a database on a server, this will also interfere with the correlation of data because disk I/O counters will be affected by the backup or restore activity.

RUN PERFORMANCE MONITOR AND PROFILER OFF THE SQL SERVER INSTANCE

Collecting a Profiler trace and a Performance Monitor counter log file simultaneously is likely to incur a significant amount of overhead. As such, it is recommended that you run both tools on a computer other than the server you are monitoring, in order to minimize the performance impact.

ENSURE BOTH CLIENT AND SERVER ARE IN SAME TIME ZONES

When you use Profiler to display a correlation graph between trace and counter data, the time stamp of each event is used to synchronize the activity. Therefore, it is important that the server being monitored, and the client computer used for the monitoring, be in the same time zones.

RESTRICT THE AMOUNT OF PERFORMANCE MONITOR COUNTER DATA COLLECTED

Just as you should limit the amount of Profiler trace data collected, you should also limit the amount of Performance Monitor counter data collected. The fewer counters selected, the lower will be the overhead of collecting the data.

RESTRICT THE NUMBER OF COUNTERS DISPLAYED IN PROFILER GUI

When you import Performance Monitor counter data into the Profiler GUI, limit the number of counters added. While adding many counters won't affect performance, it will make the correlation graph much too busy and hard to read. Keep in mind, though, that if you do add a lot of counters, you can turn them off and on as needed to make the correlation graph easier to read.

USE THE ZOOM FEATURE TO DRILL DOWN INTO TIME INTERVALS

If the correlation graph is still hard to read, even after limiting the number of counters displayed, don't forget that you can zoom into small time intervals, which can make it easier for you to see all the activity.

DATABASE ENGINE TUNING ADVISOR

This section focuses on suggestions for how to make the Profiler and The Database Engine Tuning Advisor (DTA) work more efficiently together.

ONLY INCLUDE ESSENTIAL EVENTS AND DATA COLUMNS IN DTA TRACE

As we discussed in Chapter 7, the DTA only needs a very limited set of events and data columns to produce a trace file that can be used by the DTA. There is little point in collecting any more data than the minimum required to run the DTA analysis, as it will just be ignored. An exception to this rule is if you are combining a baseline and a DTA Trace into a single trace.

RUN DTA ANALYSIS DURING TIMES OF LOW ACTIVITY

When you perform a DTA analysis, the DTA has to connect to the production server in order to run its analysis (unless you elect to run a DTA analysis on a different server). This produces a lot of overhead for the production server. To minimize the impact of this overhead on the production server, try to schedule DTA analysis during times of the day when server activity is at its lowest.

MAKE DTA TRACES A REGULAR PART OF YOUR SCHEDULED TASKS

Making a DTA trace and running a DTA analysis on it is not a one-time event for a database. It is something that should be done periodically, as data and query needs change over time. As the DBA, you need to schedule into your regular activity the periodic DTA trace, and analysis of all your production SQL Servers.

SUMMARY

As we've discovered throughout the book, SQL Server Profiler is a powerful tool that can be used to help you identify and troubleshoot many SQL Server problems. Hopefully, this chapter has summarized some guidelines that will help you use the tool in the most efficient way.

Chapter 11
PROFILER EVENTS AND DATA COLUMNS EXPLAINED

Throughout this book, we have been rather selective in terms of the events and data columns we have considered. We have only covered ones necessary for solving the problem at hand. As such, we have only scratched the surface in terms of the full range of events and data columns that can be traced with Profiler.

In fact, SQL Server Profiler can capture over 170 different events, arranged into 21 different event categories. Each event can have up to 64 data columns associated with it. Assuming every event had every available data column associated with it (not the case, fortunately), then there would be over 10,000 different pieces of data to work with. Think of a large spreadsheet with over 170 rows and 64 columns.

Because it is not practical to describe all 170 events and 64 data columns in detail, the intent of this chapter is to provide a reference source for each of the 21 event categories, how they can be used to troubleshoot specific SQL Server problems, and the events in each that will be of the most interest to the DBA. In each section I try to describe not only the events that comprise that category, but the additional "context events" that might help you when troubleshooting a SQL server problem in that category. As well as this, the chapter also provides a description of the most important data columns.

I left this chapter to last because, unlike the other 10 chapters, it's not one I expect anyone to read from beginning to end, in one go. That's not to say that it doesn't contain some very useful information. Some of the event categories described in this chapter, such as "Errors and Warnings", "Stored Procedures" and "Performance", among others, need to be understood by all DBAs. However, I expect that you will use this as a reference chapter when you need information on a given event or data column, or advice on troubleshooting in one of the areas covered by a given event category.

EVENT CATEGORIES

We begin our journey by discussing the twenty-one event categories into which SQL Server Profiler divides the 170+ events:

- Broker Events
- CLR Events
- Cursors
- Database
- Deprecation
- Errors and Warnings
- Full Text
- Locks
- OLEDB
- Objects
- Performance
- Progress Report
- Query Notifications
- Scans
- Security Audit
- Server
- Sessions
- Stored Procedures
- TSQL
- Transaction
- User Configurable

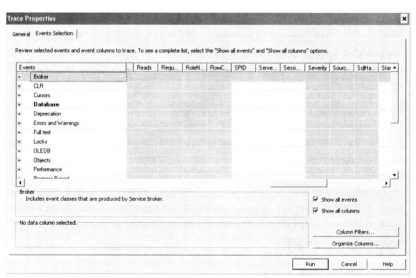

Figure 11-1: Profiler events are divided into twenty-one categories, and are selected from the Events Selection tab of the Trace Properties screen.

BROKER EVENTS

If you are like most DBAs, you probably don't use the SQL Server Service Broker, and so will have no reason to use any of the thirteen events available in this category. On the other hand, if you do support the Service Broker, or write code for it, then some of these thirteen events can be worth their weight in gold. They are:

- Activation
- Connection
- Conversation
- Conversation Group
- Corrupted Message
- Forwarded Message Dropped
- Forwarded Message Sent
- Message Classify
- Message Undeliverable
- Mirrored Route State Changed
- Queue Disabled
- Remote Message Acknowledgement
- Transmission

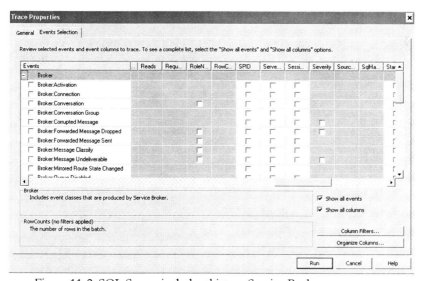

Figure 11-2: SQL Server includes thirteen Service Broker events.

Besides the above key events, Profiler also has the ability to capture two broker-related audit events, which include:

- Audit Broker Login

- Audit Broker Conversation

While one of the most obvious use of Broker events is to debug Service Broker-related code, they can also be used to provide on-going monitoring of Service Broker activities (assuming the application doesn't do this already).

Rather than to try and pick out specific broker-related events, I tend to create a trace to capture all thirteen events, including all the related data columns for each event. You would start the trace just before the start of the Service Broker activity you want to examine and stop the trace just after it completes. While this captures a lot of data, you shouldn't have to run the trace for long periods of time, preventing any excess resource usage on your SQL Server instance.

NOTE:

The purpose of collecting a lot of data at first is to get the "big" picture of what is happening. Having said this, if you are a Service Broker expert, then you may want to pick only those events you think are related to the problem at hand.

Once you identify the big picture, you should be able to determine which events and data columns are relevant, and if you need to perform additional traces to gather more information, then create traces with only the events and data columns relevant to your current problem. This way, you won't have to worry about using excessive service resources when capturing a trace.

Besides these specific Service Broker events, you may also want to capture additional events from other categories when troubleshooting Server Broker problems. For example, there are some events that, when captured with Service Broker events, can make it easier to see exactly how your code is working. These include:

- RPC:Completed
- SQL:BatchStarting
- SQL:BatchCompleted
- SQL:StmtCompleted

Seeing Server Broker events in context with the T-SQL code running in your application can make troubleshooting problems much easier.

CLR EVENTS

SQL Server provides the ability to execute .Net Common Language Runtime (CLR) objects inside SQL Server. This allows developers to use any .Net programming language to create custom functionality within SQL Server that doesn't exist by default. CLR objects are created outside SQL Server and saved in a file called an assembly. Essentially, an assembly is packaged in the form of a DLL or executable file. In order for SQL Server to use an assembly, it must be registered with a SQL Server instance, where it is hosted. Once it is hosted, T-SQL code can be used to load the assembly and execute it.

Given that Microsoft has put a lot of effort into developing the ability of SQL Server to execute CLR objects, it is odd that there is only a single CLR event that can be captured by Profiler.

The event is called "Assembly Load". Essentially all it does is tell you if a particular request to load a CLR object has successfully or unsuccessfully executed.

Figure 11-3: The CLR event category has a single, lonely event.

Used by itself, the Assembly Load event is not particularly useful. However, when combined with other Profiler events, it will help you troubleshoot CLR objects running in SQL Server.

For example, if your goal is to test, debug, performance tune, or troubleshoot CLR objects interacting with T-SQL code, you might want to consider capturing all the following events.

- CLR: Assembly Load: to see if assembly load requests are succeeding or failing.
- RPC:Completed
- SQL:BatchStarting
- SQL:BatchCompleted
- SQL:StmtCompleted

By using all of these events together, you will not only be able to see if a particular assembly fails to load, but you will also get additional information about the Transact-SQL used to execute the assembly. All this information, in context, paints a better picture of what is happening in your code and makes it easier to identify and resolve CLR object-related problems.

CURSORS

There are exceptions to every rule, but my general philosophy is: "Cursors are evil. Don't use them". Here's why:

- They use excessive server resources to execute, compared to set-based methods.
- They reduce data concurrency, contributing more to blocking and other nasty problems.
- They increase network traffic.
- They significantly hurt application scalability.
- Virtually any server-based cursor can be rewritten to be set-based, boosting performance. In other words, using a cursor is the lazy way to retrieve and manipulate data.

The focus of virtually all Transact-SQL code is set-based operations. In other words, your code grabs a set of records, and then does something to all of them in one fell swoop. It's fast, it's efficient, and it's the way SQL Server is designed to run. By default, Transact-SQL is a set-based programming language.

However, many developers are not familiar with set-based coding techniques and prefer to use the more familiar procedural coding techniques, where data is dealt with row-by-row, instead of as a set. This is not the default way Transact-SQL works, but default behavior can be changed as the developer sees fit and SQL Server allows developers to manipulate data one row at a time, using an object called a server-based cursor.

SQL Server supports two different ways to create a server-based cursor. One option is to use Transact-SQL code to create and manipulate the server cursor. The second option is to use a database application programming interface (API) to create and manipulate the server cursor directly from an application.

So how does all the above fit in with Profiler cursor events? Essentially, Profiler events track API-created cursors, not Transact-SQL cursors. Profiler provides the following dedicated events for monitoring API-created, server-based cursors

- CursorClose
- CursorExecute
- CursorImplicitConversion
- CursorOpen
- CursorPrepare
- CursorRecompile

- CursorUnprepare

Events	Applic...	Bigint...	Bigint...	Binary...	CPU	Client...	Colum...	DBUs...	Datab...	Datab...	Durati...	EndTi...	E
Cursors													
☐ CursorClose	☐					☐			☐	☐			
☐ CursorExecute	☐					☐			☐	☐			
☐ CursorImplicitConversi...	☐			☐		☐			☐	☐			
☐ CursorOpen	☐					☐			☐	☐			
☐ CursorPrepare	☐					☐			☐	☐			
☐ CursorRecompile	☐					☐			☐	☐			
☐ CursorUnprepare	☐					☐			☐	☐			

Figure 11-4: While there are a lot of cursor events, but they only work with API-created, server-based cursors.

Essentially, the above Profiler events tell you when an API-created, server-based cursor is created, compiled, executed, and destroyed. This information can be used to help debug problematic code when cursor-related problems (error messages) are occurring.

If you want to monitor the activity of Transact-SQL cursors, you won't be able to use the above Profiler events. Instead, as Transact-SQL cursor code is executed, you can monitor it using one or more of the following events:

- RPC:Completed
- SQL:BatchStarting
- SQL: BatchCompleted
- SQL: StmtCompleted

These standard events can be used to monitor any Transact-SQL code used to create and execute cursors.

DATABASE

The Database event category name is somewhat of a misnomer. Firstly, virtually every Profiler event has something to do with a database; secondly, while four of the five events are related, the fifth one seems to be lumped into this category, even though it is unrelated to the first four.

The five Database events are:

- Data File Auto Grow
- Data File Auto Shrink
- Log File Auto Grow
- Log File Auto Shrink
- Database Mirroring State Change

Database					
Data File Auto Grow	□		□	□ □	□
Data File Auto Shrink	□		□	□ □	□
Database Mirroring State Change				□ □	
Log File Auto Grow	□		□	□ □	□
Log File Auto Shrink	□		□	□ □	□

Figure 11-5: Data and log file growth and shrinkage are recorded by these events.

AUTOMATIC LOG AND DATA FILE GROWTH AND SHRINKAGE

The first four events describe when auto grow or auto shrink is automatically invoked for a data or log file. Notice that I said *automatically*. If you manually grow or shrink a data or log file using ALTER DATABASE, no event is fired.

So why would you want to know if a data or log file automatically grows or shrinks? There are two ways to answer this question, depending on how experienced a DBA you are.

If you are an experienced DBA, you should now that it is recommended *not* to use the automatic growth/shrink options to manage the size of your database. The best practice for managing data and log file size is to manage them manually so that you can control when and how long growth/shrink operations occur. This allows you to prevent automatic behavior from occurring during unexpected or inappropriate times, such as your SQL Server's busiest time of the day.

Yes, as an experienced DBA you may want to leave the auto growth database option on to prevent problems due to some unexpected file growth, as this is better than running out of space. But this feature should only be used to cover unexpected events. Routine data and log file growth/shrinkage should be managed manually. If you fall into this category, then you don't have any need to capture these four growth/shrinkage events, as they won't ever become a problem for you.

If you don't follow the best practice just mentioned, or you are a consultant who is analyzing a customer's SQL Server databases, the four growth/shrinkage events can come in handy. This is because these events tell you when such unmanaged data and log file growth/shrinkage is occurring, and how often. Excessive or unplanned growth/shrinkage events can cause resource contention on your SQL Server. These four events allow you to see if, and when, they occur.

If you check out these events and notice a lot of file growth/shrinkage activity, then you are being tipped off that data and log file management is not being managed manually, as it should be. With this information, you can then change the data and log file management so that it better meets the needs of your SQL Server.

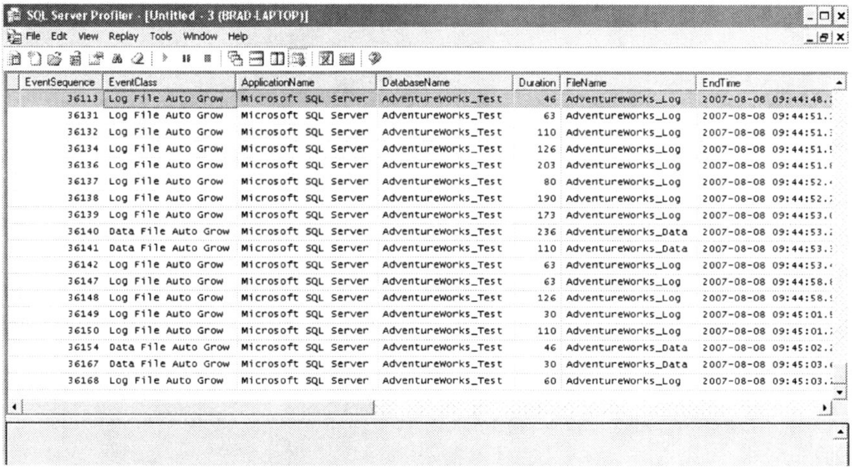

Figure 11-6: Excessive data or log growth/shrinkage can put an undue resource load on your server.

In the example above, you can see an extreme example of where both data and log file auto growth is excessive, with events occurring within milliseconds of each other. If this type of activity was typical for your server, it would be putting an excessive burden on your server's resources, hurting performance.

DATABASE MIRRORING STATE CHANGE

If you don't use database mirroring, this event will be of no interest to you. But if you do use database mirroring, it can be a handy tool to help track what is going on in your mirrored databases.

Any time a mirrored database's state changes, this state change is logged as a Database Mirroring State Change event. From this event, you can find out the following information from the State data column, which is part of the event.

Mirroring State ID Numbers:

- 0 = Null Notification
- 1 = Synchronized Principal with Witness
- 2 = Synchronized Principal without Witness
- 3 = Synchronized Mirror with Witness
- 4 = Synchronized Mirror without Witness
- 5 = Connection with Principal Lost
- 6 = Connection with Mirror Lost
- 7 = Manual Failover
- 8 = Automatic Failover

- 9 = Mirroring Suspended
- 10 = No Quorum
- 11 = Synchronizing Mirror
- 12 = Principal Running Exposed

If you are familiar with database mirroring, you should be able to see instantly how this information can be useful. For example, you can troubleshoot many different mirroring problems, and even monitor when database mirroring failover occurred. This event can be very useful and is one with which all DBAs who use database mirroring should be familiar.

DEPRECATION

Now, this is a word most people don't use in daily conversation. Essentially, deprecation means that a current feature of SQL Server will be removed in some future version.

In the context of SQL Server Profiler, deprecation refers to Transact-SQL code, commands, or functionality that will be eventually removed from the current version of SQL Server, either in the next release, or sometime after the next major release of SQL Server.

In the deprecation event category, there are two events:

- **Deprecation Announcement** – a warning that this particular code will be supported in the next major release of SQL Server, but that it will be removed sometime after the next major release.
- **Deprecation Final Support** – a warning that this particular code will definitely be removed from the next major release of SQL Server.

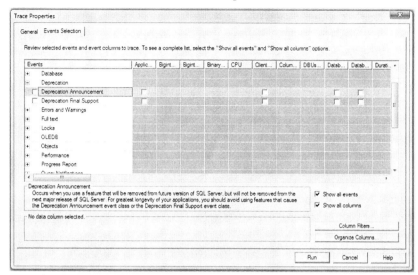

Figure 11-7: There are two types of deprecation warnings.

When you run a Profiler trace looking for deprecation warnings, they look as shown in Figure 11-8:

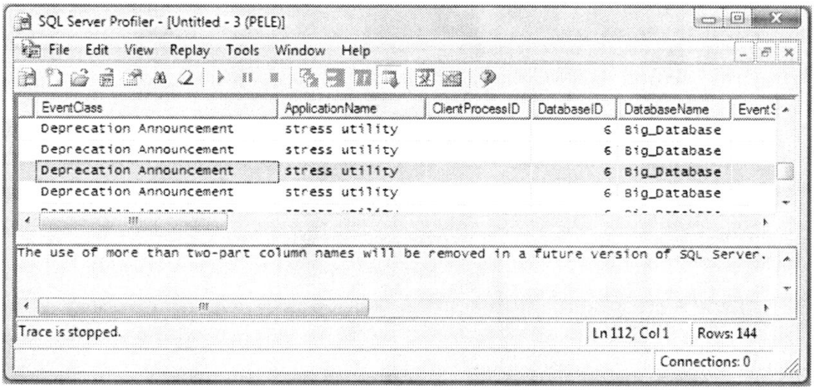

Figure 11-8: An example of a deprecation announcement.

In the above figure, you notice that many Deprecation Announcement events are being captured. The highlighted Deprecation Announcement tells us that "the use of more than two-part column names will be removed from a future version of SQL Server". Well, this message is somewhat useful, but exactly what code is causing the problem? To find out, we need to collect more than just deprecation warnings; we need to also collect the code that includes the deprecated events. This is because deprecation events don't usually include the deprecated code. If you don't know what the deprecated code is, it can be hard to identify and correct.

To make it easier to identify the code that is deprecated, you should consider including these additional events in your trace:

- RPC:Completed
- SP:StmtCompleted
- SQL:StmtCompleted

When you collect the above events, plus the deprecated events, a better picture is painted of what is going on, and what T-SQL activity caused the event to occur. For example, let's see what happens when I run the deprecated command, **sp_lock**:

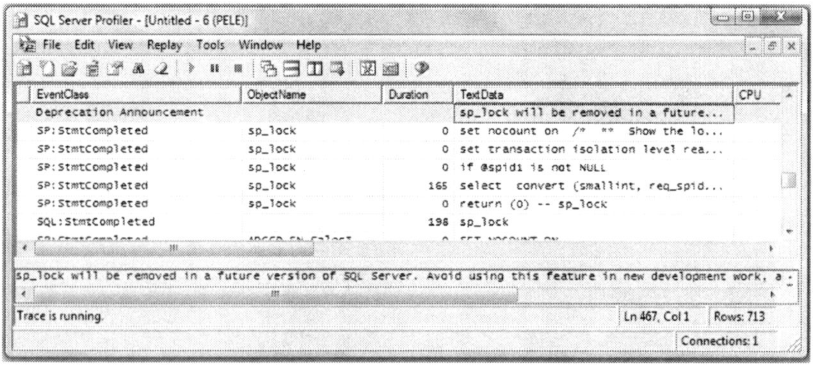

Figure 11-9: The deprecated event occurs before the actual code is run.

Notice that in figure 11-9 the deprecation event occurs *before* the actual sp_lock command is run. What does this mean? It means that when you are trying to identify what code or commands are causing deprecation events, you must look for the code immediately after the deprecation event.

If you are an administrative DBA who works with developers, it is a good idea to identify all deprecated code, commands and functionality in your current applications, and share that with developers, so that they won't use it in new code. Hopefully, they will remove it from their current code before the next version of SQL Server comes out that no longer supports the functionality. If you are a developer DBA who writes a lot of code, you also need to take the same advice. The sooner you and your organization's developers become familiar with what features are going away, the better prepared you will be for the future.

ERRORS AND WARNINGS

The Errors and Warnings event category is large, mixing both useful and not-so-useful events together in one large grouping. As you might have guessed from the event category name, Errors and Warnings are just that: events representing potential SQL Server problems that Microsoft thinks that DBAs might be interested in knowing about. As I describe each event, I will spend the most time on those events that I think are more useful to DBAs. The events in the Errors and Warnings event category are:

- Attention
- Background Job Error
- Blocked Process Report
- ErrorLog
- EventLog
- Exception
- Exchange Spill
- Execution Warnings
- Hash Warning
- Missing Column Statistics
- Missing Join Predicate
- Sort Warnings
- User Error Message

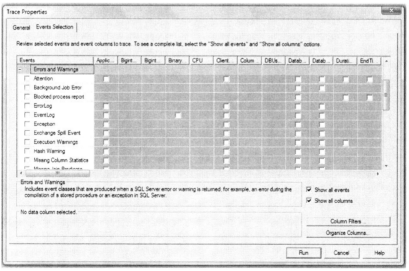

Figure 11-10: There are many events available to the DBA within the Errors and Warnings event category.

ATTENTION

Whenever a connection between a client and SQL Server is canceled or broken, for whatever reason, an attention event is created by SQL Server. This can be a useful event if you are trying to troubleshoot client connection problems. As a DBA, I sometimes receive phone calls from users telling me that their client application lost connection to SQL Server. It was then my job to help identify what was causing the problem (usually network issues), and the attention event can help provide the necessary information needed to identify the cause of the problem.

Like many events, the attention event is more useful if you also capture additional events, such as:

- RPC:Completed
- SP:StmtCompleted
- SQL:StmtCompleted

This way, you can better see what code is running when the attention event occurs. Take a look at the example trace shown in Figure 11-11:

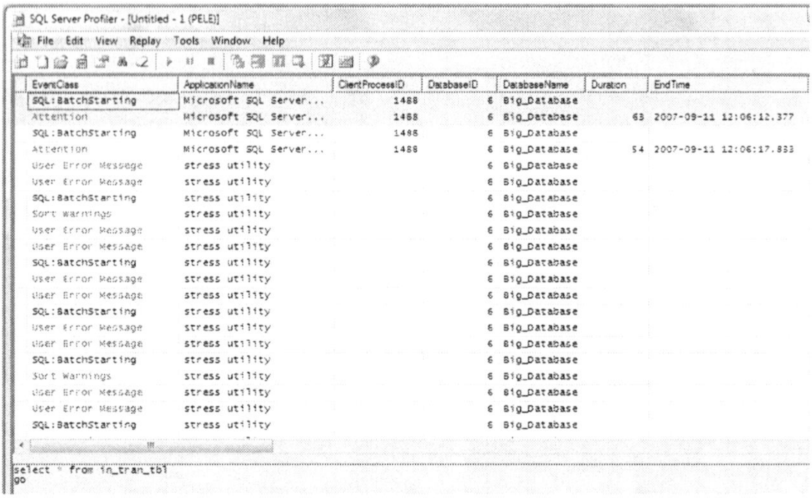

Figure 11-11: In the above trace, we see many types of Error and Warning events.

For example, look at the very first event on the screen, which is a SQL:BatchStarting event for ClientProcessID 1488. We can see that the code that was run is as follows (see the bottom of the above screenshot):

```
select * from in_tran_tbl
```

Immediately after this code is an attention event for the same ClientProcessID. This is telling us that the ClientProcessID 1488 began and was then disconnected. In addition to this, we see the same event repeated for the same ClientProcessID. Obviously, something is causing this connection to fail each time this code is run.

While Profiler is great at telling us that an error occurred, it is unable to tell us why. That's when you have to put your DBA detective hat on and begin further investigation into the cause of these broken connections. For example, if you know the time the connection attempt occurred, and the user who was disconnected, it makes it much easier to go to your network support staff and ask them if there were any network problems during this same time period for this user. Most network support staff are able to check for such problems.

BACKGROUND JOB ERROR

This is one type of error message you don't want to see. When it occurs, it means that some SQL Server-based background job has failed abnormally. Examples of background jobs include the lazy writer, lock monitor, schedule monitor, ghost clean up, auto-shrink, and so on. If you are regularly having these kinds of errors, you are probably also having a lot of other severe problems with your SQL Server, and you may want to start thinking about rebuilding your SQL Server.

In most cases, you probably won't be using Profiler to trace for these errors as these problems will be so severe, you won't need to use Profiler to find them, as SQL Server will be failing in other significant areas and it will be very obvious that something is going wrong. However, if you should decide to trace for these errors, you need to know that there are three different EventSubClass messages (found in the event's data columns) that provide you with some additional information that may be of some use to you:

- **EventSubClass message 1** indicates that a background job is ending after some(?) sort of generic failure
- **EventSubClass message 2** indicates that a background job has been dropped because some related queue is full
- **EventSubClass message 3** indicates that the background job returned a specific error message that may be of some use to you when troubleshooting problems.

BLOCKED PROCESS REPORT

This is a very powerful new feature of SQL Server 2005 that every DBA needs to become familiar with. It allows you to capture information on blocked processes that have been blocked longer than the amount of time you specified. For example, let's say that you want a Profiler trace that shows you all of the blocked processes that exceed 30 seconds. No problem. Once you turn this feature on, and start Profiler, it will automatically create the report for you. Let's find out how.

Unlike virtually all the other events available in Profiler, this particular event is turned off by default. In other words, if you want to produce a Blocked Process Report, you must first turn on the blocked process threshold. Why do I have to turn this event on, while virtually all the other Profiler events are turned on by default? Performance is the reason. The Blocked Process Report can be resource-intensive to produce. Generally speaking, when you need this report, you turn the event on, create the Blocked Process Report, and then turn the event off. Yes, this is a little extra work, but worth it.

Before we even begin using Profiler, the first step to creating a Blocked Process Report is to turn the blocked process threshold on. This is generally done by running the following code from a query window in SSMS:

```
--First, you must turn the Show Advanced Options on,
--assuming that it has not already been turned on for
your server
SP_CONFIGURE 'show advanced options', 1 ;
GO
RECONFIGURE ;
GO

--Second, you set the blocked process threshold to a
value in seconds
--The example here is for 30 seconds
SP_CONFIGURE 'blocked process threshold', 30 ;
GO
RECONFIGURE ;
GO

--When you are done running the Blocked Process
Report,
--run the following command to turn this feature off
SP_CONFIGURE 'blocked process threshold', 0 ;
GO
RECONFIGURE ;
GO
```

The blocked process threshold is a server-wide setting that is turned on and off using the SP_CONFIGURE command. Turning it on requires several steps. First, if you have not previously done so, you must turn on the **Show Advanced Options** feature of SQL Server, and then run RECONFIGURE. Second, you run the SP_CONFIGURE 'blocked process threshold' command, specifying the number of seconds you want to define as your threshold, and then run RECONFIGURE. At this point, you can start Profiler and produce the Blocked Process Report. Once you are done creating the report, you need to turn the blocked process threshold off, by resetting it to zero.

Having turned on the Blocked Process Reports event, your next step is to start Profiler and create a new trace with a single event selected:

- Blocked Process Report

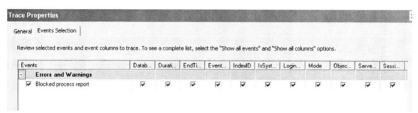

Figure 11-12: The Blocked Process Report is a very powerful tool for DBAs for identifying and troubleshooting blocking issues.

When you run the Profiler, you will get a report like the one shown in Figure 11-13:

Figure 11-13: The Blocked Process Report not only shows you excessive blocking, it shows you exactly what is causing the blocking.

Every time there is a process that is blocked for longer than the time you specified in the blocked process threshold, the block will be displayed as a row. As part of this row, you will see the code that is being blocked, together with the code that is doing the blocking.

This is a very powerful tool for troubleshooting blocking problems in your applications. With this information, you are able to see exactly what the problem is. The hard part, of course, is figuring out how to resolve the problem. I can't answer this here because each situation is different. However, by knowing exactly what code is problematic, you will be on a direct route to resolving the problem.

ERRORLOG

All the ErrorLog event does is to record an event every time SQL Server writes a message to the SQL Server error log. Generally, using Profiler to record that a message was written to the error log is not all that helpful, especially when you can go directly to the SQL Server error log and see the errors.

On the other hand, there is one useful way to use this event, and that is to help you establish the context of an error message. For example, often you will see messages in the SQL Server error log, but you aren't able to see what code was running just before the message occurred.

By creating a trace that includes the ErrorLog event, along with some additional context events, you can see exactly what is happening just before the error event occurred, and so establish a context for the problem. While you can add many different events to help you establish the context, I suggest the following three as the minimum for a ErrorLog trace:

- RPC:Completed
- SP:StmtCompleted
- SQL:StmtCompleted

EVENTLOG

The EventLog event is very similar to the ErrorLog event. Every time SQL Server writes an event to the Windows Event Log, the EventLog event is fired. In virtually all cases, when SQL Server writes an event to the Windows Event Log, it also writes it to the SQL Server error log, which means that an ErrorLog event is also fired. As such, this particular event is mostly redundant.

The one exception to this is when a developer creates a custom event log message and fires it programmatically. The EventLog event might help debug code that uses such custom event log messages.

Figure 11-14: EventLog and EventLog events generally occur together, as you can see above. The error message is displayed at the bottom of the screen.

EXCEPTION

An exception event occurs when SQL Server identifies an exception error. When an exception occurs, either the code is smart enough to handle the exception and it continues to run, or it is not and the code fails. The exceptions captured by this event can be generated by the system (SQL Server code) or a user connection (client code).

EventClass	ApplicationName	ClientProcessID	DatabaseID	DatabaseName
Exception	SQLDMO_1	2236	1	master
Exception	SQLDMO_1	2236	1	master
Exception	SQLDMO_1	2236	1	master

Figure 11-15: An example of an exception error in Profiler.

In order for this event to be useful, you need to be sure to include the Error, State, and Severity data columns. This event can be helpful when debugging code.

EXCHANGE SPILL

The name of this event is not really indicative of the data it captures. Before we can understand what this event is all about, we first need some background on parallelism. When a query is submitted to the query optimizer on a SQL Server instance that has two or more cores available to it, by default it is considered for parallelism. In other words, the query optimizer checks to see if executing the query in parallel (on two or more CPU cores) would be faster than executing it on a single CPU core. If the query optimizer thinks using parallelism is advantageous, then the query is divided into two or more data sets, and each data set is processed in parallel by multiple CPU cores. Once each data set has completed processing, the results of each data set are merged back into a single data set for return to the client.

If a query plan has multiple range scans within it (for example, the query has multiple BETWEEN operators that select from multiple ranges of rows), and the query optimizer decides to run this query in parallel, a particular event can happen, namely the Exchange Spill event. For example, if the amount of data being processed for each range is very large, it is possible for the communication buffers (in RAM), used to store the data by SQL Server, to run out of room, meaning that the data has to be written to the tempdb database. As you can imagine, this can greatly slow down a parallel query, since introducing disk I/O to the mix can greatly hurt performance. When this happens, an Exchange Spill occurs. Microsoft only considers an Exchange Spill to be a problem when more than five Exchange Spills occur within the same execution plan.

If you are still following this, I congratulate you, as this is quite obscure information and is rarely a problem for most DBAs. On the other hand, if your system runs a lot of parallel queries and they aren't performing as well as you expect, then you should consider creating a Profiler trace that includes both the Exchange Spill and the ShowPlan XML events. You may also want to include additional events, but these two are the most important. When an Exchange Spill event occurs, you want to be able to see the graphical execution plan that created it. Again, generally speaking, if you don't have more than five Exchange Spill events occurring for the same execution plan, you can ignore them.

But what if a particular query consistently creates more than five Exchange Spills every time it is run, resulting in poor query performance? If this is the case, consider one or more of the following suggestions:

- Try to avoid using ORDER BY clauses in the query.
- If you have to use ORDER BY, avoid ordering any column that is involved in the multiple range scans.
- Use an index hint to force the query optimizer to access the affected table differently.
- Rewrite the query to force the use of a different, more efficient query plan.
- Use the MAXDOP hint to turn off parallelism for this specific query.

Hopefully, you will never run into an obscure problem like this one. But if you do, you are now better prepared to handle it.

EXECUTION WARNINGS

Before a query can be executed, it must first be granted enough memory to execute. Most of the time, there is enough memory available and the memory is granted immediately. However, if the server is under intensive memory pressure, sometimes queries may have to wait their turn in order to get the amount of memory they need to execute. The Execution

Warnings event fires whenever a query has to wait one second or more before it is allocated the memory it needs.

If you think your SQL Server is experiencing memory bottlenecks that are affecting performance, you may want to trace the Execution Warnings event to see if any queries have to wait for memory (which would confirm the memory pressure you suspect).

When an Execution Warning event occurs, the EventSubClass data column specifies whether the query timed out, or if it only had to wait but ran eventually. If the query only had to wait, the Duration data column would show, in milliseconds, how long the query had to wait.

If you run this trace and notice a lot of Execution Warnings, especially ones with long durations, then you will need to take a serious look at how to add more memory to your SQL Server (or find a way to reduce the load on the current server):

EventClass	ApplicationName	ClientProcessID	DatabaseID	DatabaseName	Duration
Execution Warnings	stress utility		6	Big_Database	12000

Figure 11-16: This particular Execution Warning tells us that a query waited 12 seconds before it was able to get enough RAM in order to run.

HASH WARNING

Before we get to Hash Warning, we must first recap what a hash join is. Many kinds of JOIN statements, such as inner joins, left joins, right joins, full outer joins, and others, can cause the query optimizer to choose a hash join to join the data in two tables, especially if the tables lack adequate indexes, or the joins includes large numbers of rows. In addition, hash joins can occur as a part of an execution plan, irrespective of whether the query has a JOIN clause in it.

There are three different types of hash joins: in-memory, grace hash join and recursive hash join. An in-memory hash join is performed if there is enough memory for the hash join to occur fully in memory. This is the fastest type of join.

If there is not enough memory for the hash join to occur entirely in memory, then either a grace hash or recursive hash join is performed. In these latter two cases, since not enough memory is available, SQL Server has to go through extra steps – such as data partitioning or writing to tempdb – using additional SQL Server resources to perform the hash join. This is not an ideal situation from a performance standpoint.

A Hash Warning event occurs when a hash join is performed as a grace hash join or a recursive hash join. In other words, when an in-memory hash join is not possible, the Hash Warning event is fired. The idea behind this event is that grace hash joins and recursive hash joins are less efficient, and that the DBA should be aware of this potentially performance-harming behavior.

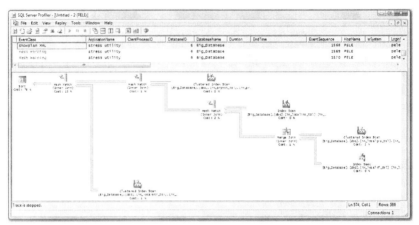

Figure 11-17: The above query (see the Graphical Execution Plan) created two Hash Warnings.

As with many other Profiler events, it is often useful to capture additional events as well as the Hash Warning event. In figure 11-17, I am capturing both Showplan XML and Hash Warning events. By capturing both types of events, not only can I see when a Hash Warning occurs, I can also see the execution plan of the query that generated the Hash Warning. In the above example, two Hash Warnings were generated from a single execution plan. If you look closely at the execution plan, you scan see that two hash matches (hash joins) were performed, and that both of them were less than optimal, causing the Hash Warning event to fire.

So how do you apply this information to your work as a DBA? Generally speaking, as a routine practice I would not run Profiler specifically looking for Hash Warnings. Instead, I would often be looking at execution plans. If I noticed that a lot of the execution plans used hash joins, and that some of these queries did not seem to be running optimally, then I would consider specifically conducting a trace looking for Hash Warnings, and follow up from there.

If your queries do suffer from many Hash Warnings, what can you do? Here are some suggestions to get you started:

- Reduce the number of rows being returned by the query.
- If a hash join has to be used, ensure that the current statistics exist on the columns being joined. Performing hash joins on table

columns with no or outdated column statistics is one of the biggest causes of Hash Warnings.

- Hash Warnings are sometimes a result of not having enough memory, so consider adding more memory to your server.

- Try to use a different type of join. Both a merge and loop join are generally more efficient than a hash join. In some cases, the reason the query optimizer uses a hash join instead of a generally more efficient merge or loop join is because the tables being joined lack appropriate indexes. By adding the right indexes, you can speed up many join operations. In addition, a query hint can be used to tell SQL Server what kind of join operation to perform, although you should be wary of trying this, as you might cause more harm than good. Be sure to experiment to see what happens.

Hash Warnings aren't generally a huge problem, so don't spend a lot of time tracking them until you have resolved the more obvious performance issues your server may be suffering from.

MISSING COLUMN STATISTICS

By default, SQL Server has the auto create and auto update statistics database option turned on for every user database. Assuming you maintain these settings, the query optimizer can identify when columns are missing any useful column statistics, or if the statistics need to be updated, and automatically add or update them as needed.

On occasion though, a DBA might determine that having auto create and auto update statistics turned on for a particular database is not a good choice. For example, automatic auto create or auto update operations may occur at inopportune times, disrupting performance on a temporary basis, causing random performance issues for users.

Now what does this have to do with the Missing Column Statistic event? If you have auto create statistics turned on for a database, you will never see a Missing Column Statistics event occur, as this event is automatically turned off when auto create statistics is on. So this event is not of use to most DBAs in most cases.

On the other hand, if you have turned off auto create statistics for a database, then the Missing Column Statistics event is turned on and you should monitor it, as it is one of the best ways to identify table columns that are missing potentially valuable column statistics that can help boost the performance of your SQL Server. Once missing column statistics have been identified, you can manually add them. Or, if you prefer, you can have the Database Engine Tuning Advisor do it for you. When you run a Profiler Trace and feed it to the Database Engine Tuning Advisor, it also looks for missing column statistics, and it can automatically create them for you.

MISSING JOIN PREDICATE EVENT

Sometimes, when a person writes a query, especially a long one with lots of joins, they forget to add appropriate join predicates within the query. This can result in an unplanned cross-join (also known as a Cartesian product). A cross-join joins every row in both of the tables, potentially creating a large result set, which is normally not what the query writer intended. When cross-joins are performed on large tables, huge amounts of server resources can be wasted.

To help identify this kind of mistake, you can use the Missing Join Predicate event. This event fires whenever the query optimizer identifies a query with a cross-join, planned or unplanned.

In my example below, I have intentionally created a cross-join query, which in turn created a Missing Join Predicate event in my Profiler trace, shown in Figure 11-18:

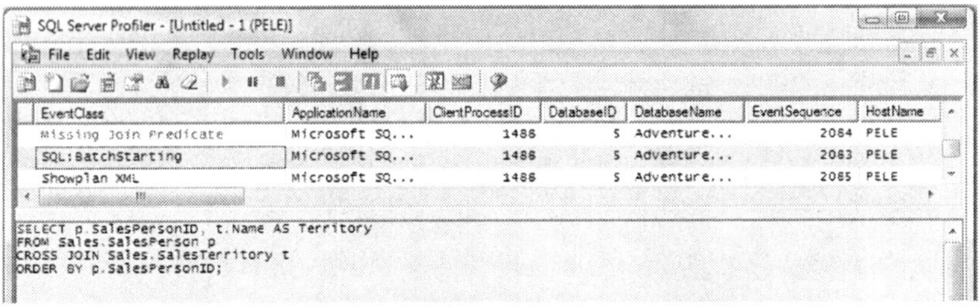

Figure 11-18: Identifying poorly performing queries due to missing join predicates is easy when using the Missing Join Predicate event.

When using Profiler to identify Missing Join Predicate events, you may also want to capture the following additional events:

- Showplan XML
- RPC:Completed
- SP:StmtCompleted
- SQL:StmtCompleted

By tracing all these events, you not only establish the context for the event firing (i.e. see the code that is causing the problem), you also can see a graphical execution plan of the code, providing additional useful information to help you identify the poorly written code so that it can be corrected.

As a DBA, if you are familiar with the queries you run, you may already know that your join code is written well, and you need not bother tracing this particular event. On the other hand, if you are new to your DBA job, or a DBA consultant, and are not familiar with the code that is running, tracing this event can go a long way to identifying poorly performing queries very quickly.

SORT WARNINGS

When SQL Server is asked to perform an ORDER BY operation, it tries to perform the sort in memory, in order to provide the best performance. But if the amount of data to be ordered is large, it might not be able to be sorted in memory, having instead to be written to the tempdb database as part of the sorting process. Because disk I/O is now involved, sort performance can suffer.

The Sort Warnings event fires whenever SQL Server is unable to complete a sort entirely in memory and has to resort to writing to the tempdb. While it is inevitable that some sorting occurs in the tempdb, it is not desirable and should be avoided if possible.

When you create a trace to identify Sort Warnings, it is a good idea to also include these additional events:

- Showplan XML
- RPC:Completed
- SP:StmtCompleted
- SQL:StmtCompleted

By collecting all these events, you will be in a better position to identify the exact code that is causing the Sort Warnings.

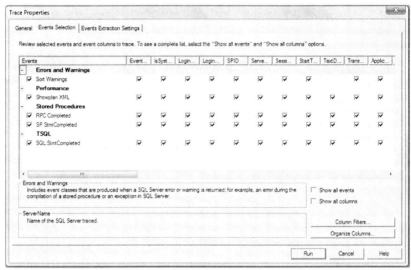

Figure 11-19: Above are the recommended events you capture to troubleshoot Sort Warning events.

Sort Warnings occur in the Profiler trace after the code that caused the problem has been executed. In the example shown in Figure 11-20, we can see that there are several Sort Warnings. If you select the Showplan XML event that occurred just *before* the Sort Warning, you can see the execution plan of the query that generated the Sort Warning. By evaluating the execution plan, you may be able to determine what, if anything, you can do to prevent future Sort Warnings for this particular query.

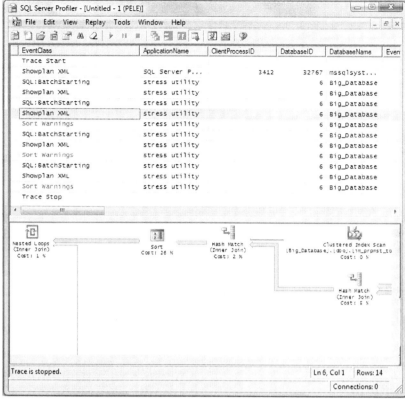

Figure 11-20: Sort Warnings occur when sorting operations are unable to be completed entirely in memory.

The Sort Warnings event is a very easy way to identify slowly performing sorts, allowing you to evaluate if there is anything you can do avoid them. Sometimes you can, sometimes you can't. So, what can you do to help avoid Sort Warnings? Some suggestions include:

- Reduce the amount of data returned, so less data needs to be sorted.
- Use data pages more efficiently. In other words, fit as many rows per data page as possible to maximize how efficiently memory is used to store rows. Be sure you run regular jobs to keep your indexes defragmented.
- Change the current fill factor to one that allows more rows to be stored per data page.
- Consider using a clustered index on the column to be sorted, in order to presort the data.
- Add more RAM to your SQL Server.
- If all else fails and you still need to sort to tempdb, locate tempdb on a faster drive all by itself, so it doesn't have to compete with

other disk I/O. Also consider dividing up the tempdb physical file into multiple files. As a rule of thumb, many DBAs create one physical file per CPU core that is available to their SQL Server instance.

USER ERROR MESSAGE

SQL Server often sends messages to the client application that is requesting data from it. These may be generic messages or specific error messages. How these messages are handled depends on how the client handles them. Some may be ignored, while others are captured and acted upon by the client application.

The User Error Message event captures all the messages that SQL Server sends to the client. Generally speaking, you will want to capture these additional events, as well as the User Error Message event, so you can see exactly what code is causing the error message to be returned.

- Showplan XML
- RPC:Completed
- SP:StmtCompleted
- SQL:StmtCompleted

This way, when you do run a trace, you can see exactly what code caused which error message to be generated, as you can see in Figure 11-22.

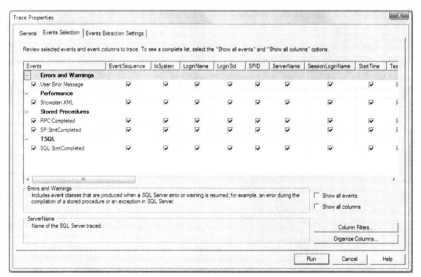

Figure 11-21: The above events are recommended for tracing User Error Messages.

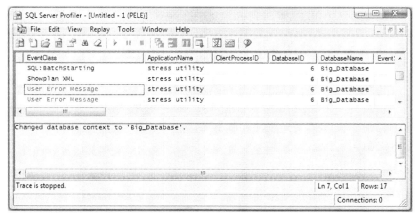

Figure 11-22: Some SQL Server activity can generate multiple User Error Messages.

We see that two User Error Messages were generated, one of which was "Changed database context to 'Big_Database'". This is an example of a user message that is normally ignored by a client application. If you look at the SQL:BatchStarting event, you can see the code that generated the event, and if you look at the Showplan XML event, you can see the execution plan for the code that generated the event.

In most cases, as an administrative DBA, you won't have a lot of need to use this particular event. On the other hand, this event can be used by developers who want a better understanding of what kind of messages that SQL Server is sending to their software, so they know how to deal with them properly.

FULL TEXT

If you don't use SQL Server 2005's Full Text service, then you can skip these three Full Text events:

- **Crawl Aborted** – indicates when a crawl has failed due to an exception error.
- **Crawl Started** – indicates that a crawl has started.
- **Crawl Stopped** – indicates that a crawl has ended because it has finished or failed.

If you do use the Full Text service, and you are troubleshooting crawling problems, then these events may be of use.

LOCKS

Locking is an integral part of preserving a database's data integrity. Most of the time, SQL Server does a great job of self-managing locks. All the work goes on in a black box that DBAs rarely have to peek into. But when locking problems arise, identifying and troubleshooting the problem can be difficult. Fortunately, SQL Server Profiler includes nine events we can use to help us out in this oftentimes difficult task:

- Acquired
- Released
- Escalation
- Cancel
- Deadlock
- Deadlock Chain
- Deadlock Graph
- Timeout (timeout > 0)
- Timeout

To keep our discussion focused, I am going to group the above nine events into these three categories, which were created for discussion purposes only:

- General Lock Events

  o Acquired
  o Released
  o Escalation
  o Cancel

- Deadlock Lock Events

  o Deadlock
  o Deadlock Chain
  o Deadlock Graph

- Timeout Lock Events

  o Timeout (timeout > 0)
  o Timeout

Before we go any further, I want to point out that a busy production SQL Server can experience thousands of locks per second. You must be very careful about how much data you collect. In other words, be sure to select only those events that are of direct interest to you, and use filters to minimize the amount of data returned. In addition, restrict your monitoring to short time periods. The worst two offenders are the Acquired and Released events. If you can avoid collecting them, you will be much better off. The other events do not present such a performance problem.

GENERAL LOCK EVENTS

The first two lock events we want to explore are **Acquired** and **Released**. Every time any sort of lock is used, an Acquired event is fired. And every time a lock is removed, a Released event is fired. In most cases, capturing this raw data is not very interesting. Figure 11-23 shows one example of each type of event:

Figure 11-23: In most cases, the Acquired and Released lock events aren't that useful.

When either event is fired, you can identify the object the lock was taken on (see the ObjectID2 data column) and the type of lock acquired (see the Mode data column). This is a normal type of locking activity and there is generally no point in monitoring it.

The **Cancel** event occurs when a lock on a resource has been cancelled, perhaps due to a cancelled query or a lock being killed due to a deadlock conflict. This is also not generally a very exciting event to track, unless you are experiencing a high volume of cancelled locks and need to investigate.

The **Escalation** event is probably the most interesting of the general lock events. It occurs when a fine-grained lock has been converted to a coarser-grained lock, such as when a record lock or a page lock is escalated. Lock escalation is SQL Server's way of minimizing the amount of resources it takes to manage the many thousands of locks at any one time, and it is a normal process. But in some cases, lock escalation, especially from page to table locks, can cause resource contention issues that sometimes have to be identified and resolved. For example, a query on a table might end up locking an entire table, preventing other users from accessing it until the lock is released.

If your server is experiencing a lot of concurrency problems, you might want to trace the escalation event to see if lock escalation is contributing to the problem. If it is, you may need to rewrite your queries to make them more efficient, or you may need to add more effective indexes. As a last resort you may need to use query hints to control locking behavior.

DEADLOCK LOCK EVENTS

A deadlock occurs when two or more spids try to lock on the same resource and therefore block each other. Neither spid can complete its task, but nor can the resource be released until each spid completes its task, so a deadlock occurs. In most cases, the spid that has used the fewest resources up to the point of the deadlock will be automatically killed by a SQL Server lock monitor thread, allowing the other spid to complete.

Profiler includes three events related to deadlocking:

- Deadlock Graph
- Deadlock
- Deadlock Chain

You can find out more about these events, in great depth, in Chapter 5 of this book.

TIMEOUT LOCK EVENTS

By default, connections from a client to SQL Server do not timeout due to blocking locks. A connection will wait for as long as it needs to wait for a blocking lock to be cleared.

NOTE:

While SQL Server will not, by default, timeout a connection between a client and SQL Server, it is possible that the client will timeout the connection, depending on how the client connection was configured by the developer.

As an option, when a connection is made, the **SET LOCK_TIMEOUT** command can be used to establish a specific timeout value, overriding the default behavior. If this option has been turned on for a connection, then either of the two Timeout Lock events – **Timeout** or **Timeout (timeout >0)** – can be captured to indicate when a lock times out due to this setting. If the **SET LOCK_TIMEOUT** command is not being used, then the Timeout Lock events won't fire.

Timeout and Timeout (timeout >0) provide almost identical functionality. The difference is that the Timeout event can fire if a Timeout event of zero occurs. A Timeout of zero can occur due to internal SQL Server activity and is not very useful. If you do use the **SET LOCK_TIMEOUT** command to control how long blocking locks exists before they timeout, you will want to capture the Timeout (timeout >0) Profiler event. Each time a timeout occurs due to a blocking lock, the Timeout (timeout>0) event will be fired so the Profiler can trace the event.

OBJECTS

The three events in the Objects event category are all DDL-related audit events. In other words, these events are fired when any object is created, altered, or deleted. The events include:

- Altered
- Created
- Deleted

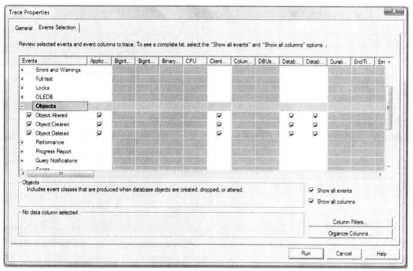

Figure 11-27: You can audit object creation, alteration and deletion activity using these events.

To see how these events track object Created, Altered, and Deleted activity, I ran the following test script. It instigates all three types of event in the AdventureWorks database:

```
CREATE TABLE MyTest
    (
        CustID INT IDENTITY(1000, 1)
                PRIMARY KEY,
        CompanyName NVARCHAR(50)
```

```
     )
go

ALTER TABLE MyTest ALTER COLUMN CompanyName
NVARCHAR(100)
go

DROP TABLE MyTest
go
```

The Profiler results are as shown in Figure 11-28:

EventClass	ApplicationName	ClientProcessID	DatabaseID	DatabaseName	EventSequence	EventSubClass	HostName	IndexID	IntegerData	IsSystem	LoginName
Trace Start											
Object:Created	Microsoft ...	1684	5	Adventureworks	412	0 - Begin	PELE		1		pele\Brad
Object:Created	Microsoft ...	1684	5	Adventureworks	413	0 - Begin	PELE				pele\Brad
Object:Created	Microsoft ...	1684	5	Adventureworks	413	1 - Commit	PELE				pele\Brad
Object:Created	Microsoft ...	1684	5	Adventureworks	412	1 - Commit	PELE				pele\Brad
Object:Altered	Microsoft ...	1684	5	Adventureworks	415	0 - Begin	PELE				pele\Brad
Object:Altered	Microsoft ...	1684	5	Adventureworks	415	1 - Commit	PELE				pele\Brad
Object:Deleted	Microsoft ...	1684	5	Adventureworks	417	0 - Begin	PELE				pele\Brad
Object:Deleted	Microsoft ...	1684	5	Adventureworks	417	1 - Commit	PELE				pele\Brad
Trace Stop											

Figure 11-28: While Object events can be useful for auditing DDL-type activity, they can be a little hard to read.

The first thing you will notice, from the EventSubClass column, is that every event is wrapped in a transaction. So, for every object Created, Altered or Deleted action, you will always see two events; one representing the Begin Transaction and one representing the Commit Transaction.

However, you still might be wondering why we see four Object:Created events instead of two. The reason for this is that implied in the table creation command is the creation of a primary key. The first Created event refers to the table and the second to the primary key.

So, how is this information useful to the DBA? Essentially, you can use these events to find out who is creating, altering or deleting objects in your SQL Server, together with when they did it. This is probably not something that you will do often, but if you have a problem with the mysterious appearance and disappearance of database objects, and nobody admits to making any changes, using this Profiler option will make it very easy to identify the guilty party.

OLEDB

The OLEDB event category includes five events specifically related to when SQL Server uses an OLE DB provider when making distributed queries and remote procedure calls. It is mostly of use to developers, not production DBAs.

If your SQL Server environment doesn't use distributed queries or remote procedure calls, then you will not find any use for these particular

Profiler events. If it does, then these events may "help" developers troubleshoot problems that can't be easily diagnosed by other tools. I emphasize the word "help" in the last sentence because the events provided are better than nothing, but they don't provide as much information as you might like when troubleshooting. The five events are:

- **OLEDB Call**: This event is fired when SQL Server calls an OLE DB provider for a distributed query or remote stored procedure, but for only those calls that do not return data or do not use the QueryInterface method

- **OLEDB DataRead**: This event is fired when SQL Server calls an OLE DB provider for a distributed query or remote procedure call, but only for those calls that return data.

- **OLEDB Errors**: This is probably the most useful event to collect; it notifies you of specific OLE DB-related errors, should they occur. It identifies the name of the instance making the call, the name of the linked server, and the specific error message, along with additional information that is useful in identifying where and when the error occurred.

- **OLEDB Provider Information**: Performance tuning distributed queries or remote stored procedure calls can sometimes be difficult. The data columns collected by this event can be used to help optimize query performance. However, this is a complex process requiring considerable experience.

- **OLEDB QueryInterface**: This event is used to capture those OLE DB events related to a QueryInterface call. It is designed to fire when an OLE DB provider returns an OLE DB error object, and is used for troubleshooting problems with OLE DB providers.

When using any of these events to collect Profiler data, keep in mind that the overhead of collecting OLE DB data can be great, especially if your instance is performing a lot of distributed queries or remote procedure calls. Be sure to limit the time period for which you collect data, ideally only starting a trace when you think a problem will occur, or is already occurring, and turning the trace off after you have captured your data.

From a production DBA's perspective, these events would only be collected if you are having problems with distributed queries or remote procedure calls and you have run out of ideas where to look next to find out the root cause.

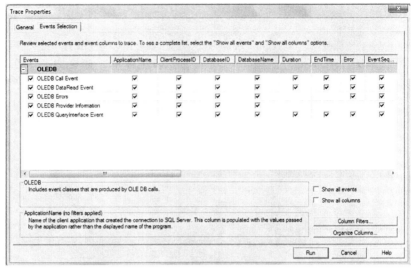

Figure 11-29: OLEDB events are used to identify problems with distributed queries or remote stored procedures.

PERFORMANCE

The Performance events category includes twelve events; a lot to consider. Fortunately, only a handful of these events are useful on a regular basis. The 12 Performance events are:

- Auto Stats
- Degree of Parallelism (7.0 Insert)
- Performance Statistics
- SQL:FullTextQuery
- Showplan All (deprecated, replace with Showplan XML)
- Showplan All For Query Compile (deprecated, replace with Showplan XML for Query Compile)
- Showplan Statistics Profile (deprecated, replace with Showplan XML Statistics Profile)
- Showplan Text (deprecated, replace with Showplan XML)
- Showplan Text (Unencoded) (deprecated, replace with Showplan XML)
- Showplan XML
- Showplan XML for Query Compile
- Showplan XML Statistics Profile

To save time, I won't be discussing the deprecated events listed above I'll cover all of the remaining seven Performance events, but will focus on those events that are of the most benefit to DBAs.

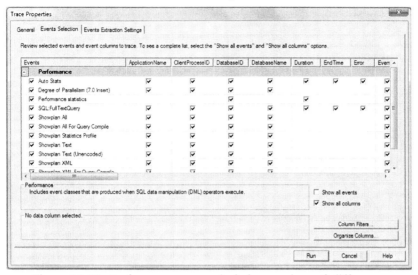

Figure 11-30: Performance events include a variety of different ways to identify performance-related issues.

AUTO STATS

The purpose of the Auto Stats event is to determine how often statistics updates occur. If you are using asynchronous auto stats, instead of synchronous stats, you can also find out about the status of the asynchronous update. This information can be used to help the DBA determine if auto stats is running more often than it needs to, if it is running at inappropriate times, or to find out how well asynchronous auto stats is performing.

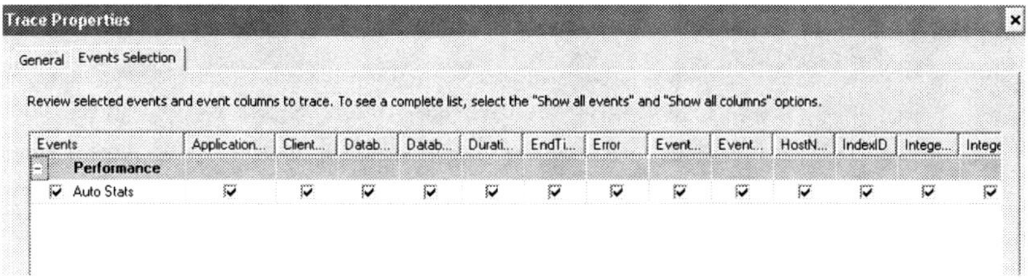

Figure 11-31: Auto Stats events are easy to capture with Profiler.

To find out how auto stats is behaving in your server, you only need to capture the Auto Stats events. Other events are not required, but might be useful in some cases.

In Figure 11-32, you can see a Profiler trace of Auto Stats events.

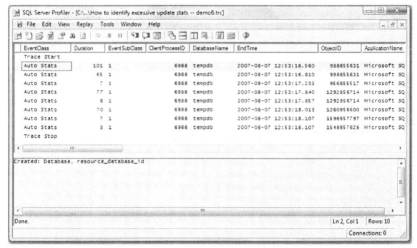

Figure 11-32: The Auto Stats event can tell you when and where auto stats are occurring in your server.

When analyzing a trace of Auto Stats, what you are looking for includes:

- How often are auto stats being run
- How long it is taking to run auto stats
- Which databases and objects are incurring the most auto stats events
- What kind of auto stats event it is – synchronous or asynchronous

Based on this information, you can troubleshoot a variety of auto stats problems.

As a general rule of thumb, the Auto Stats event is not one you will commonly use, unless you suspect an auto stats-related problem, and are specifically troubleshooting it. For example, you notice that a query normally has a fairly consistent duration, but occasionally takes much longer to run. Another example would be if you have identified a problem with excessive recompilations due to auto stats activity. Every time auto stats is run, any queries that touch the auto stats indexes or columns have to be recompiled, which can lead to excessive recompilations, hurting server performance.

What can you do if you identify auto stat-related problems? This depends on your particular problems. If you have a problem with inconsistent run times for a query, then turning asynchronous auto stats on might help. If you identify that auto stats occurs too often, or at bad times of the day, you can turn off Auto Stats and manually update index and column statistics at a time when your server is not as busy. But before you do anything, you need to determine you have a problem, and using the Auto Stats event can help you identify and troubleshoot it.

DEGREE OF PARALLELISM (7.0 INSERT)

This oddly named Profiler event is also deceivingly named. It is fired every time a **SELECT**, **INSERT**, **UPDATE** or **DELETE** statement is executed and tells you, among other things, whether or not the execution plan for the query is parallel.

The Degree of Parallelism (7.0 Insert) event is not too useful by itself and should be combined with other events to help put the event itself into context. You might want to consider collecting all the following events to make better sense of what the Degree of Parallelism (7.0 Insert) event is telling you:

- Degree of Parallelism (7.0 Insert)
- Showplan XML
- RPC:Completed
- SP:StmtCompleted
- SQL:StmtCompleted

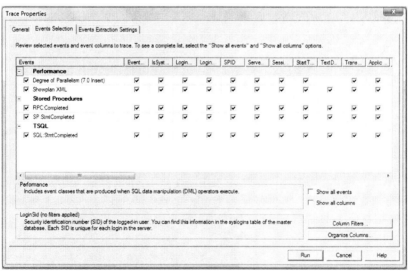

Figure 11-33: Capturing multiple events help to make sense of the Degree of Parallelism (7.0 Insert) event.

When you run the above trace, the captured events look as shown in Figure 11-34:

Figure 11-34: The Degree of Parallelism (7.0 Insert) event, by itself, is not all that useful.

In the first row of this figure, you can see that a stored procedure called ADGSP_EN_SalesInstr is starting. Next, you see the Degree of Parallelism (7.0 Insert) event, which includes two useful pieces of information:

- **BinaryData** – where the possible values are:
  - o 0x00000000 (indicates a serial execution plan)
  - o 0x01000000 (indicates a parallel execution plan running serially)
  - o >= 0x02000000 (indicates a parallel execution plan running in parallel)
- **EventSubClass** – where the possible values are:
  - o 1 - Select
  - o 2 - Insert
  - o 3 - Update
  - o 4 - Delete

From the value of the BinaryData column, you can see that in this case the stored procedure will be running a parallel plan in parallel. The EventSubClass column confirms that it is a SELECT statement that is running. Addition data columns (not shown) indicate the physical resources used by this statement.

The third row shows the graphical execution plan of the statement, which makes it easier to figure out what is going on with this plan. The fourth row indicates when the statement is completed.

So how is this information useful? In most cases, the Degree of Parallelism (7.0 Insert) event is used to help identify poorly-running queries. In some cases, a query would run more effectively in parallel than serially. In other cases, a query would run faster serially than in parallel. This event provides you basic information as to what is really happening with a query, and can be used to help decide if the query plan is as effective as it could be.

If you determine that a query is running serially when it should be running in parallel in order to be most effective (or vice versa), you may consider using an appropriate hint to modify how parallelism behaves for the particular query.

PERFORMANCE STATISTICS

The **Performance Statistics** event is similar to the **Showplan XML For Query Compile** event, which is discussed a little later. As such, you may want to read about both events and determine which better meets your needs.

Like many Profiler events, its name is deceiving. Essentially what the Performance Statistics event does is to fire when a compiled query plan is cached for the first time, compiled, recompiled, or flushed from the cache. It does not fire when a query runs that finds an execution plan already in cache.

As I often do, I like to collect other events that may be of use to me when I am analyzing the results of a trace. In particular, I will be capturing the following events in addition to the Performance Statistics events:

- RPC:Completed
- SP:StmtCompleted
- SQL:StmtCompleted

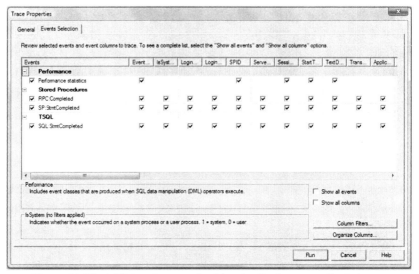

Figure 11-35: Additional events, besides the Performance Statistics event, are useful when analyzing trace data.

Before I ran my test code, I ran the **DBCC FREEPROCCACHE** command in order to remove all currently existing query plans from SQL Server cache. Next, I ran a stored procedure, followed by an ad hoc query. The trace results are shown in Figure 11-36:

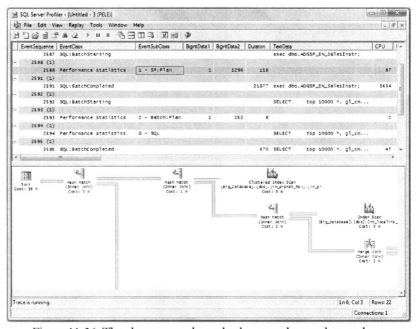

Figure 11-36: The above trace shows both a stored procedure and a query.

The first row of the trace, identified by EventSequence 2587, relates to the execution of a stored procedure named ADGSP_EN_SalesInstr. The next row, EventSequence row 2588, shows that a Performance Statistics event was fired. Last of all, we see that the query was completed in EventSequence row 2591.

So exactly what is the Performance Statistics event telling us? Unlike many other Profiler events, this event is a little harder to decipher.

In the Figure 11-36, I have clicked on the Performance Statistics event that fired for this stored procedure. First of all, notice that the execution plan for this stored procedure is displayed at the bottom of the screen. This is very similar to the ShowPlan XML event, which we will discuss in more detail later.

Second, notice that the EventSubClass for this event is "1 – SP:Plan". The Performance Statistics event can have four different values for EventSubClass:

- 0 – the execution plan for the query or batch is not present in the cache.
- 1 – queries within a stored procedure have been compiled.
- 2 – queries within an ad hoc query have been compiled. It also shows the duration, in milliseconds, for compiling the ad hoc query.
- 3 – a cached query for either a stored procedure or ad hoc query has been removed from memory.

So in our example, an EventSubClass event of 1 indicates that a query within our stored procedure was compiled. In addition:

- The **BigintData1** data column tracks the number of times this plan has been recompiled
- The **BigintData2** data column indicates the size, in kilobytes, of the compiled plan
- The **Duration** column tells you how long, in milliseconds, it took for the query to compile.

Now, let's take a look at the second query I captured, which was an ad hoc query:

```
   2592  SQL:BatchStarting                                    SELECT    top 10000 *, g1_cm...
-  2593 (1)
   2593  Performance statistics    2 - Batch:Plan    1    152    8                              2
-  2594 (1)
   2594  Performance statistics    0 - SQL                     SELECT    top 10000 *, g1_cm...
-  2595 (1)
   2595  SQL:BatchCompleted                             870  SELECT    top 10000 *, g1_cm...    47

SELECT    top 10000 *, g1_cmp_location, in_tran_type
FROM      in_tran_tbl
WHERE     (g1_cmp_location = '01') AND (in_tran_type = 'R');
```

Figure 11-37: This is an example of when an ad hoc query runs.

In **EventSequence** row 2592, we see that the ad hoc batch is starting. To the right, we see a small portion of the query. In **EventSequence** 2593, we see a Performance Statistics event, as shown in Figure 11-38:

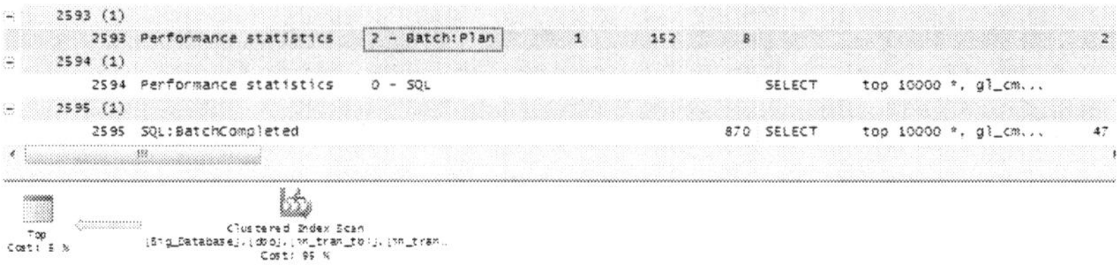

Figure 11-38: A graphical execution plan of this query is displayed above.

For this event, the EventSubClass is 2, which means that an ad hoc query is being compiled. We can also see that it took 8 milliseconds to compile and that it took 152K of memory in the cache. At the bottom of the screen, we see the query execution plan that was created for this ad hoc query. In the next row, with EventSequence 2594, we see a second Performance Statistics event for the same ad hoc query, as shown in figure 11-39:

Figure 11-39: An EventSubClass event of 0 displays the actual code at the bottom of the screen.

In this case, the EventSubClass is 0, it has no compile duration or cache size data, but it does display the ad hoc query at the bottom of the screen. What is this about? Didn't I say earlier that an EventSubClass of 0 means that the query is not in cache? This seems a little confusing given that it was preceded by an event with an EventSubClass of 2.

For whatever reason, when an ad hoc query is first compiled, it creates two Performance Statistics events, a 2 and a 0. Based on the definition of these two EventSubClasses, you would think it would list the 0 EventSubClass first and the 2 EventSubClass second. But it doesn't. These two EventSubClasses only appear when an ad hoc query is run. When a stored procedure is run and compiled for the first time, it only produces a single Performance Statistics event.

If you are really into following the lifecycle of a query, from original compilation to its removal from cache, this event can help you out, assuming you want to put up with the event's odd behavior.

SQL:FULLTEXTQUERY

The SQL:FullTextQuery event is used to troubleshoot Full Text Query problems. If you don't use the Full Text service, you can ignore this event.

If are using the Full Text service, this event can be useful by providing you the following information:

- Length of time to complete the full text query
- Error message number, if any
- The full text of the query

This event can incur a lot of overhead. Limit traces for this event to only those time periods when you want to capture troublesome queries.

SHOWPLAN XML

I've used this event throughout the book so you should be rather familiar with it. If you missed it, this event occurs every time SQL Server executes a SQL statement, producing an estimated graphical execution plan. This is a great tool for analyzing poorly performing queries. In addition, you can export the XML used to generate the graphical execution plan to an XML file.

While you can capture the Showplan XML event by itself, it is generally more useful if you capture it along with some other basic events, such as:

- RPC:Completed
- SQL:BatchStarting
- SQL:BatchCompleted

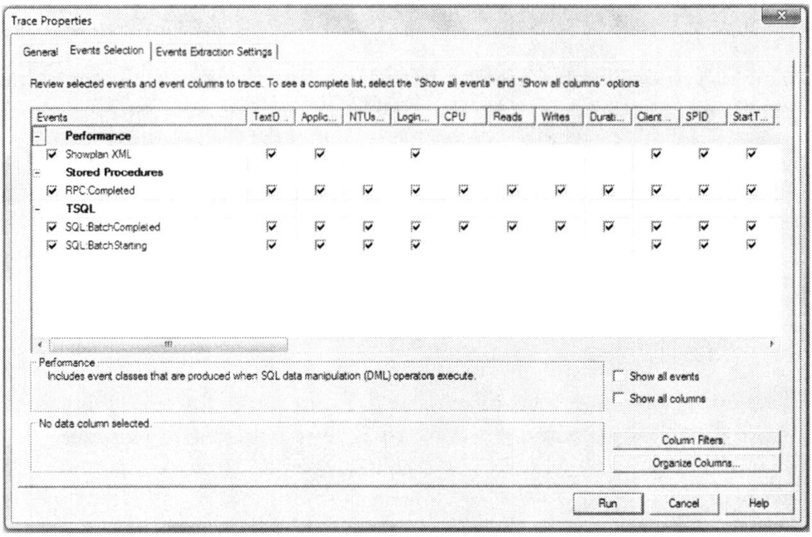

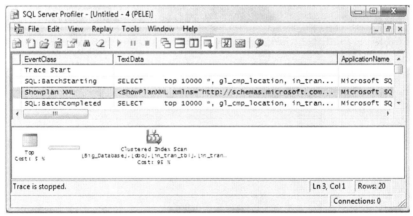

Figure 11-40: The Showplan XML event is one of the most powerful events available with Profiler.

When you capture the above events, you get a trace like the one shown in Figure 11-41:

Figure 11-41: The Showplan XML event captures the XML Showplan and displays it as a graphical execution plan in the Profiler window.

Graphical execution plans provide some of the most useful information available on how a query is executed in SQL Server. In fact, almost every Profiler trace I run includes this event.

Unfortunately, we don't have time to explain how to read graphical execution plans in this book, but if you want to learn more, check out the free e-book from Red Gate Software called *Dissecting SQL Server Execution Plans*, by Grant Fritchey.

If you want, you can save the Showplan XML code directly to a file, instead of just looking at it on the Profiler screen. There are two ways to do this. The first way is to right-click on the Showplan XML event and select "Extract Event Data", as shown in Figure 11-42:

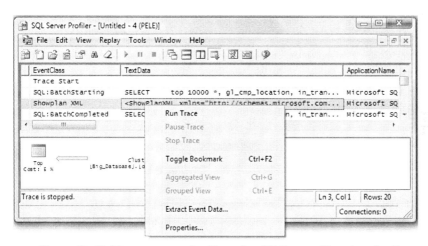

Figure 11-42: You can save the Showplan XML to a file using the Extract Event Data option.

This brings up a dialog box where you can enter the path and filename of the XML code you want to store. Instead of storing the XML code with the typical XML extension, the extension used is **.SQLPlan**. Why? When you double-click on the a .SQLPlan file from within Windows Explorer, the XML code will open up in SSMS in the form of a graphical execution plan. This means that you can share graphical execution plans with other DBAs if you want. However, if you really want to be a geek, you can also open the file in Notepad and see the raw XML code. In fact, there is hidden query performance information stored in the RAW XML. A discussion of this is beyond the scope of this book.

The second way to save the raw XML from Profiler is a little more ambitious. Instead of selecting one Showplan XML event at a time and saving it as a single file, you can have Profiler do this for you automatically for every Showplan XML event. To do this, go to the Trace Properties screen and select the Events Extraction Settings tab, as shown in Figure 11-43:

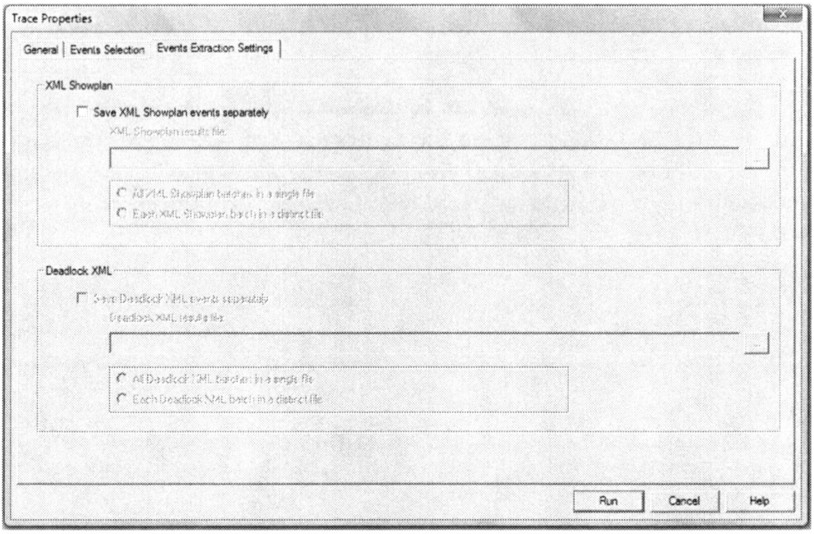

Figure 11-43: The Events Extraction Settings option allows you to save the Showplan XML code automatically for every event captured by Profiler.

Here, you can specify that you want to collect all Showplan XML events, the location in which to store them, and whether you want to store them as one large file or as separate files for each event.

NOTE:

If you don't see the Events Extraction Settings tab, then you haven't selected the Showplan XML event under the Events Selection tab.

As you might guess, using this option produces overhead for a busy server, so use it sparingly.

If you get anything out of this chapter, it should be that the Showplan XML event is one of the most useful and powerful events available to DBAs. You need to take the time to learn how to use it, along with learning how to read graphical execution plans.

SHOWPLAN XML FOR QUERY COMPILE

The Showplan XML for Query Compile event is actually a subset of the Showplan XML event. While the Showplan XML event is fired every time a query is executed, the Showplan XML for Query Compile event only fires when a query is first compiled. If a query is executed that already has an execution plan in cache, then this event does not fire.

Because the Showplan XML for Query Compile is so similar to the Showplan XML event, I don't want to repeat myself, so let's jump into a specific example to show how the two events are different.

For the trace shown in Figure 11-44, I first cleared the cache of all currently existing execution plans and then ran the same ad hoc query as in the Showplan XML example:

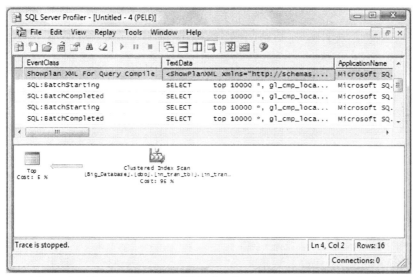

Figure 11-44: The Showplan XMP for Query Compile event only fires when a query is compiled just before it is executed.

Just before the query executes, the Showplan XML for Query Compile event fires and you can see the graphical execution plan for the query. Once the plan for the query compiles, the query is executed. I executed the query multiple times but since the plan for this query is already in cache, the Showplan XML for Query Compile event doesn't fire again.

The Showplan for Query Compile is useful for troubleshooting query compilations, and uses less overhead than does the Showplan XML event (as fewer events are captured). And just as for the Showplan XML event, you can extract the raw XML and save it to disk.

SHOWPLAN XML STATISTICS PROFILE

By now, I bet you are getting tired of Showplan XML events. But wait, there is one more to consider. The Showplan XML Statistics Profile event is like the Showplan XML event in that it fires every time a query is executed. It also produces a graphical execution plan that can be exported to a raw XML file. So what is the difference between the two?

The difference is that the Showplan XML Statistics Profile includes additional statistics not included in the Showplan XML event.

The curious thing is that if you run the Showplan XML and Showplan XML Statistics Profile events at the same time, the data returned in Profiler looks virtually identical in each case. If this is the case, how are these events different? In fact, the differences are there, just hidden. The Showplan XML Statistics Profile event hides the additional statistics within the raw XML code, which can't be seen from Profiler. In order to see the differences in the data collected, Showplan XML Statistics Profile events need to be stored in a local database table and viewed there. Then you have to write an XML-based query to extract the statistics data. As you can imagine, this is beyond the scope of this book. However, if you are an XML fan, you can find out more about how to write this code here:

http://blogs.msdn.com/sqlqueryprocessing/
rss_tag_Statistics+Profile.xml

As it is implemented currently, the Showplan XML Statistics Profile event is not very convenient to use.

PROGRESS REPORT

This event category includes a single event: Online Index Operation. It is used to monitor online index activity that results from creating, rebuilding or dropping indexes. Online indexing is only available on SQL Server 2005 Enterprise Edition.

A significant performance issue with an online index operation should be a rarity. However, if you do experience issues, you may want to investigate, using the Online Index Operation event.

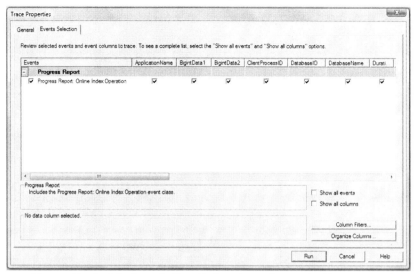

Figure 11-45: Monitor Online Index Operation only if your are having performance problems during online indexing activities.

If you decide to capture a Profiler trace of online indexing activity, you will want to start the capture just before the online indexing activity actually starts, and end it when it is complete. Otherwise, you are just wasting server resources.

The key information provided by the Online Index Operation event is found in the EventSubClass data column. In this column you will see the status of the online index activity. The available subclass events are:

- 1 = Start
- 2 = Stage 1 execution begins
- 3 = Stage 1 execution ends
- 4 = Stage 2 execution begins
- 5 = Stage 2 execution ends
- 6 = Inserted row count
- 7 = Done

While the Online Index Operations event is useful to identify the status of the online index activities, it is more useful if you combine this event with other events, such as those related to blocking and performance. In addition, you may want to run a concurrent Performance Monitor trace in order to determine where, if any, bottlenecks are occurring during the online index activity. By correlating the Profiler results with the Performance Monitor results, you can more easily identify problem areas.

NOTE:

Correlating Profiler and Performance Monitor results is covered in Chapter 8.

If you discover that online index operations are indeed contributing to unacceptable performance problems, you may need to reschedule when they occur.

QUERY NOTIFICATIONS

SQL Server 2005 introduced a new feature called Query Notifications, which is built on the Service Broker. Essentially, Query Notifications allows applications to be notified automatically when data in the database has changed. If you are not using Query Notifications in your applications, then you can skip this event category. If you are, then the four events in the Query Notification category can help you to identify performance issues and to debug application problems. The four events are:

- **QN: Dynamics** – Provides information on the background activity SQL Server performs to support query notification. This includes: clock run started, clock run finished, master cleanup task started, master cleanup task finished, and master cleanup task skipped.

- **QN: Parameter Table** – Provides information on the internal tables used to store parameter information, including: table created, table drop attempt, table drop attempt failed, table dropped, table pinned, table unpinned, number of users incremented, number of users decremented, LRU counter reset, cleanup task started, cleanup task finished.

- **QN: Subscription Event** – Provides information on subscriptions, including: subscription registered, subscription rewound, subscription fired, firing failed with broker error, firing failed without broker error, broker error intercepted, subscription deletion attempt, subscription deletion failed, and subscription destroyed.

- **QN: Template** – Provides information on the use on query templates, including: template created, template matched, and template dropped.

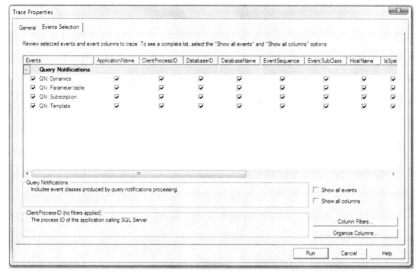

Figure 11-46: Query Notifications can be traced by using the above four events.

Since Query Notifications is built upon the Service Broker and also involves queries, you will probably want to trace the following events in addition to the Query Notification events:

- Broker Events (all that are appropriate)
- RPC:Completed
- SQL:BatchStarting
- SQL:BatchCompleted

When collecting so many events, it is important to run only such a Profiler trace for as short as time as you can in order to minimize its performance impact.

SCANS

Index and table scans are a fact of life. It is not always possible, or even efficient, for a set of data to be retrieved by an index seek. In other words, the appearance of index or table scans in an execution plan is not necessarily a reason to assume the query is performing inefficiently. In effect, some scans are "good", and the queries they are found in don't need to be tuned; and some scans are "bad," and the queries they are found in need performance tuning. While the discussion of how to tell a "good" scan from a "bad" one is outside the scope of this book, a high level of scan events in a Profiler trace may be an indication that you have more "bad" scans that would be optimal for the performance of your server.

The Scans event category includes two events:

- Scan: Started
- Scan: Stopped

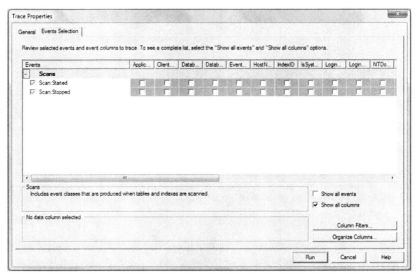

Figure 11-47: Both index and table scans are identified using the Scan events.

The scans identified by these two events can be either index or table scans and you can use the IndexID data column to determine which are which.

First of all, collecting both the "Scan:Started" and "Scan:Stopped" events are somewhat redundant, as both events indicate that a scan is being performed, which is all we really want to know. You may sometimes want to capture both events and calculate the duration, but this won't be common. What we really want to know is how many scans, of any type, are being performed, and to identify those that appear to be excessive.

Besides the single Scan:Started event, I also like to include the following context events when I am performing a Profiler trace with the goal of identifying excessive scans:

- Showplan XML
- RPC:Completed
- SP:StmtCompleted
- SQL:BatchStarting
- SQL:BatchCompleted

This way, when a trace is collected, you can see exactly what Transact-SQL is causing the scans. In addition, you get to see the execution plan of the offending query, which provides you with additional information that can help you determine if the scan you have identified is a "good" or a "bad" one.

When I perform a Scan trace, I also like to group the scan by the EventClass data column, which produces a screen like the following:

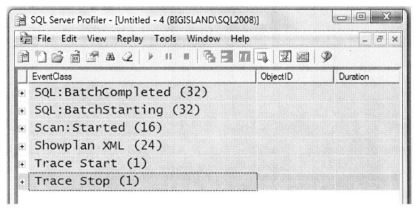

Figure 11-48: Grouping by the EventClass data column makes it easy to determine if scans are a problem.

For example, in the above trace it is very easy to see that there were only 16 Scan:Started events that occurred during the capture. If this data was captured over an hour, I would be very happy, as only 16 scans happening in a single hour would be a very good thing. On the other hand, if I discovered 124,843 Scan:Started events in a single hour, then I would want to investigate why there are so many. At this point, I would then drill down into the trace data, identifying what Transact-SQL code is contributing to the most scans, and then analyzing the code to see if the scans were "good" and could be ignored, or "bad" scans that indicated I need to review the code and look for ways to boost its performance.

SECURITY AUDIT

The Security Audit event category has more events than any other, a total of 43.

NOTE:

If you want to learn more about how to audit SQL Server activity using Profiler, see Chapter 6, "Using Profiler to Audit Database Activity."

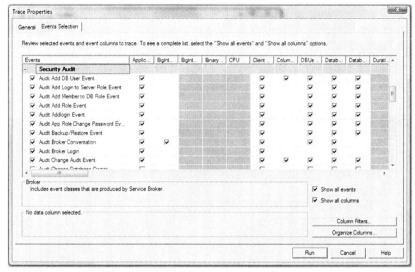

Figure 11-51: The Security Audit category has 43 events.

Typically, you use Security Audit events to track what users are doing inside a SQL Server instance. While Profiler can do this, there are several disadvantages to using Profiler for this purpose on anything but a part-time basis. For example, using Profiler to audit SQL Server instances can be very resource-intensive. A busy server can create thousands of Security audit events per minute, which means resources have to be diverted from SQL Server to Profiler. If your SQL Server is not particularly busy, this might not be a problem.

Profiler also doesn't make it particularly easy to extract the information you want from the collected data. Essentially you need to store the data in a database and then create queries to extract the data you want, which is all a manual process.

Lastly, configuring what audit events to collect, along with which data columns, is not convenient using the included GUI interface.

Yes, you can perform security auditing with Profiler, but it is far from ideal if you need to do security auditing on a continuing basis. On the other hand, if you only need to perform security auditing for short periods, then Profiler can work well for you.

SERVER

The Server event category is another one of those categories that encompasses an odd collection of events. The three events in this category are:

- Mount Tape

- Trace File Close
- Server Memory Change

We'll take a brief look at the first two, and spend a little extra time on the Server Memory Change event, which is of more interest – and use – to DBAs.

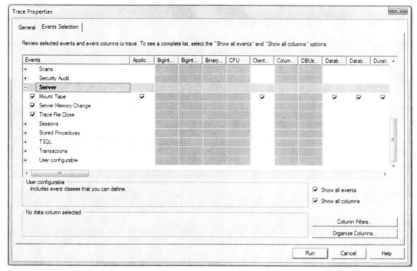

Figure 11-52: The Server event category includes widely varying event types.

MOUNT TAPE

This event will tell you when a tape mount request on your SQL Server was requested, completed, or cancelled. While I am sure there are some DBAs who use this feature on SQL Server, I have never personally met one.

TRACE FILE CLOSE

This event fires when a trace file has been closed during a rollback. This can occur when you are playing back a trace file in Profiler. I have not personally found any reason to want to trace this.

SERVER MEMORY CHANGE

Of the three events in the Server events category, this event is the most interesting. This event fires when the memory of a SQL Server instance increases or decreases by either 1mb or 5% of the maximum server memory allocated to SQL Server, whichever is greater.

When you collect this event, all it shows is when the event occurred, if the event was a memory increase or a memory decrease, and the new memory size, in mb's. There is no indication why the event occurred.

To put the Server Memory event in context, I usually capture some additional events, such as:

- RPC:Completed
- SQL:BatchStarting
- SQL:BatchCompleted

In the trace shown in Figure 11-53, there are four Server Memory events, grouped in two sets of two:

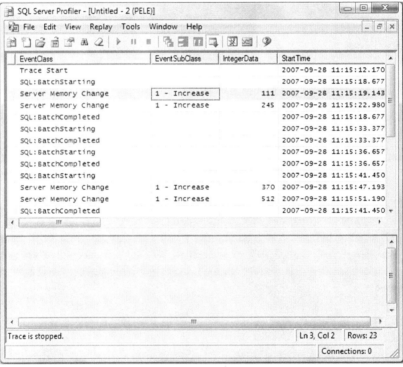

Figure 11-53: You can trace when SQL Server increases or decreases its need for memory.

In the first Server Memory Change event, the amount of memory was raised to 111mb. Almost immediately afterwards, it went up to 245mb. About 27 seconds later, memory went to 370mb, then to 512mb. I have my test system limited to a maximum of 512MB, so memory can't increase any further. However, it is already obvious that the code I was running was consuming a lot of memory, very quickly.

Fortunately, this example is not typical. Once a server has been up and running for a while, you're unlikely to see this sort of activity. In other words, once SQL Server has started and begins to use memory, it grabs the amount it needs and memory requirements generally don't change a whole lot, unless unusual activity occurs.

I don't collect this event on a regular basis because when I want to track memory usage of SQL Server, I generally use Performance Monitor instead. While Performance Monitor might not provide the exact data (the increases or decreases of 5%) it provides a wealth of other useful memory-related counters that generally provide all the memory data I need to troubleshoot problems.

SESSIONS

The Sessions event category has a single event: **ExistingConnection**. Its sole purpose is to provide a list of currently existing user connections (at the time the Profiler trace started), providing connection data for each connection.

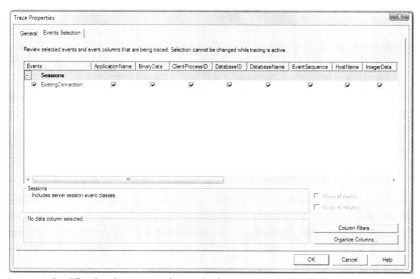

11-54: The Sessions event has a single event: ExistingConnection

Whenever you begin a Profiler Trace, using the ExistingConnection event, a list of all currently existing connections appears as rows at the top of the Profiler window. When you click on any of the connections, you see the connection information at the bottom of the screen, as shown in Figure 11-55:

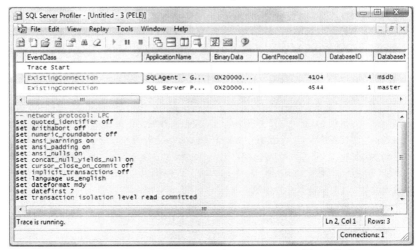

Figure 11-55: The ExistingConnection event provides all the connection settings for all current connections at the time the Profiler trace begins.

This event only fires when Profiler first starts. Once Profiler starts and all existing connections are displayed in Profiler, this event does not fire any more and any new connections made after a Profiler trace begins are not added to the list.

The connection information provided by the ExistingConnection event can be handy when troubleshooting connection problems, and to help identify the differences between connections. Different connection settings can affect how a query is processed and sometimes the only way to troubleshoot such a problem is to see what the connection settings are.

STORED PROCEDURES

The Stored Procedures event category includes 12 events and is probably one of the most useful set of events available in Profiler. These events can be used to troubleshoot many different types of stored procedure-related problem. Because of this, we will take our time in this section. The 12 events are:

- RPC:Output Parameter
- RPC:Completed
- RPC:Starting
- SP:CacheHit
- SP:CacheInsert
- SP:CacheMiss
- SP:CacheRemove

- SP:Completed
- SP:Recompile
- SP:Starting
- SP:StmtCompleted
- SP:StmtStarting

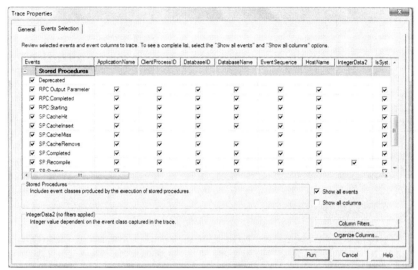

Figure 11-56: There are 12 events available in the Stored Procedures event category.

You have probably already noticed that several of these events above have been discussed previously in this chapter, and throughout the book. This is because many events in the Stored Procedure events category are useful to collect together with other events, giving you a better view of what is happening in your server.

Before we jump into the discussion of individual events, let's first take consider the RPC and SP prefixes found before each of these events. Three of the events begin with RPC, and the rest begin with SP. RPC stands for Remote Procedure Call, and SP stands for Stored Procedure. The two prefixes refer to different ways in which a stored procedure can be called.

If a stored procedure is called using an ODBC CALL escape sequence or an OLE DB RPC escape sequence, then it is picked up by the RPC events. If you create a .NET SqlCommand object and assign it a CommandType of "StoredProcedure," this will also create an RPC event.

If a stored procedure is called by the Transact-SQL Execute statement, then it is picked up by the SP events. If you create a .NET SqlCommand object and assign it a CommandType of "Text," this will also create an SP event.

You won't always know how an application will call a stored procedure, so it is a good idea to capture both RPC and SP events to ensure that you don't miss anything. More often than not, you will find SP events much more common than RPC events.

RPC:OUTPUT PARAMETER

When a stored procedure executes, an output parameter can be returned, which can be used by the called application. The RPC:Output Parameter event is designed to capture the output parameters from a stored procedure executed as a remote procedure call. This can be handy when debugging application code, checking to see if the stored procedure is outputting what you expect it to output. This event does not return output parameters from a stored procedure called by the Transact-SQL EXECUTE statement.

RPC:COMPLETED

The RPC:Completed event fires after a stored procedure is executed as a remote procedure call. The default data columns collected for this event include useful information about the execution of the stored procedure, including the CPU time used to execute the stored procedure, the total length of time the stored procedure ran, logical reads and writes that occurred during its execution, along with the name of the stored procedure itself.

RPC:STARTING

The RPC:Starting event fires when a stored procedure is first executed as a remote procedure call. In many cases, DBAs don't even bother tracing this event as the information it provides is a subset of what the RPC:Completed offers.

SP:CACHEHIT

When a client application requests that a stored procedure be executed, one of the first things the query optimizer does is to determine if the stored procedure's execution plan has been cached or not. If it has, then the stored procedure can most likely reuse the plan, saving time. The SP:CacheHit event is fired every time that a stored procedure is about to be executed and the query optimizer has determined that there is a matching execution plan available in cache.

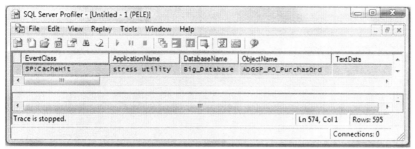

Figure 11-57: SP CacheHit indicates that the query optimizer has determined that the execution plan for the stored procedure is already in cache.

In the example shown in Figure 11-57, you can see that an SP:CacheHit event occurred when the ADGSP_PO_PurchasOrd stored procedure ran, because the execution plan for this stored procedure was already in cache. When a SP:CacheHit event occurs, the EventSubClass data column can take one of two values:

- 1 = Execution Context Hit – a free execution plan was found in the plan cache.
- 2 = Compplan Hit – a compiled plan was found in the plan cache.

This event is handy when you are trying to identify if a particular stored procedure's execution plan is being used over and over. In most cases this is a good thing, but at other times it can be a bad thing. This event, in the context of others in this event category, can make this kind of troubleshooting easier.

SP:CACHEINSERT

When the query optimizer has to create an execution plan, because one doesn't already exist in the plan cache, it has to take that plan and insert it into the plan cache so that it can be used the next time the stored procedure is executed. When this happens, an SP:CacheInsert event is fired.

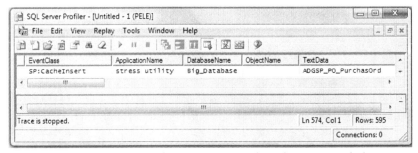

Figure 11-58: An SP:CacheInsert occurs when the query optimizer puts an execution plan into cache.

The SP:CacheInsert event can be used to help identify stored procedures that are being recompiled too often, or that are being removed from the cache too soon due to a lack of available memory to store cached plans. Each SP:CacheInsert event indicates that a stored procedure had to be compiled for some reason. The reason for this is not provided by the event.

SP:CacheMiss

The SP:CacheMiss event indicates that an execution plan for a stored procedure is not in the plan cache, causing the query optimizer to create a new execution plan.

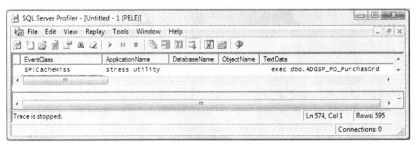

Figure 11-59: An SP:CacheMiss occurs when a stored procedure that is to be executed does not have an execution plan currently in cache.

One of the implications for the SP:CacheMiss event is that this stored procedure's execution plan could have been in the plan cache, but wasn't. This could mean that this is the first time the stored procedure has run. Or, it could mean that the stored procedure was moved out of the plan cache by SQL Server because there was not enough memory to retain it.

If you see a lot of SP:CacheMiss events for a particular stored procedure throughout the day, and this procedure runs often, it may mean your server is low on memory, forcing the execution plan to be constantly moved out of the plan cache due to lack of memory to retain it.

SP:CACHEREMOVE

Sometimes, SQL Server decides that it needs memory for a particular internal need, and because of a lack of available memory, decides to reduce the amount of RAM given to the plan cache. When this happens, currently existing execution plans are removed from the plan cache and the SP:CacheRemove event fires. If you see a lot of these events, it is a strong indication that your server needs more RAM for the existing workload.

SP:COMPLETED

Aptly named, the SP:Completed event fires when a stored procedure completes executing. The data columns return some very useful information, including the name of the stored procedure, the total duration for which the stored procedure ran, the number of rows it returned from all statements included in it, and more.

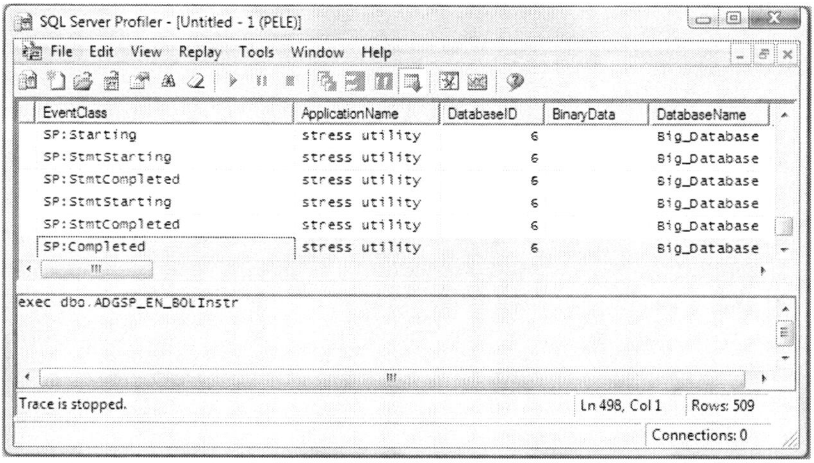

Figure 11-60: The SP: Completed events occurs when a stored procedure has complete executing.

In the example in Figure 11-60, the first row shows a SP:Starting event, which tells us that a new stored procedure has begun to execute. Then there are several statements within the stored procedure that execute and, finally, the SP: Completed event occurs, letting us know that execution of the stored procedure is complete.

SP:RECOMPILE

This event is deprecated. Instead, you should instead use the SQL:StmtRecompile event, which is included in the TSQL event category.

SP:STARTING

Like the SP:Completed event, the SP:Starting event is aptly named and fires whenever a stored procedure begins executing.

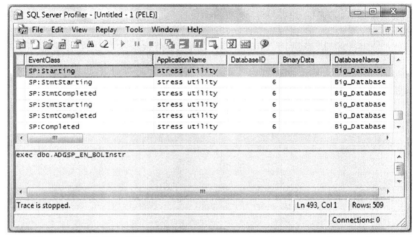

Figure 11-61: The SP: Starting events signals when a stored procedure begins execution.

While the SP:Starting event is a handy way to indicate the beginning of the execution of a stored procedure, the event's data columns don't provide a lot of useful information beyond this. Many DBAs consider this event optional when they collect trace data, as this information is essentially a subset of what the SP: Completed event provides.

SP:STMTCOMPLETED

Stored procedures are made up of one or more SQL statements. In SQL Server, each statement within a stored procedure creates a separate event. As you have already guessed, the SP:StmtCompleted event indicates when a statement within a stored procedure has ended.

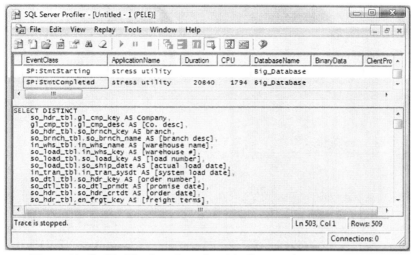

Figure 11-62: SP: The StmtCompleted indicates when a statement within a stored procedure ends.

The SP:StmtCompleted event's data columns provide lots of useful information about the statement, including the actual code in the statement, the duration for which the statement ran, the amount of CPU time used, the number of logical reads and writes, and the number of rows returned by the statement, among others. This is a very commonly collected event and is very useful to the DBA.

SP:STMTSTARTING

The SP:StmtStarting event, as you may have guessed, indicates when a statement within a stored procedure begins.

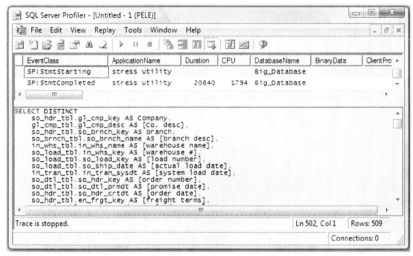

Figure 11-63: The SP: StmtStarting event indicates when a new statement within a stored procedure begins.

Like the SP:Starting event, the SP:StmtStarting event is useful to help place a statement in context of what else is going on in a server, but is of little further use. As such, many DBAs also consider the SP: StmtStarting event an optional event because it is essentially a subset of the SP: StmtCompleted event.

TSQL

While the previous section focuses on stored procedure activity, the TSQL event category focuses on Transact-SQL activity, as found in batches and individual SQL statements.

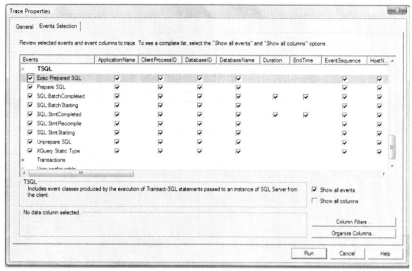

Figure 11-64: The TSQL event category has three distinct types of event.

The TSQL events fall into three distinct subcategories, so I will discuss them as three separate groups.

Batch and Statement Level Events

- SQL:BatchStarting
- SQL:BatchCompleted
- SQL:StmtStarting
- SQL:StmtCompleted
- SQL:StmtRecompile

Prepare/Execute Model Events

- Prepare SQL
- Exec Prepared SQL
- Unprepare SQL

XML Event

- XQuery Static Type

BATCH AND STATEMENT LEVEL EVENTS

A batch is a group of Transact-SQL statements that run as a single unit. A batch might include a single Transact-SQL statement, or it might include many separate Transact-SQL statements. The TSQL event category includes both batch starting and completion events, along with statement level starting and completion events. As you might expect, when a batch (with one or more statements) is executed, the batch starting event occurs first, then the statement level starting and completion events (one for each statement); when all the statements are run, a batch completed event occurs.

SQL:BATCHSTARTING

An SQL:BatchStarting event is fired whenever a new batch begins. Once a batch begins, then one or more individual Transact-SQL statements are executed.

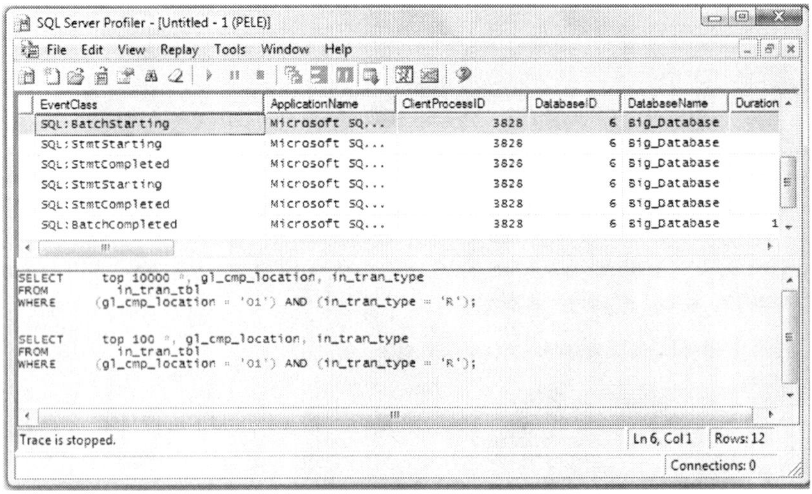

Figure 11-65: All batches begin with an SQL:BatchStarting event.

Like the SP:Starting and SP:StmtStarting events, the SQL:BatchStarting event allows you to see clearly where a batch begins. Other than this, it is not particularly useful.

SQL:BATCHCOMPLETED

The SQL:BatchCompleted event occurs when a batch completes. This means that one or more Transact-SQL statements within this batch have completed execution.

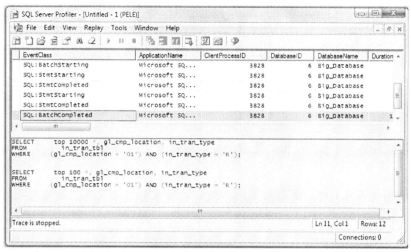

Figure 11-66: The SQL:BatchCompleted event fires when a batch is done.

The SQL:BatchCompleted event is more useful than the SQL:BatchStarting event because it includes useful information like the duration of the entire batch, the logical number of reads and physical writes caused by all the statements inside the batch, the total number of rows returned by the batch, and more. Many DBAs use the SQL:BatchCompleted event, but not the SQL:BatchStarting event, as the latter is just a subset of the SQL:BatchCompleted event.

SQL:StmtStarting

Once a batch starts, then the individual statements within the batch are executed, one at a time. The SQL:StmtStarting event is fired as the execution of each individual statement begins.

Notice in the batch that there are two SQL:StmtStarting events, indicating two Transact-SQL events in this batch. Like the SQL:BatchStarting event, the SQL:StmtStarting event is useful to identify when a new statement is being executed.

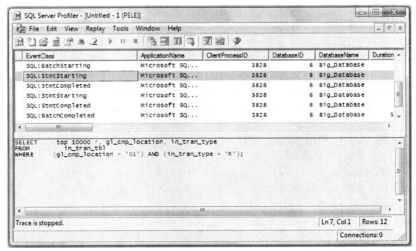

Figure 11-67: The SQL:StmtStarting event occurs at the beginning of every new Transact-SQL statement.

SQL:STMTCOMPLETED

The SQL:StmtCompleted event occurs when an individual SQL statement completes execution.

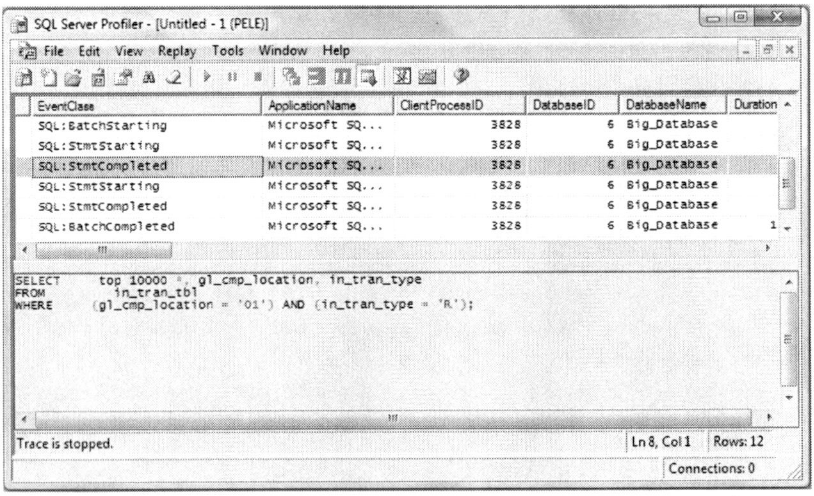

Figure 11-68: The SQL:StmtCompleted event occurs after each SQL:StmtStarting event.

In the example shown in Figure 11-68, you see two SQL:StmtCompleted events because there are two Transact-SQL events in this particular batch. Once again, the data columns that accompany the SQL:StmtCompleted event provide useful information regarding the duration of the entire statement, the logical number of reads and physical writes caused by the statement, the total number of rows returned by the statement, and so on.

SQL:STMTRECOMPILE

Starting with SQL Server 2005, recompilation of Transact-SQL code occurs at the statement level, not at the batch or stored procedure level. Because of this, the SQL:StmtRecompile can be used with both Stored Procedure and TSQL events to identify Transact-SQL code that recompiles.

Generally speaking, when the a Transact-SQL statement is sent to the query optimizer, it first checks to see if the Transact-SQL statement already has an execution plan in the plan cache. If it does not, then a new execution plan is created. If it does find an execution plan, then it is usually reused.

Occasionally, an execution plan exists in the plan cache, but the query optimizer doesn't want to use it, preferring instead to recompile the statement. Why? There are a variety of possible reasons, including:

* Schema changed
* Statistics changed
* There is a deferred compile
* A SET option changed
* A temp table changed
* A remote rowset changed
* For Browse permissions changed
* The query notification environment changed
* A partition view changed
* Cursor options changed
* A recompile request was made

If you check the EventSubClass data column for this event, it will tell you for which of these reasons the Transact-SQL statement was recompiled.

If any table or view accessed by the Transact-SQL code is subject to any of the above changes, between the time the code is first recompiled and the time it needs to execute again, then the Query Optimizer will force the code to recompile. This is because any of these changes could negatively affect the performance of the existing execution plan, so a new plan needs to be created in order to ensure an optimal execution plan is used.

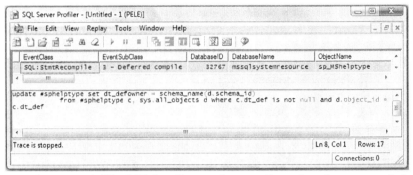

Figure 11-69: The SQL:StmtRecompile event fires when the query optimizer identifies a reason why a particular statement should be recompiled.

In many cases, a recompile is a necessary event, so seeing SQL:StmtRecompile events in a trace file is normal. On the other hand, excessive recompiles indicates a potential problem. So, if you see a lot of these events, you will want to investigate them, especially if they are occurring over and over for the same Transact-SQL statement.

PREPARE/EXECUTE MODEL EVENTS

In some cases, applications that use the SqlClient, ODBC, OLE DB, or DB-Library prepare a SQL statement that is sent to SQL Server to be executed. This can involve up to three steps:

1. Preparation of the SQL statement into an execution plan (Prepare SQL)

2. The execution of the SQL statement (Exec Prepared SQL)

3. Removing the execution plan from the plan cache (Unprepare SQL).

This occurs for applications that use the prepare/execute model to communicate with SQL Server. For too many reasons to discuss here, the prepare/execute model is not the ideal way to communicate with SQL Server and should be avoided. Most applications do not use this model, so it is not much of an issue, and you will not have to worry about tracing the three related TSQL events: Prepare SQL, Exec Prepared SQL, and Unprepare SQL.

On the other hand, if you have poorly-performing applications and notice that it is using the Prepare/Execute model to communicate with SQL Server, then you can use these three TSQL events to monitor how effectively this model is working.

PREPARE SQL

This event fires when a prepared Transact-SQL statement has been sent to SQL Server via SqlClient, ODBC OLE DB, or DB-Library. This event only occurs when the Transact-SQL statement is first compiled.

EXEC PREPARED SQL

This event fires when the Transact-SQL statement is actually executed. In a typical trace you should see three to five times more Exec Prepared SQL events than Prepare SQL events. This is because the Transact-SQL statement should be compiled only once, and then executed over and over again without being recompiled each time it is run. If you notice that the number of Prepare SQL events is about the same as the Exec Prepared SQL events, this means that the Transact-SQL statement is being recompiled over and over again, and is a strong indicator that the application code used to execute the Transact-SQL using the Prepare/Execute Model is poorly designed and is running inefficiently.

UNPREPARE SQL

This event fires when the application has specifically removed a prepared Transact-SQL statement from the plan cache. This should be a rare event.

XML EVENT: XQUERY STATIC TYPE

The last event in the TSQL event category is XQuery Static Type. The XQuery Static Type event fires whenever SQL Server executes an XQuery expression. To manipulate XML data in SQL Server, the XQuery language must be used. It is a subset of Transact-SQL and is executed by the query optimizer in a very similar way to standard Transact-SQL statements. This event can be used when troubleshooting problems with the XQuery language.

TRANSACTION

The Transaction event category has 13 events, three of which may be of some use to DBAs, while the other 10 are client software specific. The 13 events are:

- DTCTransaction Event Class
- SQLTransaction Event Class
- TM: Begin Tran Completed Event Class
- TM: Begin Tran Starting Event Class

- TM: Commit Tran Completed Event Class
- TM: Commit Tran Starting Event Class
- TM: Promote Tran Completed Event Class
- TM: Promote Tran Starting Event Class
- TM: Rollback Tran Completed Event Class
- TM: Rollback Tran Starting Event Class
- TM: Save Tran Completed Event Class
- TM: Save Tran Starting Event Class
- TransactionLog Event Class

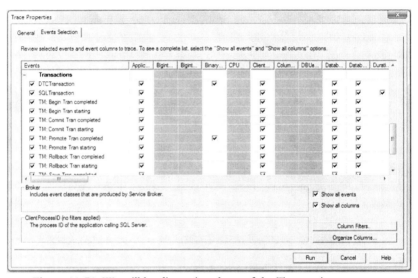

Figure 11-71: We will be discussing three of the Transaction events.

Of the above 13 Transaction events, ten are preceded by the letters "TM". These ten events only collect data if your client application is using a Transaction Management Interface to communicate with SQL Server. Because this is not common, and because these events are of more interest to developers than DBAs, we won't discuss them here. However, we will discuss these 3 Transaction events:

- DTCTransaction
- SQLTransaction
- TransactionLog

DTCTRANSACTION

Distributed transactions, or transactions that occur between two databases on the same or different servers, are notoriously difficult to troubleshoot. While this is mostly a developer debugging issue, often DBAs get caught up in helping to resolve these problems.

The DTCTransaction event can be used to monitor the status of transactions flowing through the Microsoft Distributed Transaction Coordinator (MS DTC). It is fired every time a distributed transaction occurs. While the data columns for this event provide a lot of useful troubleshooting information, the most useful data is found in the EventSubClass data column. This column describes the status of the distributed transaction, and can report back the following states:

- 0 = Get address
- 1 = Propagate Transaction
- 3 = Close connection
- 6 = Creating a new DTC transaction
- 7 = Enlisting in a DTC transaction
- 9 = Internal commit
- 10 = Internal abort
- 14 = Preparing Transaction
- 15 = Transaction is prepared
- 16 = Transaction is aborting
- 17 = Transaction is committing
- 22 = TM failed while in prepared state
- 23 = Unknown

Armed with the above information, the developer should be able to see what is happening with the code and troubleshoot the problem. If your server is running many distributed transactions, capturing this event can put an undue burden on the SQL Server's resources. Be sure to collect data only for limited periods of time.

SQLTRANSACTION

Of the three Transaction events, this one is probably of the most interest to DBAs and developers. The SQLTransaction event fires each and every time a SQL Server transaction begins and ends.

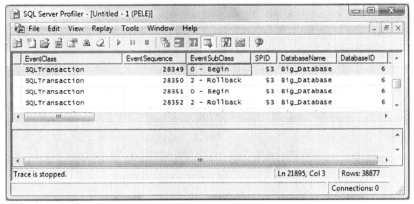

Figure 11-72: The SQLTransaction event reports back on all SQL Serve transactions.

When it fires, the SQLTransaction event provides a wealth of usefu information for DBAs and developers trying to troubleshoot specifi transaction problems. The information provided by this event includes:

- The duration of the event
- Username of the transaction
- The name of the object being referenced in the transaction
- The state of the transaction

  - 0 = Begin
  - 1 = Commit
  - 2 = Rollback
  - 3 = Savepoint

Because the SQLTransaction event fires at least twice for ever transaction, collecting this event can be quite burdensome on the serve so only collect this event if you absolute need to, and only collect it fc the duration of the specific transactions in which you are interested.

TRANSACTIONLOG

The TransactionLog event is used to track activity in a database transaction log, and is supposed to record when transactions are actuall written to a transaction log. Unfortunately, this event is not very usefu because the most of the data it provides is not documented by Microsof

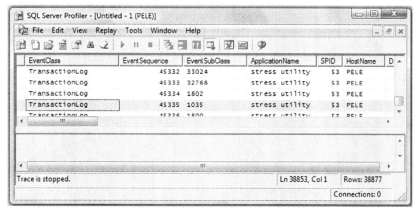

Figure 11-73: The TransactionLog Event is poorly documented and not too useful.

In addition, this event can generate thousands of events per second, putting a huge burden on your server. Until Microsoft decides to document this event, it is not much use to anyone.

USER CONFIGURABLE

The User Configurable event category allows the DBA or developer to create up to ten user-defined Profiler events. That's right: you have to define these events yourself if you want to use them!

User Configurable events can be used to debug an application, or within an application to provide useful information on the behavior of your application.

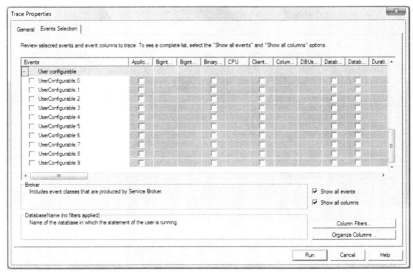

Figure 11-74: Create your own profiler events that can be captured with Profiler.

Other than to say that these events are created with the sp_trace_generateevent command in SQL Server, we will not be discussing the topic further in this book, as it would require a lengthy chapter to cover all there is to know about it.

Believe it or not, we have finished our discussion on useful Profiler events. If you have any attention span left at this point, we are ready to dissect the various data columns that are available for Profiler events.

PROFILER DATA COLUMNS

SQL Server Profiler offers up to 64 different data columns per event, although not every column is used for every event. In this section, we will take a quick look at each of the available data columns, including a discussion of which ones are more useful than others.

NOTE:

When I describe the data columns below, I often refer to how often a particular data column is used, such as rarely or often. When I make such a statement, I am referring to how commonly the data column is used by the various events, not by how commonly the data columns are used by DBAs to troubleshoot problems.

APPLICATIONNAME

Assuming that the client application passes SQL Server its name (and often no name is passed from the application), this data column lets you know which application is associated with this event. On some occasions, the name of the application that is passed to SQL Server may not match the name normally associated with the application, making it difficult to determine exactly which application is creating the event. When multiple applications are running on the server and you only need to see trace results of a single application, it is often useful to filter on this column.

BIGINTDATA1

This seldom-used data column includes event-specific data.

NOTE:

Event-specific data means that the contents of a particular data column will vary, depending on the event. Often, the only way to find out event-specific data is to look it up in Books Online.

BIGINTDATA2

This even less seldom-used data column includes event-specific data.

BINARYDATA

A few events include this column, which stores event-specific binary data. In most cases, as the data is in binary form, it is not too useful. One exception to this is the Showplan XML event. The actual XML data is stored as binary data. While we can't read the data directly, we need to capture it so that Profiler can display the graphical execution plan.

CPU

This useful data column shows the amount of CPU time used by the event (in milliseconds). This is a commonly-used data column.

CLIENTPROCESSID

This the ID number assigned to the client process that is communicating with SQL Server and that has created this event. It is only populated if the client passes the ClientProcessID to SQL Server. Most events include this data column, and it can be used to filter events so that you only capture those events relating to the client process in which you are interested.

ColumnPermissions

This rarely-used data column is available for audit events only and is used to help you track column permission activity.

DBUserName

This is the SQL Server user name used by the client. It may or may not be very useful, depending on the granularity of user security used by the client. For example, if a client application uses DBO to access a database, then DBO will be put into this data column, which is generally not very useful information.

DatabaseID

This is the internal database ID used by SQL Server, as expressed by a single integer. You can use the DB_NAME() function to find out the name of the database associated with this integer. Generally, however, it is easier to use the DatabaseName data column. For most events, both the DatabaseID and DatabaseName data columns are available, so you only need to capture one or the other. However, for those few events that only return the DatabaseID, and not the DatabaseName, will you need to use this data column to identify which database is being affected by the event.

DatabaseName

Many events include the DatabaseName data column, which makes it easy to identify which database is being affected by which event. If this column is available for an event, there is no point collecting the DatabaseID, as it is redundant. Filters are often created on the DatabaseName column, restricting events to those relevant to the database you are investigating.

Duration

This very useful data column provides the length of time that an event has taken from beginning to end, in *microseconds*. Curiously, when Duration is displayed from the Profiler GUI, it is shown in *milliseconds* (although you can change this by going to Tools | Options from within Profiler, and changing the default setting). So internally, SQL Server stores Duration data as microseconds, but, by default, displays it in milliseconds in Profiler. In addition, when trace data is written to a file or a database, the data is also written in the form of microseconds.

The Duration column provides DBAs with valuable information on the performance of the event. You can also filter on Duration, which allows you to select only those events that fall into a timeframe of interest to you. For example, when I look for long running queries on a SQL Server, I often only return those queries that exceed a duration of 5000 milliseconds (5 seconds). This helps me to focus on only those queries that are causing the biggest performance problems.

ENDTIME

The EndTime data column is used for those events associated with a specific end time. It can be used to help identify when a particular query or transaction completes.

ERROR

Some events are associated with specific errors. If an error occurs, this data column is populated with the error number. While not always true, you can search for the text message associated with the error message in the sys.messages system view.

EVENTCLASS

This is the name of the event you are capturing. You will always want to capture this data column so you know what events you have captured.

EVENTSEQUENCE

Every event produced by SQL Server Profiler trace is assigned a sequence number. This data column is useful to see the order in which events were fired. Much of the time, you will capture traces in default order, which means that the events are displayed in the order they occurred in the Profiler GUI, and the EventSequence numbers will be displayed in ascending order. However, if you choose to capture traces grouped differently from the default order, then the EventSequence data column makes it easier for you to see whether an event occurred before or after another event.

EVENTSUBCLASS

This is a very useful, but often overlooked data column. Many events have sub-events which, rather than have their own row, are displayed in the EventSubClass data column. In this column, assuming the event has sub-events, you will see some indication of what the sub-event is. Most of the time the sub-events are fairly self-explanatory; if they are not, you can research them in Books Online. If an event has an EventSubClass data column, I highly recommend that you always capture it, as it can contain valuable information.

FILENAME

Some of the events refer to a logical name of a file that has been modified. If this is the case, the name of the file is stored in the FileName data column.

GUID

This seldom-used data column contains a GUID value that is specific to the event being traced.

HANDLE

This seldom-used data column stores an integer value, used by ODBC, OLE DB, or DB-Library to coordinate server execution.

HOSTNAME

This common and useful data column includes the name of the host running the client application. Unfortunately, this column has to be provided by the application, which does not always do this. A filter on this column allows you to focus your trace on only those events from the specific host you are troubleshooting.

INDEXID

A handful of events refer to specific indexes that have been affected by an event. The value returned is an integer that identifies the logical number of the index. You can find the name of the index by looking up the index ID number in the sys.indexes system view of the database where the index is located.

INTEGERDATA

This seldom-used data column includes event-specific data.

INTEGERDATA2

This even less-used data column includes event-specific data.

ISSYSTEM

This very common data column tells you whether an event occurred on a system process or a user process. A value of 1 refers to a system process, and a value of 0 refers to a user process. It is sometimes handy to filter out the system process so you can focus on user processes instead.

LINENUMBER

This data column can be helpful when debugging application code. For a limited number of events, it contains the physical line number of the statement in a batch or stored procedure that is affected by the event.

LINKEDSERVERNAME

If you are tracing any of the limited number of events that relate to linked servers, this data column stores the name of the linked server.

LOGINNAME

Most events include the LoginName data column. It stores the login of the user that caused the event. Depending on the type of login used, this column can contain either the SQL Server login ID or the Windows Login ID (domain\username). This useful data column helps you to identify who is causing potential problems, and is also a good column to filter on. This way, you can limit trace results to those of a specific user.

LOGINSID

This commonly-used data column contains the security identify (SID) of the user that caused the event. In most cases, you will probably not need it, as the LoginName data column provides essentially the same data and is easier to read. If you need to find out the login name of a SID, you can do so by querying the sys.server_principals view in the master database.

METHODNAME

This seldom-used data column contains the OLE DB method that was used when this event was created. You might find it useful for debugging applications.

MODE

This seldom-used data column includes event specific state data.

NTDOMAINNAME

This commonly-used data column contains the name of the domain in which the user responsible for the event resides. In most cases, you won't care about this information.

NTUSERNAME

This is also another commonly-used data column and contains the Windows user name of the user responsible for the event. In many cases this data duplicates the data found in the LoginName column.

NESTEDLEVEL

This data column is used for those events that return a value based on the @@NESTLEVEL function. It can sometimes be useful for debugging applications.

OBJECTID

Many events are directly related to specific objects, such as a table or index. The ObjectID data column stores the system-assigned ID of the object being affected by the event. To identify the name of an object ID, query the sys.objects system view of the database where the object is located. This can be a very useful data column, helping you to identify specific objects that might be troublesome. In addition, you can filter on this column so that you focus exclusively on particular objects of interest. Many events that include the ObjectID also include the ObjectName data column. If this is the case, using both of these data columns would be redundant.

OBJECTID2

In a limited number of events, the ObjectID2 data column is used to indicate the system-assigned ID of an object related to the object found in the ObjectID column.

OBJECTNAME

In some events, the ObjectName is stored in the ObjectName data column. There is no point in returning data for both ObjectID and ObjectName data columns. Instead, pick one and use it.

OBJECT TYPE

Occasionally, when an ObjectID or ObjectName column is used in an event, the type of the object is stored in this column. The type value is a number, not a name. You can query the sys.objects system view to find out what object type the number refers to.

OFFSET

This seldom-used data column indicates a starting offset number of a statement within a batch or stored procedure. You might find it useful for debugging applications.

OWNERID

This data column is deceivingly named. It is only used for lock events and refers to the type of the object that owns the lock. This can be useful information when troubleshooting locking issues.

OWNERNAME

This data column, which is used for some Broker and Audit events, lists the database user name of the object owner.

PARENTNAME

This rarely-used data column appears in some Broker and Audit events, and contains the name of the schema in which an object resides.

PERMISSIONS

This data column is only available for selected Audit events. It contains values representing the type of permissions affected by the event. If you are auditing events for security purposes, this is a useful data column.

PLANHANDLE

The PlanHandle data column is only available for a single event: Performance Statistics. It contains the plan handle to the corresponding compiled plan stored in cache.

PROVIDERNAME

This uncommon data column includes the name of the OLE DB provider used for this event.

READS

This very useful data column contains the number of logical page reads performed for the event. It is very useful in determining how a particular event affects performance.

REQUESTID

This common, but rarely used, data column contains the request ID of the statement shown in the event.

ROLENAME

If the event is caused by a client running under a SQL Server database role, the role name is located in this data column.

ROWCOUNTS

The RowCounts data column is only found in a few Stored Procedure events. It contains the number of rows returned from a query.

SPID

This required data column exists for every event, and contains the number of the server process ID (SPID) that is assigned to the client process creating the event. It is used to identify what connections are being used for an event, and can also be used as a filter to limit the number of events returned to those that are of particular interest.

SERVERNAME

This common data column lists the name of the SQL Server instance that is being traced. In most cases, this is redundant information and does not need to be collected.

SESSIONLOGINNAME

This common, but seldom-used, data column contains the login name of the account that started the session that produced the event. This can be useful to know if the event was fired using an account other than the account original login account.

SEVERITY

When an event produces an error message, it also produces a severity code, which is stored in the Severity data column. If you are tracking error messages, you will also want to track the message's severity.

SOURCEDATABASEID

This data column is only available for certain Stored Procedure events. It contains the ID of the database where the object exists that is directly related to the event. You can use the DB_NAME() function to find out the name of the database associated with this ID.

SQLHANDLE

This seldom-used data column includes a 64-bit hash based on the code of an ad hoc query, or it can contain the object ID of an object. To make use of this value, you must query sys.dm_exec_sql_text() in order to identify the text associated with this handle.

STARTTIME

Virtually every event has a StartTime data column and, as you would expect, it includes the time the event started. Often, the start time of an event can be matched to other related events to identify their order of execution. It can also be compared to the stop time of events to determine the differences in time between when one event started and another event completed.

STATE

This seldom-used data column contains an error state code that is related to the particular event that occurred.

SUCCESS

Many events indicate whether they were successful or not. A value of 1 means success, and a value of 0 means failure.

TARGETLOGINNAME

Used only for Broker and Audit events that target a login, this data column contains the name of the targeted login.

TARGETLOGINSID

Used only for Broker and Audit events that target a login, this data column contains the SID of the targeted login.

TARGETUSERNAME

Used only for Broker and Audit events that target a database user, this data column contains the name of the targeted user.

TEXTDATA

This commonly-used data column is one of the most useful data columns you can collect. The value stored in this column varies according to the event, but often includes the text of the code that fired the event. You should almost always include this data column in your traces.

TRANSACTIONID

The TransactionID data column exists for most events and contains the system-assigned ID of the transaction firing the event. Unless you are troubleshooting transactions, this column is not all that useful.

TYPE

Used mostly for Lock events, this data column contains an integer value that is dependent on the event.

WRITES

Like the Reads data column, the Writes data column is not used often by events. But when it is available, it provides useful information on the number of physical disk write operations that are performed on the server as a result of the event. This information is useful when troubleshooting performance problems.

XACTSEQUENCE

While a commonly-used data column, it does not provide information of much use to the DBA. It contains a token used to describe the current transaction.

SUMMARY

Now that you know the basics of Profiler events and data columns, you can apply them to real world situations, as appropriate.

I hope you have enjoyed your journey to becoming a Profiler Master. By reading this book, and using what you have learned in your day-to-day task as a DBA, you are well on your way to becoming an Exceptional DBA.

INDEX

SQL Backup   from $295

Compress, encrypt and monitor SQL Server backups

- ↗ Compress database backups by **up to 95%** for faster backups and restores
- ↗ Protect your data with up to 256-bit AES encryption (SQL Backup Pro only)
- ↗ Monitor your data with an interactive timeline, so you can check and edit the status of past, present and future backup activities
- ↗ Optimize backup performance with multiple threads in SQL Backup's engine

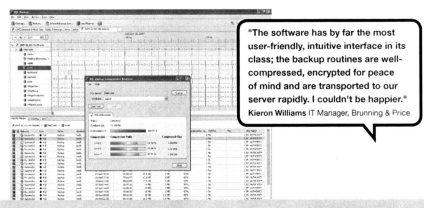

"The software has by far the most user-friendly, intuitive interface in its class; the backup routines are well-compressed, encrypted for peace of mind and are transported to our server rapidly. I couldn't be happier."
Kieron Williams IT Manager, Brunning & Price

SQL Response   from $495

Monitors SQL Servers, with alerts and diagnostic data

- ↗ Compare your database contents
- ↗ Automatically synchronize your data
- ↗ Simplify data migrations
- ↗ Row-level restore
- ↗ Compare to backups

"Very impressed! It's an easy installation and the tool is light weight. It doesn't measurably impact my servers, and still provides great monitoring for all aspects of my server's health"
Chris Miller Senior DBA, Kansas City, MO
(Release Candidate tester)

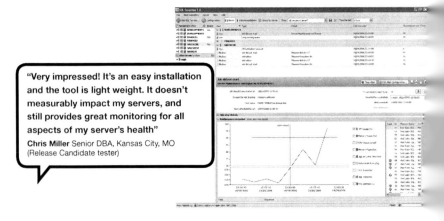

SQL Compare

from $395

Compare and synchronize SQL Server database schemas

- ↗ Automate database comparisons, and synchronize your databases
- ↗ Simple, easy to use, 100% accurate
- ↗ Save hours of tedious work, and eliminate manual scripting errors
- ↗ Work with live databases, snapshots, script files or backups

> "SQL Compare and SQL Data Compare are the best purchases we've made in the .NET/SQL environment. They've saved us hours of development time and the fast, easy-to-use database comparison gives us maximum confidence that our migration scripts are correct. We rely on these products for every deployment."
>
> **Paul Tebbutt** Technical Lead, Universal Music Group

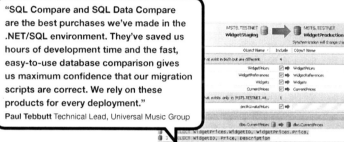

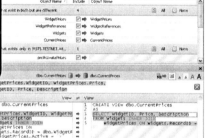

SQL Data Compare

from $395

Compare and synchronize SQL Server database schemas

- ↗ Automate database comparisons, and synchronize your databases
- ↗ Simple, easy to use, 100% accurate
- ↗ Save hours of tedious work, and eliminate manual scripting errors
- ↗ Work with live databases, snapshots, script files or backups

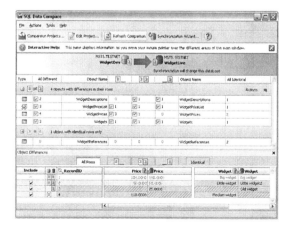

SQL Prompt

from $195

Intelligent code completion and layout for SQL Server

- ↗ Write SQL fast and accurately with code completion
- ↗ Understand code more easily with script layout
- ↗ Continue to use your current editor – SQL Prompt works within SSMS, Query Analyzer, and Visual Studio
- ↗ Keyword formatting, join completion, code snippets, and many more powerful features

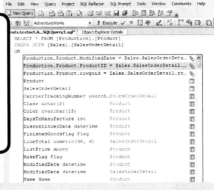

"It's amazing how such a simple concept quickly becomes a way of life. With SQL Prompt there's no longer any need to hunt out the design documentation, or to memorize every field length in the entire database. It's about freeing the mind from being a database repository - and instead concentrate on problem solving and solution providing!" **Dr Michael Dye** Dyetech

SQL Data Generator

$295

Test data generator for SQL Server databases

- ↗ Data generation in one click
- ↗ Realistic data based on column and table name
- ↗ Data can be customized if desired
- ↗ Eliminates hours of tedious work

"Red Gate's SQL Data Generator has overnight become the principal tool we use for loading test data to run our performance and load tests" **Grant Fritchey** Principal DBA, FM Global

▣ Preview of data to be generated (first 100 lines)

TitleOfCourtesy / Title	BirthDate / datetime	HireDate / datetime	Address / Address Line (Stre...	City / US City	Region / Region	PostalCode / ZIP Code	Country / Country	HomeF / Phone
Dr	23/08/1963 04:0...	25/04/1992 20:0...	37 Fabien St.	Richmond	IA-CT	58907	Gibraltar	12353:
Miss	10/01/1960 23:2...	16/02/1976 11:2...	850 White Nobel...	NULL	NV-EW	39330	Tajikistan	69862:
Mr	27/07/1970 13:5...	03/12/1953 15:3...	45 Green Milton...	New York	TN-OH	60387	Liberia	529-89
Mr	27/01/2002 04:3...	24/07/1958 00:5...	43 Milton Boulev...	Sacramento	NM-JR	13294	Côte d'Ivoire	984-11
Mr	31/05/1994 04:1	12/01/1964 04:4...	592 Rocky Cowl...	Santa Ana	MI-UU	NULL	Jersey	417-47
Mrs	17/11/1975 10:1...	27/10/1968 18:5...	69 Clarendon Pa...	San Jose	IL-TC	41768	New Caledonia	11305(
Dr.	16/05/1974 06:1...	25/11/1998 14:5	207 Fabien Blvd.	Houston	AL-GE	04937	Belgium	89687E
Dr	27/12/1999 19:4...	03/05/1972 13:1...	53 Rocky Oak R...	Baton Rouge	MA-RT	65364	Swaziland	076-87
Dr	14/10/1971 03:1...	28/06/1978 10:0...	260 East Rocky...	Charlotte	AL-AR	97727	Benin	546845
Mr	09/11/1981 13:2...	26/12/2001 15:0...	476 North Fabie...	Akron	MA-IU	94269	Palau	875611
Dr	28/06/1987 01:3...	30/10/1972 00:0...	48 South Hague...	Norfolk	VT-UV	66365	American Samoa	89085(
Mr	20/10/1962 04:4.	07/09/2005 17:1...	939 Fabien Park...	Grand Rapids	HI-YT	86033	Swaziland	58415(
Mr	25/01/2001 08:0...	18/08/1983 12:0...	348 North Green...	Wichita	FL-IV	32302	Zambia	124-42
Mr	05/01/1955 10:0.	12/08/1983 22:5...	32 Cowley Boule...	Spokane	WV-DI	45980	Chile	457-22

SQL Toolbelt™ $1,795

The twelve essential SQL Server tools for database professionals

You can buy our acclaimed SQL Server tools individually or bundled.
Our most popular deal is the SQL Toolbelt: all twelve SQL Server tools in a single installer, with **a combined value of $5,240 but an actual price of $1,795**, a saving of more than 65%.

*Fully compatible with SQL Server 2000, 2005 and **2008!***

SQL Doc

Intelligent code completion and layout for SQL Server

↗ Produce simple, legible and fast HTML reports for multiple databases
↗ Documentation is stored as part of the database
↗ Output completed documentation to a range of different formats.

$295

SQL Dependency Tracker

The graphical tool for tracking database and cross-server dependencies

↗ Visually track database object dependencies
↗ Discover all cross-database and cross-server object relationships
↗ Analyze potential impact of database schema changes
↗ Rapidly document database dependencies for reports, version control, and database change planning

$195

SQL Packager

Compress and package your databases for easy installations and upgrades

↗ Script your entire database accurately and quickly
↗ Move your database from A to B
↗ Compress your database as an exe file, or launch as a Visual Studio project
↗ Simplify database deployments and installations

from $295

SQL Multi Script

Single-click script execution on multiple SQL Servers

↗ Cut out repetitive administration by deploying multiple scripts on multiple servers with just one click
↗ Return easy-to-read, aggregated results from your queries to export either as a csv or .txt file
↗ Edit queries fast with an intuitive interface, including colored syntax highlighting, Find and Replace, and split-screen editing

$195

SQL Comparison SDK

Automate database comparisons and synchronizations

↗ Full API access to Red Gate comparison tools
↗ Incorporate comparison and synchronization functionality into your applications
↗ Schedule any of the tasks you require from the SQL Comparison Bundle

$595

SQL Refactor

Refactor and format your SQL code

Twelve tools to help update and maintain databases quickly and reliably, including:

↗ Rename object and update all references
↗ Expand column wildcards, qualify object names, and uppercase keywords
↗ Summarize script
↗ Encapsulate code as stored procedure

$295

How to Become an Exceptional DBA
Brad McGehee

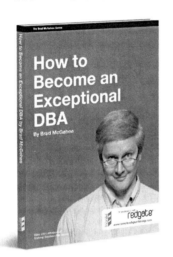

A career guide that will show you, step-by-step, exactly what you can do to differentiate yourself from the crowd so that you can be an Exceptional DBA. While Brad focuses on how to become an Exceptional SQL Server DBA, the advice in this book applies to any DBA, no matter what database software they use. If you are considering becoming a DBA, or are a DBA and want to be more than an average DBA, this is the book to get you started.

Brad's Sure Guide to SQL Server 2008
Brad McGehee

Learning SQL Server 2008 is not as steep a learning curve as learning SQL Server 2005 was, but neither is it a simple task that you can expect to accomplish overnight. This book describes the top ten most important new features for Production DBAs in SQL Server 2008, and covers many of the key features Production DBAs will find interesting. Brad walks you through each feature, gives examples, and makes sure you're ready to tackle SQL Server 2008.

SQL Server Execution Plans
Grant Fritchey

Execution plans show you what's going on behind the scenes in SQL Server and provide you with a wealth of information on how your queries are being executed. Grant provides a clear route through the subject, from the basics of capturing plans, through their interpretation, and then right on to how to use them to understand how you might optimize your SQL queries, improve your indexing strategy, and so on. All this rich information makes the execution plan a fairly important tool in the tool belt of pretty much anyone who writes TSQL to access data in a SQL Server database.

The Art of XSD
Jacob Sebastian

This book will help you learn and use XML Schema collections in SQL Server. Prior knowledge of XSD is not required to start with this book, although any experience with XSD will make your learning process easier. A lot of applications exchange information in XML format, and this book will take you from the basics of XML schemas and walk you through everything you need to know, with examples and labs, in order to build powerful XML schemas in SQL Server.

LaVergne, TN USA
20 August 2010
194084LV00001B/11/P